W9-AEI-104

The Carlos Complex

The Carlos Complex

a study in terror

CHRISTOPHER DOBSON

and

RONALD PAYNE

G.P. Putnam's Sons · New York

First American Edition 1977

Library of Congress Catalog Number: 76-57878

SBN: 399-11903-5

Printed in the United States of America

Contents

Introduction

LOOKING BACK OVER THE DECADE OF THE 1970S WHEN INTERNATIONAL terrorism established itself as a force to be reckoned with and a true disease of the age, people will be struck by the paunchy figure of a young Venezuelan named Ilich Ramirez Sanchez, better known as Carlos the Killer. By means of the bomb and the machine-pistol, through assassination and kidnapping, Carlos captured the public imagination. People may be horrified by him, but they are also enthralled by his exploits. His eagerness to kill, his contempt for the normal rules of civilised behaviour, his sexuality, are all a part of his spell. And then there is the belief that the day of retribution will come and he will soon meet a violent death.

He has become a television show anti-hero translated into real life, a star on the world stage. He is the bad man in the black hat surrounded by his henchmen from the Baader-Meinhof gang, the Japanese Red Army, and the Palestinian groups. Wadi Hadad, the terror master, makes his bookings. And his financial backer, Moammer Gaddafi, makes him rich with oil money.

As such he is a natural subject for a book. But it is our belief that his importance goes much beyond his notoriety, for, as the symbol of international terrorism, he has made ordinary people aware that there is a worldwide network of revolutionaries determined for a variety of reasons to destroy the fabric of modern society. Carlos is also important because most of the strands of this network come together in him. In this book we have set out to use him as our guide through the network. It has been an exciting journey through many dark paths and we have encountered extraordinary characters on the way, men and women who at first sight appear to have no connection with terrorism. But the network is so comprehensive, with its "hit-men", its support groups, and its intellectual sympathisers, that every turning had its surprises. Wherever we trod we came across the footprints of the heavy-booted men of the KGB – for the Kremlin, even when it is not involved, wants to know what is going on.

Our own interest in terrorism stems from our careers as foreign correspondents in which between us we have covered virtually every war since the end of the Second World War. Starting with Ronald Payne's coverage of the Algerian revolution and its effects on France twenty years ago, and Christopher Dobson's accounts of Castro's fight against Batista, we have amassed a huge amount of information about various revolutionary groups and the way in which they have fought. Eoka in Cyprus, the Irgun Zvai Leumi in Israel, the Viet Cong, Black September – each in their turn filled our notebooks. But it was not until we were assigned by the *Sunday Telegraph* to write about Carlos following his shooting of four men in the rue Toullier in Paris in 1975 and the subsequent disclosure that he was the leader of a terrorist group that we realised that we had the basic ingredients of this book. And it was not until we had organised the material that we knew that we had so much – or that so much still needed to be done.

There followed nearly a year of research in which, happily, the interests of the *Sunday Telegraph* coincided with our own. Payne had an extraordinary interview with Colonel Gaddafi and Dobson covered the Entebbe raid. We were able to draw on friendships made on both sides in the Middle East, with diplomats and those men belonging to discreet government agencies whom every foreign correspondent meets on his travels. We talked to many people, most of whom would rather not be named, and had the usual quota of good luck and bad, of following up leads which collapsed and others which blossomed into beautiful flowers of knowledge.

At the outset, for example, we never for a moment suspected that we would uncover a link between Carlos and the British traitor George Blake, who, after being sentenced to forty-two years' imprisonment, escaped and now lives in Moscow. There were many other surprises. We discovered that Joachim Klein, the German anarchist who was wounded during Carlos's kidnapping of the OPEC oil ministers in Vienna, had once acted as chauffeur to Jean-Paul Sartre.

We learnt that among the terrorists killed by the Israelis at Entebbe were two senior PFLP men – not young gunmen but the "diplomats" responsible for the liaison between the PFLP and the Japanese and South American revolutionaries. And we found out how Carlos was taught to seduce innocent young women to act as cover for him.

Our research was in one way a treasure hunt for those intriguing little jewels of fact. But there was also more solid, and no less valuable, matter to be mined. The most important theme that emerged throughout our research was the way in which young middle-class men and women of good education and bright prospects – like Carlos himself – abandoned everything they had been taught to believe in and turned to the gun and to violence. We consider that it is important at the start of this book to establish the basis for understanding why young people who proclaim their love of peace and their passionate need to reform the world should choose brutal violence as their method.

To understand this phenomenon one must go all the way back to 1945, to the blighted hopes of the peace agreement which failed to bring the justice and tranquillity so fervently desired by the world after the horrors of the Second World War.

World politics after 1945 were dominated by two main themes: the disintegration of the old colonial empires and the stalemate between the super-powers brought about by the threat of mutual destruction in an atomic war. The situation was one not of peace but of unwar, with Russia and the United States using revolutionary movements of both the right and the left as surrogates, to fight on their behalf battles which neither dared fight themselves. Colonial uprisings which in the old days of empire might have been put down with a swift decisiveness were allowed to linger on because the European colonial powers were too tired by five years of war to use the traditional methods effectively while the revolutionaries more often than not enjoyed the support of one of the super-powers. Strong currents of violence began to run in countries which had once been firmly administered. The Mau Mau in Kenya, Eoka in Cyprus and the Communists in Malaya turned to terrorism, using guerrilla techniques which had been taught to them during the war. Mao Tse-Tung's triumph of a People's War in China, with his guerrillas "swimming like fish in the sea of the people", showed what could be done by dedicated fighters as long as the political and geographical conditions allowed them to operate. Later, Fidel Castro and his bearded guerrillas created a new religion of revolution with

Che Guevara as its high priest, evangelising the world's youth in the cause of the new creed.

But the real catalyst which turned young idealists into terrorists was Vietnam.

The long war there destroyed the old empire of France and the new empire of America. Torture and terror were an everyday business in Vietnam and the French took the techniques they had learned from the Indo-Chinese back to Algiers to fight the National Liberation Front. The Americans took over from the French in Vietnam and they, too, learnt the techniques of torture and terror. It was a situation which either disgusted or degraded the young conscripts of both the French and American armies. At the same time the postwar generations of students and intellectuals in the West, the brave new wave, gave increasing sympathy to the colonially exploited nations of the Third World. The French left wing supported the Algerians. The Americans were slower in their opposition to the war in Vietnam: it took mounting casualties and the realisation that the war could not be won before the opposition crystallised. Nevertheless, when that opposition came, it was devastating to a country which up to that time had been so sure of itself.

All round the world the liberal ideas and democratic socialism of the new wave began to tilt towards the non-classic styles of communism vaguely defined as Maoism and Trotskyism, or to the even vaguer theories of the flower people and the hippies who wanted to contract out.

The activists wanted to reform Western society, in which they no longer believed. To them capitalism and colonialism marched hand in hand as forces of evil. They looked on parliamentary democracy as the handmaiden of those forces and they sought new ways to bring about their nebulous ideas of Utopia. Mostly middle-class, their often noble and generous aspirations to help the poor at home and the oppressed abroad bred the New Left of the middle 1960s.

Nor were these views confined to the West. They spread to Czechoslovakia and Hungary and took root among the young people of Eastern Europe, who suspected Communism in the same way that their counterparts in the West suspected capitalism. But behind the Iron Curtain they were put down with a savagery which no Western Government with a parliamentary tradition would dare attempt.

In 1968 in Paris the student revolution erupted which almost ended the reign of Charles de Gaulle. The black flag of anarchy flew on the boulevards next to the hammer and sickle. The prophets of this revolution were Herbert Marcuse, Régis Debray and Frantz Fanon. Its heroes were Che Guevara, Daniel Cohn-Bendit and Red Rudi Dutschke. This revolution had repercussions all round the world and one of its results was that it became acceptable for students to attack the forces of law and order. In the eyes of the students, it was the authorities who were the oppressors and it was right and proper to answer state violence with revolutionary violence.

One of the incidents which confirmed them in this belief came two years later in the United States when National Guardsmen opened fire without warning on students who were rioting at Kent State University in Ohio in protest against President Nixon's invasion of Cambodia. The Guardsmen killed four students and wounded ten. Nixon dismissed the killings as the inevitable consequence of "the resort to violence" – meaning violence by the young. But to young people, not only in America but throughout the world, it was a perfect example of violence by the state.

Thus the young idealists, many of them experienced in warfare in Indo-China and the Middle East, found themselves moving almost unknowingly towards violence themselves. They reached for the Kalashnikov and the bomb to strike back and destroy what they hated so much. They became intellectuals "with a pistol in the drawer". Revolution and terror became the first priority and eventually ends in themselves for people who no longer had clear ideas about what sort of world they would try to build once they had torn down the old system. The very act of destruction was sufficient, they argued. Something better was certain to emerge from the ruins.

We are not now discussing the agents and agitators of the Communist powers who so gratefully battened onto the discontent in the West while stamping out the same discontent in their own lands. Neither are we talking about the psychopaths who get pleasure from killing. The people we are talking about are the idealists, the young nuclear disarmers and moderate socialists who were sucked into violence, the gentle people who wanted to remake the world and turned to murder in order to do so. These are the saddest of the terrorists and in the end the most ruthless because their ideals slip through their fingers and only blood is left. They are like the old-style Communists who, in the Stalin show trials, willingly confessed to crimes they did not commit because to have denied the charges would have meant the denial of Communism and their whole world, everything they had lived for, in fact. Ulrike Meinhof, one of the founders of the Baader-Meinhof gang, was precisely like this. She began her activist life as an idealist, progressed through Communism to terrorism and then, during her trial, committed suicide – apparently because she began to have doubts about the justice of her cause. The misery of the Palestinian people was evident – even though their misery had become a tool of policy. The Palestinian guerrillas were fighting what in New Left terms was a genuine anti-Colonialist war. And Israel for them was an American creation, a bastard child of capitalist imperialism.

But they had more than a cause. The Palestinians had money, weapons, organisation and safe hiding-places. They were dedicated to striking, not only at Israel, but also at the United States; and the PFLP in particular promised world revolution. What more could any young activist want?

And so the strands knitted together. The Palestinians needed the revolutionaries from other countries to help carry out their terror operations, and the revolutionaries, harried by the authorities in their own countries, felt secure, both ideologically and physically, with the Palestinians.

There is a third strand, more sinister and hidden, that runs from Moscow to Havana. The KGB has always relished disorder, seeking to gain advantage from other peoples' misfortunes. In every Palestinian group, in every terrorist organisation, there is at least one man who is ultimately controlled by the Kremlin. And it is no coincidence that most of the weapons used by the terrorists come from Communist arsenals.

The Cuban end of the line was knotted together in Havana in January 1966. The Dirección General de Inteligencia, Castro's intelligence service, was already serving virtually as a branch office of the KGB, but both Castro and the Russians were looking for something more active in the way of subversion. And so they called the "First Conference of Solidarity of the Peoples of Africa, Asia and Latin America" which has since become known as the Tricontinental Conference. The Cuban government and Communist Party were the hosts. Delegates came from eighty-two countries and the Soviet delegation, forty strong, was the largest.

The language of the conference was revolutionary: "Struggle

against imperialism ... Struggle for complete national liberation ... Intensification of all forms of struggle ..." The theme of the conference could be summed up in the resolution: "The Conference proclaims the inalienable right of the peoples to total political independence and to resort to all forms of struggle that are necessary, including armed struggle, in order to conquer that right." All peoples, that is, except those under Communist rule.

Two permanent organisations grew out of the conference. The first was the Organisation of Solidarity of the Peoples of Africa, Asia and Latin America whose purpose was to "unite, co-ordinate and further the struggle" on those three continents. The second, formed after the conference ended and against the wishes of the Russians, was the Latin American Organisation of Solidarity. It was composed of twenty-seven Latin American delegations, and its purpose was to "utilise all the means within its reach in order to support the movements of liberation".

The Russians' opposition to this organisation was based on a question of tactics rather than objectives. They preferred to work through the official Communist parties in Latin America rather than the independent guerrilla movements which were more nationalistic than Communist. This situation had, as will be seen later, an important effect on the modern terrorist movement.

When the Tricontinental was held, Che Guevara was already engaged on the revolutionary adventure in Bolivia which was to end in his death. But he was made "President of Honour" in his absence and he sent a message calling for the creation of "two, three, or many Vietnams" in order to strangle the United States with a rope of guerrilla wars.

The Tricontinental was, quite simply, a conference designed to coordinate worldwide revolution and terrorism. One of its most effective results was to formalise the training of young Latin Americans in Cuban camps under both Russian and Cuban instructors. They were taught the arts of guerrilla warfare and terrorism, and the brightest students were sent on to Lumumba University in Moscow for further training and indoctrination.

It is here that the trail brings us back directly to Carlos. He is a Latin American revolutionary, imbued with the ideals of the Tricontinental. He was trained first in Cuba and then at Lumumba University. And then he moved on to involvement with the Palestinians and his notoriety as an international terrorist. At first sight he seems the classic example of the disillusioned youth turning to violence. But there are certain things about Carlos which make him different from the others. And all show how his family background and the shadowy aspects of his Moscow connections made that difference, turning him into what his admiring Communist-millionaire father describes as "a professor of terrorism".

We have chosen to start our story with the Munich massacre in the summer of 1972, a Palestinian operation in which Carlos had no hand. This is not perversity on our part. It is because that event provides the logical beginning to an account of modern terrorism and of the Palestinian cause which is the hub round which it revolves.

Chapter One
"Terrorism is theatre"

THE MUNICH OLYMPICS WERE DESIGNED TO MARK THE REACCEPTANCE of the German people by the rest of the world. The ugly memories of Hitler's Olympics in Berlin in 1936 were going to be wiped away in a festival of brotherhood and friendly competition. Germany, rich and self-confident, was to be host to the world's sportsmen and women and, through the medium of television, to the whole of the world. It was to be a ceremony of reconciliation.

Instead, what the world saw was a paroxysm of violence, the slaughter of eleven members of the Israeli Olympic team by eight young Arabs, five of whom also died. The games continued, but the world had been forced to recognise in the most brutal manner what most people wanted to ignore: that hatred and cruelty are still part of the human condition.

The young Arabs, operational members of the Black September Organisation, had a more specific objective in mind. They were determined to use the Olympics to shock the world into acknowledging the Palestinian cause. Brian Jenkins, Research Analyst in Terrorism at the Rand Corporation and adviser to the US State Department on political conspiracy and violence, argues that "terrorism is aimed at the people watching, not at the actual victims. Terrorism is theatre."

The Palestinians put it another way. An old Arab, sipping coffee from a tiny cup while watching the sun go down behind Amman's honey-coloured hills, patted the head of his grand-daughter and said: "We recognise that sport is the modern religion of the Western world. We knew that the people of England and America would switch their television sets from any programme about the plight of the Palestinians if there was a sporting event on another channel. So we decided to use the Olympics, the most sacred ceremony of this religion, to make the world pay attention to us. We offered up human sacrifices to your gods of sport and television. And they answered our prayers. From Munich onwards nobody could ignore the Palestinians or their cause."

That cause – and the origins of the modern terrorist movement – came into being in 1948, with the founding of the state of Israel. In 1948, when Israel was born, three quarters of a million Palestinian Arabs fled or were forced to flee from their homes. The position was exacerbated after the Six-Day War which brought the West Bank of the Jordan and the Gaza Strip under Israeli control and turned another four hundred thousand Palestinians into refugees, many of them living in miserable tents and shacks on handouts from UNRWA (The United Nations Relief and Works Agency).

Conditions in the refugee camps were deplorable. There was little work for the men and no pride of home for the women. Each camp seethed with discontent and bitterness. Many of the men moved on. The Palestinians are the best educated and most technically minded of the Arabs and they were welcome in the Gulf States where the oil boom was getting into its stride. Today the oil industries of those states depend on Palestinians for their technicians and office workers. But the militant Arab states also pursued a deliberate policy of keeping the camps in being and keeping them in poverty.

If Egypt or Saudi Arabia had spent one fraction of the money that they spent on arms on resettling the refugees, the camps would have ceased to exist. But the Arab governments would not pursue this course. "Why should we," ran the argument, "do the Israelis' work for them? As long as we keep the camps in being the Palestinians will remain a people. Get rid of the camps and the Palestinians will cease to exist."

It is difficult for Westerners to understand the depth of the hatred that the Palestinians feel for the Israelis. No conversation can be held with a Palestinian which does not come full circle to a discussion of their iniquities. The bitterness is blind and unreasoning and the logic of the arguments so conditioned that any act of violence is justifiable as long as it is seen to harm Israel.

The refugee camps, with young men and women growing up in this atmosphere of bitterness and with nothing to do but hate, became the breeding grounds, recruiting centres and training fields of the various resistance groups, groups which were often at war with each other, fighting for control of particular camps.

With the frustration of the Arab armies, slapped down by the Israelis every time they pointed their guns, it fell more and more to these groups to salvage pride, to offer some reason for continuing the fight. They began to strike across the borders, in pinprick raids, killing border settlers and blowing up water pumps. It was such raids from the Gaza Strip which gave the Israelis an excuse for sending their tanks into the Sinai Desert in 1956 (an operation, incidentally, which enabled them to open up the port of Eilat in the Gulf of Akaba and therefore both to export to the East and to import oil from Iran). Similar incursions from Jordan and Syria caused the escalation of tension which led directly to the Six-Day War. Every success of the guerrilla gangs led to a punitive raid by the Israelis designed not only to punish the guerrillas, but also the country which gave them arms and sanctuary.

The Syrians kept a very tight hand on Palestinian operations. They made sure that any raid launched from Syrian territory had to pass through Jordan first, so that if there was any retaliation it would be the Jordanians who would suffer. And suffer they did. The Egyptians, after a taste of the Israelis' punitive techniques, refused to allow the guerrillas to operate from their territory. In effect, this meant that fighting activity against Israel was confined to operations mounted by small groups crossing into the West Bank of the Jordan from bases on the Jordanian side of the valley.

By this time the Palestinian resistance movement had developed into a number of organisations, and although there was much movement from one group to another the groups themselves and their aims became definable. The largest, about seven thousand strong, was Fatah, led by Yasser Arafat and Salah Khalef, better known under his codename of Abu Iyad. Fatah is essentially a political movement, but it does have a military arm, Assifa (The Storm), which has carried out a number of small military-type operations and has played a major role in the inter-Arab fighting in Beirut.

Fatah also developed a terrorist arm under the control of Abu Iyad. It was this collection of killers that came to be known as Black September and was responsible for the Munich massacre. Fatah's politics are hazy, veering from extreme right to extreme left according to the prevailing circumstances. It is, however, dedicated to the return of Palestine to the Palestinians, a dedication which entails the destruction of the state of Israel.

Smaller than Fatah, but far more important in the terms of international terrorism, is the Popular Front for the Liberation of Palestine (PFLP), led by Dr. George Habash and his chief of operations, Wadi Hadad. This small but fierce group is committed not only to the destruction of Israel but to a fundamental Marxist-Leninist revolution throughout the Arab world. Its targets are Israel first, then the "feudal" Arab states, and then world revolution. With this programme it is inevitable that it has attracted the following of the "Progressive" movements around the world. And it is the PFLP which has provided the organisation, training, finance and safe bases for the international terror movement. Habash's philosophy is that it is useless for the Palestinians to attempt classical military-style operations against the Israelis. Only terror, he argues, is effective. Bassam Abu Sherif, PFLP's spokesman, who was hideously scarred by an Israeli parcel bomb, told Dobson in Beirut: "We intend to attack imperialist and Zionist interests wherever we find them in the world. They are legitimate targets." It was when Fatah's leaders saw how effective PFLP's operations could be that they set up Black September – although they refused to acknowledge its provenance in case its activities harmed Arafat's political campaign.

Wadi Hadad's name looms large in this story. He is the one man whose death would have a significant effect on international terrorism. A doctor and a Greek Orthodox Christian, he has dedicated his life to revenge and killing. Ostensibly, he is Number 2 to George Habash, who is also a Greek Orthodox Christian and a doctor – they once ran a children's clinic together – but Habash suffers from heart trouble and his role as leader has been increasingly taken over by Hadad. They have quarrelled more than once on strategy because Habash thinks in "pure" Marxist-Leninist terms while Hadad is an opportunistic revolutionary.

The Israelis put him high on their death list and one of their assassination teams rented an apartment opposite his in Beirut in order to kill him. The Israelis set up a battery of explosive rockets at their window, aimed them at Hadad's bedroom and set a timing device for late at night. But luckily for him, Hadad stayed up later than usual – talking to Leila Khaled – and he had not gone to bed when the rockets crashed into his bedroom and destroyed it. He was unhurt but shaken and very frightened.

He went to ground after that, first in the security of the Baddawi refugee camp, outside Beirut, surrounded by armed guards, and then, when the Israelis demonstrated that they had agents inside the refugee camps, he moved to Baghdad. There he was secure and could rely on the support of the Iraqis in his campaign against Israel and its friends. However, the Iraqi price for sanctuary was a measure of control and so he left for Aden, the Red Sea port which is now the capital of the Peoples' Democratic Republic of Yemen. In the past few years this former colonial base which rose to importance as a coaling station for the Royal Navy on its Imperial missions has achieved a new role as a sanctuary for revolutionaries, who are cosseted and encouraged by its Marxist government. This government owes a special debt to the PFLP which played a large part in the emergence of its National Liberation Front when Aden was still controlled by Britain. It expresses its thanks to Hadad by allowing him absolute freedom to plot and plan. Hijacked planes land there and the hijackers are given sanctuary. Baader-Meinhof terrorists released by hostage blackmail have been welcomed there. The Yemenis take their cut of hijack ransoms. Aden has become the centre of the web of international terrorism and there Hadad has his base. He directs the "Department for Military Action Abroad" which picks targets, sets up the operations and chooses the men and women to carry them out. It was Hadad who recruited Carlos, arranged his further training and provided him with the organisation and funds that resulted in the Carlos Complex.

Other organisations have also come into being. As-Saiqa (The Thunderbolt) was created by the Syrians under the leadership of Zuhair Mohsen largely to oppose Fatah's ambitions. The Popular Democratic Front for the Liberation of Palestine is an offshoot of the PFLP from which it differs on matters of doctrine. Its leader is Naif Hawatmeh, who claims he is the only "pure" revolutionary leader. Another break-away from the PFLP is the Popular Front for the Liberation of Palestine – General Command, led by Ahmed Jibril. Then there is the Arab Liberation Front set up by the Iraqis under Dr. Zaid Haydar to give the Iraqis a voice in Palestinian councils.

All these organisations, and some other even smaller splinter groups, come under the umbrella of the Palestine Liberation Organisation whose chairman is Yasser Arafat, the recognised political leader of the Palestinians. His political ambitions and Habash's philosophy of terror, translated into action by Wadi Hadad, made their first spectacular impact in 1968.

In March of that year a party of schoolchildren from Tel Aviv were being taken by bus on an outing to the Negev desert. The bus hit a mine planted in the road and two children were killed and twenty-eight injured. The enraged Israelis determined on a once-and-for-all punitive raid: they set out to destroy the Fatah base at Karameh, a village taken over by the Palestinians on the East Bank of the Jordan river. The Israelis gambled on the Jordanian army staying out of the fight. But they lost their bet and the Jordanians came to the help of the guerrillas who, though putting up a spirited resistance, were being badly mauled. The Israelis, taken in the rear by a Jordanian armoured force and unwilling to escalate the raid into a full-scale battle, pulled back, leaving wrecked armour behind. Arafat, ignoring the Jordanian army's role, immediately claimed Karameh as a great victory for the Palestinians. Fatah had taken on the might of Israel and defeated the vaunted Israeli army – that was the message that rang round the refugee camps. The Arabs, anxious to grasp at any crumb of military comfort after the defeat of 1967, swallowed it whole. The guerrillas became the standard-bearers of the Arab world. Recruits, anxious for glory, hurried to Jordan to join the fight. Arafat grew confident. His men, carrying their Russian-made Kalashnikov assault rifles – the weapon of revolution – and girded with belts of ammunition, moved out of the Jordan Valley and into the main cities. King Hussein, beset by severe domestic political problems and suffering from the fact that his army had been virtually wiped out in 1967, could do little about them. Soon, the Palestinians moved into Amman itself, operating out of the refugee camps, setting up their own roadblocks, taking what they wanted from the shops and refusing to pay, setting up their own courts of rough justice. They formed a state within a state and Arafat looked forward confidently to the day when Hussein would be deposed and the Palestinians would take over Jordan as the first step on the road back to Jerusalem. This was the situation in September 1970 when Wadi Hadad went too far by mounting his terrorist spectacular, the hijacking of a fleet of airliners, and – in true Arab fashion – turned victory into defeat.

PFLP had been carrying out a campaign of terror with two or three incidents every month. There were hijackings, bombings and the blowing up in mid-air of a Swiss airliner on its way to Tel Aviv, which killed forty-seven people. The bomb had in fact been posted by the terrorists, who planned it to explode at a given height on board an El Al flight to Tel Aviv. Their calculations were right but confusions in the Swiss Post Office ensured that the bomb package found itself on board a Swissair flight. Habash justified this act with his customary twisted logic: "Non-Israeli passengers are on their way to Israel. Since we have no control over the land that was stolen from us and called Israel, it is right that no one may go to Israel without our permission."

Now the PFLP determined to prove to the world that they were, as Habash said, "the joker in the pack". Hadad planned his operation with great care. On September 6th 1970 four of his hijack teams struck simultaneously. One, attempting to seize an El Al Boeing 707 over the Thames Estuary, failed. One of the hijackers, a Nicaraguan-American named Patrick Arguello, was killed in a mid-air gun battle with Israeli security guards, and the other, Leila Khaled, was captured and handed over – reluctantly because the Israelis wanted to take her back to Tel Aviv – to the British authorities. Another hijack team flew its prize, a Pan-American Boeing, to Cairo, where the passengers and crew were set free and the jet was blown up. Two other planes, belonging to TWA and Swissair, were flown with their passengers to Dawson's Field, an abandoned wartime RAF airfield in the wilds of the Jordanian desert. They were joined a few days later by a BOAC VC 10 hijacked to secure the release of Leila Khaled. There they remained with 425 hostages sweltering under a merciless sun until eventually the governments concerned – except Israel – agreed to PFLP's demands. Leila Khaled and a number of other imprisoned terrorists were released and all except forty of the hostages were set free. The unlucky forty were imprisoned in a refugee camp while the airliners were blown up.

It was a bold stroke, a daring piece of "theatre". But it was too much for Hussein. His loyal Bedouins had been given new tanks and artillery and they were itching to get at the cocky Palestinians who had virtually taken over their country. On September 17th Hussein slipped the leash and his men roared into the refugee camps. There was bitter and bloody fighting during which Hussein had to counter a thrust from the north by a Syrian armoured column moving to help the guerrillas. But by the end of that "Black September" the guerrilla presence in Jordan had been virtually destroyed. Palestinians died in their hundreds, and thousands more fled. They fled to Syria, some even crossed the Jordan and surrendered to the Israelis. But most crossed over into the Lebanon.

There they nursed their hatred – and by now they hated Hussein almost as much as they hated the Israelis. They licked their wounds and turned once more to the only weapon that was left to them: terrorism. Fatah formed Black September, choosing the name to commemorate those who had died that month in Jordan. It was a loose organisation under the control of Abu Iyad and several other chieftains. They picked men from the ranks of Fatah and other organisations for specific operations, they were helped by Arab embassies, especially the Libyan embassies, in foreign countries, and they drew on the sympathy of foreign revolutionaries.

They killed Wasfi Tell, Hussein's Prime Minister, on the steps of the Sheraton Hotel in Cairo; they wounded Zeid Rifai, Jordan's Ambassador to London, as he drove to the Embassy in his Daimler. They killed for revenge and in desperation, to prove that despite the disaster in Jordan they were a force the world dared not ignore.

But, as usual, it was the PFLP that stole the headlines. With their dreams of world revolution, they had always been more internationally involved than Fatah, and Habash saw the way to use the terrorist movements which were blossoming in various countries not only to augment his own small force, but also to provide an international network of killers who would carry out operations on each other's behalf in the name of revolution. In May 1972 he organised an international symposium of terrorists at the PFLP-controlled Baddawi refugee camp in the Lebanon where the leaders of the various groups he had been cultivating met to discuss the establishment of what amounted to a multi-national corporation of terrorism. Andreas Baader of the Baader-Meinhof anarchist gang of Germany was there, so was Fusako Shigenobu, leader of the Japanese Red Army. Black September sent Abu Iyad and another leader, Fuad Shemali. There were representatives from the IRA, from the Turkish "People's Liberation Army", from the "Liberation Front" of Iran and from various South American organisations.

At the end of the month PFLP counted its first profit from its new terrorist corporation. Three young members of the Japanese Red Army sprayed the arrival hall at Tel Aviv's Lod airport with bullets and grenades and killed several people. PFLP hailed this massacre as a great victory, as proof that nowhere was safe for the Israelis. Three months later Black September attacked at Munich. This time the "hit team" were all Arabs, but essential support was provided by French sympathisers with the Arab cause and by PFLP's Baader-Meinhof allies in Germany, loaned to Abu Iyad for the occasion by Wadi Hadad.

Again, the slaughter was acclaimed throughout the Arab world as a heroic achievement. Only King Hussein among the Arab leaders called it a crime.

Chapter Two
After the games — the chase

AFTER THE MUNICH OUTRAGE THE ISRAELIS DECIDED TO TAKE A terrible revenge, to kill every Arab who had taken part. The Israelis had sworn "Never again" after six million Jews had entered Hitler's gas chambers without putting up a fight. Now, nobody could harm a Jew and not expect retaliation. An eye for an eye, a tooth for a tooth, was the old saying. After Munich it was to be a life for a life. Drawing on the hard men of Arik Sharon's "Unit 101", the Israeli equivalent of the Special Air Service, they built a small but highly efficient killer squad known as the "Wrath of God". Its members were expert in killing with their favourite weapon, the high velocity .22 pistol, and they were set loose to avenge Munich. This Israeli decision transformed, by extending it, the whole range of terrorist operations in Europe.

Wael Zwaiter was the first man to die. Employed as a clerk at the Libyan Embassy in Rome, he was actually Fatah's representative. He was shot twelve times by two men armed with .22 pistols who ambushed him as he entered the elevator leading to his apartment. He was mourned by his friends as a peaceful intellectual, but the Israelis claimed that although he might have been an intellectual he was far from being peaceful and was Black September's agent for Italy.

The next man on the Israeli death list was Mahmoud Hamshari, officially the PLO's representative in Paris, but in fact Black September's Number 2 for France. He was killed by a bomb wired to his telephone. "Is that you Monsieur Hamshari?" asked a caller. "Yes, this is Mahmoud Hamshari," he replied. And the telephone exploded in his face.

Then it was the turn of Dr. Bassel Rauf Kubeisy, Professor of Law at the American University in Beirut and a leading member of the PFLP. He was killed in the shadow of the Madeleine Church in Paris by two young men who pumped ten bullets into him from .22 pistols as he cried: "Non! Non! Ne faites pas cela."

The Israelis did not have it all their own way. In January 1973, Baruch Cohen, their chief agent in Madrid, was shot dead as he sat talking to an Arab outside a pavement café. The Arab, who Baruch thought was working for him, put his hand in his pocket ostensibly to bring out a list of names, but instead of the list he produced a pistol and shot Baruch four times.

This bitter game of kill and counterkill went on all over the Middle East and Europe. It even reached Norway and the United States. The Israelis launched a daring raid on Beirut and killed three leading Palestinians, men were blown up by bombs in their beds in Cyprus, shot down in restaurants in Paris and mutilated by letter bombs. It was in this doom-laden atmosphere, with the Palestinians under intense pressure from the Israelis and with their overseas groups breaking down as their regional chiefs were killed one after the other, that Mohamed Boudia was efficiently, if somewhat messily, despatched from this life by an Israeli car-bomb.

Boudia, a forty-one-year-old Algerian, was a prime target for the Israelis. He was Black September's chief operative in France and had been so successful that his authority had penetrated into other countries.

He knew he was being hunted and he kept on the move, rarely spending the night at his own home, preferring to stay, both for safety and for pleasure, with one of his harem of mistresses. But at eleven o'clock on the morning of June 28th 1973, after a night spent in one of these "safe houses", he climbed into his metal-blue Renault 16 which had been parked all night in the rue des Fosses St. Bernard. As he settled his weight into the driving seat there was a flash and a roar. The car's doors were blown open, the roof was peppered with holes like a colander. Little other damage was done to the car, but Boudia died instantly.

The police investigators were considerably puzzled. For some convoluted reason, another of Boudia's women friends told them that he had spent the night with her on the other side of Paris. If this was true, and if a bomb had been planted in the car during the night, it would have been impossible for Boudia to travel across Paris without setting it off. Furthermore, no sign could be found of any wiring mechanism attached to the ignition. The usual way of setting a car-bomb is to arrange for a lump of plastic explosive, or several sticks of gelignite, to be detonated by the car's own electrical system when the ignition is switched on.

The police were also puzzled by the fact that Boudia, a trained agent who knew he was in danger, had apparently made no effort to make sure his car was "clean".

It was thought, therefore, that he had "scored an own goal" – that he had killed himself with explosive which he was delivering to an Arab bomb factory and which had gone off accidentally. Later, how-ever, it was discovered that a bomb had been placed under the driver's seat and that it had been actuated by pressure, just like a war-time landmine. It needed no wiring, but when Boudia sat on the driver's seat his weight forced a plunger into the detonating mechanism and the "mine" went up. Just to make absolutely sure, it had been packed with what is known in Ireland as "shipyard confetti", a deadly type of shrapnel composed of nuts and bolts. It was this which peppered the car's roof.

An ingenious device, and bad luck on any terrorist. Indeed, Boudia may well have been more careful than the police thought. Perhaps he did check his engine to make sure there was no gelignite wired to the ignition. Perhaps he did look at his exhaust pipe to make sure there was no plastic explosive moulded round it. It is unlikely that even an accomplished agent would think of looking for a landmine under his seat.

Boudia had led a many-sided life in Paris. His cover was his post as administrative director of the state-subsidised Théâtre de l'Ouest Parisien. In this capacity he was constantly in touch with left-wing intellectual circles in which he was known as a Marxist opponent of President Houari Boumedienne of Algeria. Boudia had been a sup-porter of Ahmed Ben Bella; and when Ben Bella was deposed and imprisoned by Boumedienne, Boudia was forced to flee the country. His Marxism and opposition to Boumedienne took him to the dismal "bidonvilles", the Arab shanty-towns on the outskirts of Paris, where he plotted with other exiled Algerians.

He drew on both intellectuals and slum dwellers to provide recruits for his essential activity, Black September. His "cell" was built round Mahmoud Hamshari, who was combined adjutant, quartermaster and finance officer, and the Algerian brothers Mohamed and Amine Ben Mansour, who were his technical wizards. Working in their makeshift laboratory-workshops in villas at Igny and Fontenay-sur-Roses, they were able to turn out a weird but deadly array of explosives ranging from a conventional time-bomb to an incendiary Tampax.

Boudia was a busy man. In the one month of February 1972 his team of saboteurs and hit-men carried out at least four operations. They set fire to more oil tanks in the Netherlands; murdered five Jordanians in West Germany on the grounds that they were collaborating with the Israelis; blew up a factory making motors for Israel in Hamburg; and damaged an oil pipeline, also in Hamburg.

From then on there were so many incidents in Europe, many of them aimed at multi-national corporations accused of aiding Israel, that it is impossible yet to sort out which were Boudia operations and which were carried out by rival organisations. The Italian police, however, were in no doubt about whom they considered responsible for blowing up the Transalpine oil pipeline at Trieste on August 5th 1972. They issued a warrant for Boudia's arrest.

That warrant was never executed, for just three weeks later Black September struck at Munich. And the Israelis, sure that Boudia had played an important part in planning the operation, marked him down for death.

It has been important to write in some detail about Boudia because not only did his death bring Carlos into the act like some demon appearing on the stage with a loud bang and a puff of smoke, but also he left Carlos a valuable legacy, a truly international network of agents. What Carlos did thereafter was to build on that legacy, using many of Boudia's techniques – the use of innocent women as cover is one, and involvement in left-wing student affairs in Paris is another – to develop his own brand of international terrorism.

Boudia had contacts with the Turkish Dev Gench (Popular Army) group and the Baader-Meinhof gang along with various splinter groups of anarchists in France and Italy. For operations he used a mixture of Arabs and French leftists. One of his most successful agents was a glamorous blonde, Evelyne Barges, who was not only an agent but also his cashier at the theatre. On Boudia's orders, she blew up three oil tanks belonging to Gulf Oil at Rotterdam in March 1971. It was a spectacular success, a sign of things to come, although its importance was not fully recognised at the time.

After Rotterdam, Boudia set about planning for what should have been his most audacious operation: a series of attacks on Tel Aviv's tourist hotels and restaurants, at a time when they would be crowded with visitors for the Christian Easter and the Jewish Passover celebrations. To carry out these attacks he put together the "Easter Commando". This consisted of Evelyne Barges, the committed terrorist; two Moroccan sisters, Nadia and Marlene Bardali, the daughters of a rich merchant, who were by no means committed to terrorism and later told an Israeli court that they had acted out of love for their Arab boyfriends and were described in Lebanese newspapers as "nymphomaniac terrorists"; and an elderly French couple who had been paid £850 and given return tickets to smuggle detonators and timing devices into Israel.

The Mansour brothers had equipped this unlikely commando with an astonishing variety of pyrotechnics. The three young women had explosives in liquid and powder form hidden in the false lining of their brassières, girdles, hollowed-out shoe-heels and lipsticks. Even their Tampax had been soaked in inflammable fluid. The linings of the Moroccan girls' long, fashionable coats were impregnated with a liquid which, when combined with another chemical carried by Evelyne Barges, would have turned the girls into walking napalm bombs.

The members of the "Commando" set off separately only a month after Evelyne's Rotterdam exploit. But the Israelis are far more security-conscious than the Dutch. They picked up the Bardali girls immediately and they quickly confessed. Then Evelyne and the French couple were arrested and all were put on trial. Evelyne told the court: "I considered the Palestinians' cause against Israel the same as that created by French colonisation in Algeria. That's why I wanted to help them."

She was sentenced to fourteen years' imprisonment, and at the age of twenty-five her prospects seemed dark. However, the sentences on all five were commuted and they are now free. One of the reasons for this leniency was that they wrote out full confessions, naming Boudia as their boss, and the Israelis later used photocopies of these confessions to justify Boudia's assassination. The girls also gave the Israelis details of the Mansour brothers' explosive factories. This information was passed on to the French authorities, but when the police raided the two villas they found that their birds had flown. Because their policy was to woo Arab opinion the French adopted a hands-off policy towards Boudia and although his activities were now well known they allowed him to go about his business. It must be remembered that all this took place before Lod and before Munich.

Boudia was killed while Evelyne was still in prison, but it was her flat, let to another friend, that he had been visiting. It seems, however, that what happened did not lessen her revolutionary ardour. At the time of writing she is again in prison, jailed by the French police for planning three bombings in Paris in May 1976. The bombs were ineffectual. One, planted at the Exhibition Centre at Porte de Versailles where a Zionist meeting was to be held, failed to explode after passers-by accidentally trampled on its fuse. Evelyne's group gave itself the grand title of the "International Revolutionary Front" but it seems to have been composed of small-time crooks. However, the *Journal du Dimanche*, describing her as "a true revolutionary, a professional of clandestinity and of terror attacks", calls her "Carlos in a skirt".

Chapter Three
Enter Carlos

THE WANTED NOTICE FOR CARLOS PUT OUT BY INTERPOL SAYS OF HIM: "Individu Très Dangereux. N'Hésite Pas A Faire Usage De Ses Armes."

How did it happen? How did it come about that the podgy, guitar-playing womaniser who was so well known as a playboy on the diplomatic party roundabout in London turned into this trigger-happy public enemy? To answer this question one must look at his father, José Altagracia Ramirez Navas, a millionaire and revolutionary, for few sons have been fashioned by their fathers so completely as Carlos has been by his.

Small and frail-looking, with white hair cut in the Roman style, and a fanatic's eyes gleaming from deep-set sockets, he is now in his sixties. In his youth he was deeply religious and spent two years training for the Roman Catholic priesthood. But, tortured by doubt, he decided that he had no vocation for the Church and fled the seminary to study law in Bogota, Colombia. As so often happens when a man flees from one set of convictions and disciplines, the swing of the pendulum took him to the opposite extreme and he became a Communist of the mos' fervent variety, finding his true vocation in the convictions and disci-plines of this other religion. He became a Stalinist and the Soviet dictator could do no wrong in the young lawyer's eyes. At the same time he did not neglect the material side of his life and in a series of property deals, particularly in the Venezuelan port of Barcelona, he became rich.

His conversion to Communism was in itself part of the process which made his then unborn son into a terrorist, for it was carried out by two men who played a large part in Latin American revolutionary politics. One was Jorge Eliecer Gaitan, the Colombian Populist leader who was murdered in 1948, shot down while he was walking to a meeting with a group of students among whom was the young Fidel Castro.

This killing led to the mob taking over Bogota for three days in an uprising which became known as the "Bogotazo". It left the capital in ruins and brought about five savage years of terrorism and repression which became notorious as the time of "La Violencia". Gaitan was a natural leader who commanded passionate loyalties and it is possible that if he had lived he would have filled the role of a Fidel Castro in Colombia, years before Castro fought his way to power.

The other man who made young Ramirez see the Communist light was Gustavo Machado who, with his brother, Eduardo, led the then outlawed Venezuelan Communist Party. In an interview soon after the OPEC affair, Machado said: "The oddest thing is that Ramirez, who for a long time played an important role in the Party, finally broke with us. After the Krushchev Report [Krushchev's secret speech to the 20th Communist Party Conference in 1956 in which he repudiated Stalin] and the beginning of the détente he began saying that we were too soft and too conservative. He was tempted by the far left which he considered more truly revolutionary."

The background to Ramirez's break with the Communist Party lies in the equivocal stand on revolution taken by the official Communist Parties in Latin America. The Communists did nothing, for example, to bring the "Bogotazo" to a successful revolutionary conclusion, and most of its leaders went into hiding while the mob rampaged through the city. And, in particular, the Venezuelan branch of the Party has turned its face against revolution. As Richard Gott in his *Guerrilla Movements in Latin America* says somewhat disdainfully: "The Communist Party of Venezuela at its Seventh Plenum in April 1965, decided to give priority to the legal struggle. The other parties in the continent followed suit during the course of the next three years." Castro, the advocate of guerrilla warfare, quarrelled bitterly with the Venezuelans at the Tricontinental conference and accused them of betraying the Venezuelan "freedom fighters". Castro's arguments prevailed and the conference, at which the "freedom fighters" were heavily represented, defeated the cautious views of the Russian-sponsored official parties.

Ramirez was on the side of the activists from 1956 onwards. He argued that Machado and his colleagues had become too closely tied to Moscow, too conformist and too staid, and he broke with them. He moved far to the left and toyed with Maoism even before the quarrels at the Tricontinental.

Carlos, who was born on October 12th 1949, the eldest of the three sons of José Ramirez and his plump, good-looking wife, Elba Maria Sanchez, grew up in this fevered political atmosphere. His father named the three boys Ilich, Lenin and Vladimir after the Bolshevik leader and set about bringing them up as good revolutionaries, yet making sure that his wealth meant that they lacked for nothing. Carlos told Zaki Yamani, while he and the kidnapped Saudi Arabian Oil Minister were flying to Algiers, that he had begun his terroristic activities at the age of fourteen.

He would certainly have had every opportunity at that age, for when he became fourteen, in 1963, Caracas was engulfed in urban guerrilla warfare. Régis Debray in his book *Latin America: the Long March* described what the city was like at that time:

Not a day went by without simultaneous armed engagements in different ranchos. At nightfall the shooting began, to die away only with the dawn. The operations included harassing the forces of repression, ambushes, full-scale battles against the army, and even complete occupation of a neighbourhood which became for a few hours a liberated territory until the concentrations of armed groups in a small area became untenable and they evaporated. The aim was to pin down the military in Caracas, to wear them out, to divide them in order to hasten demoralisation and desertion ...

Debray was, of course, writing from a committed revolutionary viewpoint but, nevertheless, the situation he described must have been an ideal training ground for the young terrorist.

There is another aspect of Carlos's development which should also be considered. His father remembers him as a shy, quiet child with much less self-assurance than his brothers. He was even then tending to put on weight and his thinner, sharper brothers teased him about it. Someone gave him the nickname Muchacho Gordo, the Little Fat One, and even today he is still called El Gordo, the Fat One, although some of the local Venezuelan papers have taken to calling him, with some pride, El Gran Carlos. He retaliated to the teasing by promising that one day the world would take notice of him.

Dr. Jacques Leauté, Director of the Institute of Criminology in Paris, analyses him in this way: "There exists in him a number of fascinating paradoxes. By the very nature of his work the terrorist must shun, at all costs, publicity or exposure of his identity. Yet here we have this Carlos who thrives on international exposure and attention." He thinks this need to mix murder with a craving for juvenile attention can be traced to the family training.

Carlos left school in 1966 and his father sent him abroad to finish his education. He travelled in the Caribbean and went to Mexico and then, late in the year, arrived in Cuba to attend one of Castro's training camps for young guerrillas.

Orlando Castro Hidalgo, a defector from Castro's secret service, tells in his book *Spy for Fidel* how these camps are run:

One of the first functions of DGI [Dirección General de Inteligencia] was the running of special schools for the training of Latin Americans in guerrilla warfare and subversive techniques. At one time, early in the sixties, as many as 1,500 men a year were being brought to Cuba for training ... Cuba's virtual exclusion from the hemispheric political system sharply cut down transportation means to and from the island. Nevertheless, flights have continued between Havana and Mexico City and Madrid and there are also flights to and form the island. Nevertheless, flights have continued between were utilised to bring Latin Americans to Cuba, and use was also made of clandestine methods: Communist freighters and Cuban fishing boats. Once in Havana, the trainees were grouped by nationality. Usually there were fifteen to twenty-five men in each group, although there might be as few as three. The various nationalities were generally kept apart, for security reasons as well as because the courses given to the different groups varied. Venezuelans concentrated on guerrilla operations and sabotage techniques. Chileans, coming from a country with a strong Communist Party, were coached on furthering the Communist cause through political methods. [This was written before Allende achieved power with the first elected Marxist government to be voted freely into office anywhere in the world.] Guerrilla warfare courses lasted three to six months, but occasionally as long as a year. Trainees showing particular promise were sometimes given additional training to become intelligence agents when they returned to their home countries.

In June 1967 a Venezuelan, Manuel Carrasquel, told an investigating committee of the Organisation of American States about the training his group had received in various subjects. They included tactics, weapon training, bomb making – particularly how to blow up oil pipelines – map reading, cryptography, photography, the falsification of documents, and disguise.

Carlos went through his training at Camp Mantanzas, one of three such camps around Havana. He was one of a hundred young Venezuelans being educated in the art of subversion. Their professor was the notorious General Viktor Simenov of the KGB who had been posted to Havana to become the operational boss of the Cuban secret service.

John Barron in his authoritative book on the KGB says the organisation has intensified its recruitment of DGI personnel as Soviet agents and ensconced General Simenov in an office next to that of the DGI chief. Simenov must approve the annual operational plans for all DGI divisions. He and his KGB subordinates monitor all operations and communications involving any DGI agent of sensitivity or importance.

Another instructor was Antonio Dages Bouvier, an Ecuadorian expert in guerrilla warfare.

Carlos's involvement in this scene of international communist skulduggery is known because when Castro Hidalgo defected from the Cuban Embassy in Paris and was debriefed by the CIA, he named Carlos as one of the Venezuelan "students" in Cuba.

This early training, along with his experience in the Caracas rioting and the political indoctrination carried out by his father, should have made of Carlos a formidable operator. As it was, his first operation was a hopeless shambles. For some time the Cubans had been landing small parties of insurgents on the Venezuelan coast. In May 1967 the Venezuelan army rounded up a group which included four Cubans. A year later the Cubans tried again and this time they sent Carlos. But he was picked up almost immediately by the police. They questioned him, could prove nothing, and turned him loose to flee back to Cuba.

Later that same year the Cubans tried again. Carlos was sent back to Venezuela to help stir up trouble at the University of Caracas in imitation of the student revolt in Paris. But again he failed. He was arrested for the second time and on this occasion the police grilled him for twelve hours. He was released only after the intervention of his father. These two episodes are referred to rather delicately in one Caracas newspaper which mentions that he entered Venezuela "on at least one occasion without leaving any record with the Venezuelan Immigration Service".

Carlos's exact movements at this time cannot be plotted. His mother and father had separated, and his mother, considerably younger than his father, had moved to London with Lenin and Vladimir. They lived in a series of flats in Kensington and Paddington and Mrs. Ramirez-Sanchez, well provided with money from her husband who had retired to the old-world town of San Cristobal in the foothills of the Andes, entered with some gusto into the Latin American diplomatic whirl in London.

The next move by Carlos which can be positively assigned is to Lumumba University in Moscow, where the Russians gather in students from all over the Third World, teach them ordinary university subjects, indoctrinate them in Communism and, if they show sufficient aptitude and loyalty, train them as members of the KGB. Then there is a further selection and the élite go on to be trained by Department V, the KGB's Assassination and Sabotage squad. A Russian defector who had been a teacher at Lumumba told us that ninety per cent of the staff are KGB members and that all the Russian students who are sent there to leaven the Third World mixture are either agents or stooges of the KGB. These Russian students, who form twenty-five per cent of the student body which now averages around 20,000, are handpicked and thoroughly briefed on their responsibility to spread the Communist word among the foreign students, and to report back on the students' attitudes. But there is more to it than that. Very few of the Third World students are chosen to become members of the KGB. Most of them finish their courses and go home to become doctors, engineers, civil servants and take their place among the new leadership of the developing countries. Only later, when they have achieved positions of power, do they find that Russian students with whom they were friendly at Lumumba suddenly turn up as diplomats and journalists and seek to renew the friendship. Then the pressure is on. It can be done gently on the old-boy basis, or it can be done roughly on the basis of blackmail through some sexual indiscretion committed in Moscow. And that must apply to almost everybody, because the students spend several years at Lumumba without their families and girlfriends, unable to afford the fare home. The KGB are expert at blackmail and do not hesitate to use it.

Carlos, however, was a different proposition. Along with his brother Lenin, who had joined him at the university, he received a large allowance from his father and revelled in his indiscretions. Gustavo Machado says rather ruefully: "Before accepting him Moscow asked us for more information. I told them that I would stand as his guarantor. Later I had to change my tune. With his knack of drawing attention to himself he began leading a dolce vita life, chasing the girls. They didn't like that in Moscow. He once had himself photographed in Russian folklore costume strumming a balalaika. I saw him in Moscow and tried to reason with him."

But Carlos would not listen to reason and when the Soviet authorities asked his father to send him less money the bourgeois revolutionary refused, saying: "My sons have never lacked for anything."

Students in Moscow still use old-fashioned fountain pens and the only ink available is a bright violet colour. Most of the embassies in Moscow are painted either a custard yellow or apple green and when pots of violet ink are hurled against them there is gaudy but otherwise harmless evidence that someone has taken exception to the policies of that embassy's government. Violet ink, therefore, became the permitted weapon for Russian students in their carefully staged demonstrations. Sometimes, however, demonstrations are mounted which are not arranged by the authorities and then the police move in and break them up. This happened in 1969 when the Libyan students at Lumumba marched on their embassy in protest against their new government's refusal to renew their visas – Colonel Gaddafi had just brought off his coup in Libya – and Carlos marched with them in a gesture of solidarity. The police stopped the Libyans, but allowed the white man, Carlos, through. He picked up an inkpot and threw it at the embassy. But he missed and the inkpot went flying through the window of a private house. The occupants were none too pleased, and Carlos once again found himself under arrest. The police gave him a stiff warning and he was summoned to appear before the university disciplinary committee. Shortly afterwards he was expelled from the university and from Russia "for anti-Soviet provocation and leading a dissipated life".

The question that must be asked is: can this be accepted at face value, or was it an elaborate charade? The KGB love these little games.

For instance, there was the case of the foreign ambassador who unwisely decided to take a Russian woman to bed. She assured him that it was quite safe, her husband was a geologist and he was somewhere in the Urals digging up rocks. But no sooner were they in bed than the door burst open and a burly KGB man wearing a bush jacket burst in brandishing a geologist's hammer. The ambassador was beaten up and subsequently blackmailed, while the KGB congratulated themselves on producing another successful scenario. There is every probability that Carlos's expulsion was similarly contrived, with the aim of wiping out his police record in Caracas by enabling him to pose as a "ne seriosnik", a playboy who has rebelled against Communism. The evidence in support of this theory is circumstantial but persuasive.

In the first place there are persistent reports from a number of sources that he returned to Russia in 1974 with a PFLP group undergoing special training at a Russian camp. Some of these reports come from Arab terrorists who have been captured by the Israelis and swear that they saw Carlos in the camp.

Certainly the Russians are encouraging non-Arabs to join the terror squads of the Palestinian organisations, for two good reasons. In the first place, the Russians consider these squads to be the best form of active service training for international subversion; and in the second, with their own men in squads, they will not only be kept informed about developments but will also have a voice in making decisions.

As is customary with their planning they are taking a long-term view as well as looking for immediate advantage and they are trying to build into the Palestinian organisations a second generation of leadership in anticipation of the natural or violent disappearance of the present leaders. They are doing this by the infiltration of Palestinian Communist Party members into the rank and file of the organisations and through the indoctrination of Arab students at Lumumba and the ideological courses which are run parallel with the military courses for Palestinians belonging to the left-wing organisations.

While Carlos as a non-Arab will never be one of the political leaders of the Palestinians, nevertheless his position as chief hit-man for the PFLP gives him a degree of influence and a continual flow of information, both of which are invaluable to the Kremlin. And who knows? he may one day return to his home continent to serve the cause through Latin American terrorism.

Another factor which makes his continued involvement with the

Russians likely is his close association with members of the Cuban DGI. The KGB has been using Cubans for operations in places such as Portugal where they merge more easily into the background than Russians. The use of Cuban troops as a surrogate Red Army in Angola is simply a military extension of this long-standing practice.

The consensus among the many people we have consulted about Carlos's Russian links is that while he is not directly controlled by the KGB and has developed into what Brian Jenkins describes as a "free-lance type of individual who is in terrorism as a vocation as opposed to dedication", he nevertheless maintains a close contact with the Russians on a number of levels: through the PFLP's official contacts; through the Cubans; and through his own "case officer".

Zaki Yamani, who spent long, frightening hours talking to his kidnapper, says: "He has some activities the dimensions of which were set for him by Moscow. But he grew bolder and went beyond the limits. His ambition spurred him to establish his own identity . . . Carlos sits now on the throne of a terroristic organisation which has an international structure and he offers his services to those who need them and whose aims are either directly or indirectly in tune with his . . . He is not a committed Communist, and when he talked to us he did not hesitate to describe contemporary Bolshevik principles as demagogic. Carlos does not believe in the Palestinian cause or in Arab nationalism, but, as he said, he considers them as a phasial step or as a factor helping the spread of the International Revolutionary Movement."

Whatever doubts there might be about his connections with the KGB, there are none about his involvement with the most militant Palestinians. The PFLP boasts that he belongs to them and is "an agent of the Palestinian revolution". After his "expulsion" from Lumumba he stayed for some weeks in East Berlin, which has become a staging post for terrorists on the move to and from European targets. He returned to London and spent some time with his mother, about whom he is most solicitous and whom he resembles facially. Then he moved on to the Middle East in time for Black September, fought with the guerrillas against Hussein's army, and did so well that he was taken into the PFLP by Wadi Hadad.

After his stay in the Middle East, Carlos returned to London where he built up his cover as an irresponsible playboy. His mother – quite ignorant, it appears, of his other life – put his name down for entry to the London School of Economics. But he did not do much studying.

He taught languages for some time at the Langham Secretarial College where he is remembered as a conceited womaniser. He escorted his mother to diplomatic parties and cut a dash in the Latin American community in London. He played poker, sang to his guitar, spent his generous allowance from his father and led an apparently carefree life. Nevertheless, he was making his preparations. He had long since been taught by his instructors in subversion to "surround yourself with pretty young girls". It was a counsel he followed with much pleasure and assiduity. The women he seduced were mostly innocent ones, not at all involved in terrorism. But he intended to use them to provide him with cover, and with "safe houses" where he could store guns, money and false documents.

During this period Antonio Bouvier, who had been one of his instructors in Cuba, arrived in London and they set up a headquarters together in a Kensington flat. Carlos at this stage was often short of money despite the allowance of between £1,000 and £1,500 a month which his father made to the family. Señora Sanchez liked the social life and developed an expensive taste for antique furniture so that Carlos, himself a big spender, was often short. However, he had an additional source of funds: he was able to draw on an account opened by Bouvier – possibly Carlos's "case officer" and working for the KGB – in his middle name of Dages.

So Carlos continued his pleasant double life in London. But soon something happened which brought the world close to war, changed the course of Middle East politics and, consequently, altered the conduct of international terrorism.

At two in the afternoon of October 6th, the Day of Atonement, the holiest day in the Jewish calender, the Egyptian and Syrian armies, equipped with the most modern Russian weapons, struck at Israel. It was a deadly little war. The Israelis, made over-confident by twenty-five years of military success, were caught by surprise. Their vaunted tanks and fighter bombers wilted under the fire of Russian missiles bravely handled by the Egyptians and Syrians. The Israeli Southern Command and the Government itself, plagued by quarrelling generals, came close to panic. But the Israelis, almost miraculously, pulled themselves together and the war ended with their tanks on the road to Damascus and with a task force, led by Arik Sharon, across the Suez Canal and into Egypt proper with little standing between them and Cairo. So great was this danger to the stability of the Egyptian régime that the Russians threatened to send in an airborne force, and the United States declared a worldwide state of alert which had its men and missiles preparing for war. This situation obviously could not be allowed to persist and so Russia and the United States imposed peace on the Middle East.

It was a peace which left Palestinian politics even more confused than before and made the Palestinians even more fearful for their future. The secret underground war of kill and counterkill had already been dying out before the big war started. Black September had ceased operations after the murder in Khartoum, on March 2nd 1973, of the American Ambassador Mr. Cleo Noel and his deputy Mr. George Curtis Moore, along with Belgian diplomat M. Guy Eid. It was now accepted that Black September was a branch of Fatah, and the shocked reaction to these killings convinced Arafat that Black September as an organisation had outlived its usefulness and had become a threat to his political plans.

The Israelis, too, had given up the game of assassination after one of their operations in Norway had gone sour. Their first team of assassins, worn out by the strain of killing and trying to stay alive, was being rested when the news arrived in July 1973 that Ali Hassan Salemeh had been spotted in Lillehammer. Salemeh was one of the men most responsible for Munich. He was marked for death. And so the Israelis scraped together a second eleven to kill him. But the operation went disastrously wrong. The man they killed with their .22 pistols was a Moroccan waiter married to a Norwegian. Six of the hit-team were caught by Norwegian police, two of them in the home of Yigal Eyal, the security chief of the Israeli Embassy. In the trial, which caused great embarrassment to the Israelis, the full story was told and five of the group were sent to prison. It was to be the last operation carried out by the Wrath of God. Both Fatah and the Israelis had found the war of assassination too costly in diplomatic terms.

The situation was altered further by Secretary of State Henry Kissinger's step-by-step negotiations with Egypt, Syria and Israel in his attempts to bring about a permanent settlement in the Middle East. Arafat, scenting that a Palestinian state with himself at its head could emerge from such a settlement, took the majority of the PLO along with him in agreeing to the negotiations. However, he was bitterly opposed by George Habash and Wadi Hadad who, with Ahmed Jibril's PFLP General Command, the Iraqi-sponsored Arab Liberation Front and the tiny, ineffective Palestine Popular Struggle Front, formed the Front of Refusal which rejects any sort of compromise with the Israelis. Arafat also had to put down opposition in his own organisation from those who wanted to fight Israel to destruction. His principal opponent was his second in command Abu Iyad who, even when agreeing to give up terrorism and to negotiate, still mounted an assassination attempt against King Hussein of Jordan at the Rabat summit conference of Arab leaders.

Abu Iyad's hatred for Hussein is pathological. It stems from an incident during the Black September period when he was captured by Hussein's men. He was taken before Hussein who treated him kindly and persuaded him to make a broadcast calling on his comrades to stop fighting. Furthermore, when the fighting was over Hussein released him. Abu Iyad has never forgiven Hussein for publicising his display of weakness and even after the Rabat attempt had failed and he had incurred the wrath of the Arab leaders, he swore to a group of students in Beirut: "We failed this time, but we will try again and again until we get him."

By the end of 1973 the Arab kaleidoscope had come to rest for a time and the picture showed the opposition to any form of agreement with the Israelis centring round the newly formed Front of Refusal and militant members of Fatah. For them the fight was still on and any form of terrorism was justified. They got the backing they needed from another Arab who rejected any form of deal with Israel. This was President Moammer Gaddafi of Libya, a religious and nationalistic fanatic. Gaddafi stopped his payments to Fatah and gave them to the Rejection Front instead. He also formed his own terrorist band and we shall reveal more about him and his personal terrorists in a later chapter. The division between Arafat and his followers on the one hand and Gaddafi's men and the Rejection Front on the other was so deep and so bitter that open warfare broke out between them.

It was in this atmosphere that Carlos was let loose to do what he could, not only to strike at the Israelis, but also to damage the prospects of any settlement in the Middle East which would leave the state of Israel in being. He was being used to further political ends by terroristic means.

His first known act of terrorism was carried out in London on Sunday evening, December 30th 1973, when he shot Mr. Joseph Edward ("Teddy") Sieff, the President of Marks and Spencer.

The shooting was carefully planned and boldly carried out in the style which has become recognisably his own. He knocked on the door of the Sieff home in Queen's Grove, St. John's Wood, shortly before seven o'clock and pointed a 9 mm pistol at the man who answered the door, Sieff's butler, Manuel Terloria. Carlos was wearing a parka with the hood pulled over his head and had covered the lower part of his face with a dark scarf. He ordered the frightened Terloria to take him to Mr. Sieff. The butler tried to gain time by leading the gunman into the lounge, but Carlos threatened him and he was forced to lead the way to the first-floor bathroom where victim and gunman confronted one another. Carlos fired immediately and, expert shot that he is, hit Sieff full in the face. Sieff was saved by the fact that he has good, strong teeth. The bullet, its force spent by knocking out his two front teeth, lodged in the back of his neck, missing his jugular vein by a fraction of an inch. He survived, but the gunman escaped and at that time no one had any idea who he was. Nobody had heard of Carlos, and Sieff himself told us: "I neither saw him nor heard him speak, and I know nothing about him other than what I have read in the press." It was quite obvious, however, that Carlos knew all about his intended victim. Sieff is a keen gardener, a music lover and a patron of the arts. He is also a passionate Zionist and he and his family are revered in Israel for their support and generosity to the state and the people. Later, when Carlos's death list was found, Teddy Sieff's name was near the top. Soon after this attempted assassination PFLP claimed responsibility for it because "the British Zionist billionaire Joseph Sieff . . . gives every year millions of pounds to the Zionist usurper and his war machine . . ." Carlos was linked with the Sieff shooting when the gun that fired the shot was found among a cache of his weapons nearly two years later.

One month after the Sieff shooting a young man held open the door of the Israeli Hapoalim Bank in Cheapside in the City of London and threw in a bomb packed in a shoe box. He did not get his aim quite right, the bomb bounced off a door and exploded in front of the counter, injuring a typist. Another woman employee gave a description of the bomb thrower. It matched that of Carlos precisely. Again PFLP claimed responsibility for the attack.

It was at this time that Carlos met Angela Otaola, a twenty-three-year-old Spanish waitress who arrived in England in 1973 to learn English while working in restaurants and clubs in Piccadilly. Although she is a Basque, she has no connection with any terrorist organisation. Pert and pretty, she is, in fact, a classic example of the kind of harmless young girl from a good family Carlos frequently used to provide cover for him. He picked her up in the Ducks and Drakes pub in Bayswater and invited her out to dinner. She, as she confessed later, "became spellbound by his charms" and they became lovers. He moved into her flat on the top floor of an unfashionable house in Hereford Road, Bayswater. He took with him a black suitcase which he kept locked. The relationship lasted for eighteen months and Carlos explained his frequent absences by saying that he was an economist engaged on projects which meant that he had to travel throughout Europe. He was certainly travelling to Europe, but the projects on which he was engaged had nothing to do with economics. What Miss Otaola was not to discover until later – and it was a discovery that was to cost her a year in jail – was that her chubby lover's black suitcase contained a miniature arsenal of guns and grenades and a list of men and women to be killed, and that his absences were arranged for him so that he could carry out terrorist missions in France. When Carlos the economist left Miss Otaola's arms it was to become Carlos the killer.

The many-sided pattern of his existence was now emerging. He lived one life as a dutiful son with his attractive mother; he had his headquarters with Antonio Bouvier, the professor of terrorism, and he had his cover with Angela Otaola. He used a number of passports. We have traced five different sets of travel documents used by him. He has been Cenon Clarke of New York; Hector Hugo Dupont, an Anglo-Frenchman; Glenn Gebhard, an American; Adolf Bernal from Chile and Carlos Martinez-Torres, a Peruvian economist. Using these identities he flitted in and out of the country and nobody imagined for one moment that he was a terrorist. When he was in London he lived the good life, dancing the night away, smoking cigars and eating richly until he grew even more sensitive about being El Gordo.

Somebody who knew him then says: "He had a ball here, always out with the birds. But his mother was always in the background. He adored her and never went against her wishes." Little did his mother know what the darker side of his life involved.

There was another important strand to his life in London and that was his association with Mrs. Maria Nydia Tobon di Romero, a thirty-nine-year-old Colombian lawyer. Their friendship began at the Colombian Centre in London where she worked. But there was less innocence about this association than the affair with Angela, for Nydia Tobon had been a member of the secretariat of the pro-Soviet Colombian Communist Party, and her ex-husband, Alonso Romero Buj, was a senior Party member who worked closely with the international Communist front organisation, the World Federation of Democratic Youth. Mrs. Tobon acted as banker and a minder of false documents for Carlos, Bouvier and Moukharbel. She later told the British police that she and Carlos were both Maoists who thought that Russia was too bourgeois: "We had a certain rapport in our political thinking." She denied that she knew Carlos was a terrorist, but said she thought he was working for political exiles. At all events, Carlos was completely unsuspected by the authorities in London of any involvement with terrorism. And he hoped to follow precisely the same tactic when he was called to Paris in June 1973.

Chapter Four
Mischief in Paris

CARLOS WAS "ON ICE" IN LONDON, A "SLEEPER" WAITING FOR THE CALL
to arms, when Mohamed Boudia was killed, leaving vacant the post
of chief terrorist in Europe. Carlos got the job because he had the right
qualifications. He was an assassin and a saboteur, trained in the best
Cuban, Russian and Arab schools. He had good connections in the
diplomatic world and, capable of speaking several languages, he could
travel easily around Europe. So far as the police were concerned he
was clean and without a record; and he was a man of some presence
and culture without any of the stink of the refugee camp about him.
Above all, he was clearly not an Arab, which was an advantage at a
time when the Israeli assassination squads were prowling Europe. This
fitted him well for the initial task in France, to rebuild the network
which had been shattered by the deaths of Hamshari and Boudia, so
that it would be ready when the policy decision was made to resume
use of the terror weapon.

Carlos also had certain disadvantages. Despite later protestations,
he was not as devoted to the Palestinian cause as Boudia had been – no
non-Arab who had failed to experience their own peculiar mixture of
pride and humiliation could achieve such devotion. Furthermore, he
was quite capable of taking a "contract" for jobs on the side.

Even more important, the terror masters could not trust Carlos to
keep up the inevitable paperwork, for terrorism like any other activity
has its own kind of bureaucracy. Accounts have to be kept and
expenses must be justified. For this reason it was decided that Carlos
would be used as the chief operator, the hit-man, but that administra-

tive control would be given to a thin-faced Lebanese called Michel Moukharbel. An interior decorator who had some training in account-ancy, Moukharbel sported a moustache and was a bit of a dandy. He knew the ropes, having been used by Boudia as a courier between Paris and Wadi Hadad's headquarters. It now became his job to convey orders to Carlos, to keep the books and to maintain watch over the hot-headed Venezuelan.

He was meticulous. He kept his accounts scrupulously, entering the most minute expenditures, and indenting for their reimbursement. He also wrote a diary in which he detailed his movements and many of Carlos's. It was this diary which was eventually to give the French police a detailed picture of the ramifications of their activities. One of the first entries reads: "Marseilles. 12 August, train tickets and hotel 500 francs." An innocent enough record, but it conceals a small drama which almost brought their partnership to an end only a month after it had started. Carlos and Moukharbel went down to Marseilles to observe French anti-Algerian riots which had broken out but, inadvertently, they became involved in a race fracas and were arrested. The police, not knowing who they were, let them go and they fled back to anonymity in Paris.

There they set about their real task of building an international cell. They made contact with a Turkish People's Liberation Army group which had its headquarters at a villa in the pleasant suburban town of Villiers-sur-Marne, south of Paris. This group was organised by the widow of the man who, as a favour to the PFLP, had murdered Ephraim Elrom, the Israeli Consul General in Istanbul, in 1971. The killer was himself shot dead later by the Turkish police. The villa, a large nineteenth-century edifice with a fake Gothic tower that made it look like a Charles Addams drawing, lay in a secluded position, and a large garden protected its inmates from prying eyes, although a neighbour did report later that she had noticed a number of "students" there.

The villa provided a useful "safe house" for Carlos. He stored arms and grenades there and used it as a communications centre. But it was not as safe as it appeared to be. The Israelis suggested to the French police that they might be interested in stopping a Dodge car, peculiarly painted red with black mudguards. The police picked it up at Modane on the Franco-Italian frontier and questioned its occupants, among them a German woman.

After some persuasion they revealed that they had delivered a cargo of explosives and equipment from Bulgaria by way of Belgium to the villa at Villiers-sur-Marne. The police raided it on December 20th 1973 and arrested ten Turks, two Palestinians and one Algerian. Although they found documents showing that terrorist raids were being planned, the French authorities took no action other than to expel their prisoners, escorting them to the frontier of their choice.

As far as the Carlos complex is concerned, the most interesting discovery at the Turkish villa was of sophisticated radio transmitters and receivers. They meant nothing at the time but later they were found to match those left behind by Carlos at one of his hiding-places in Paris. The DST (Direction de la Surveillance du Territoire) is now convinced that the villa was an important operational base for Carlos and his group as well as for the Turks who manned it.

There was nothing at the villa to lead the police to Carlos. To the authorities he was absolutely unknown. But Carlos and Moukharbel decided to take no chances once they heard about the raid, and they fled across the Channel to London. It was there that Carlos was ordered into action in the militant Palestinians' campaign to wreck the Kissinger initiatives for a Middle East settlement following the Yom Kippur war. Eager to prove himself, he tried to assassinate Mr. Sieff, and followed up with the bomb attack on the Hapoalim Bank in the City of London. Neither he, nor Moukharbel, nor Bouvier, operating in London, had yet come under suspicion. This was the time of greatest freedom. Leaving Bouvier behind, Carlos and his adjutant headed back across the Channel and spent the next few months travelling round Europe, making contacts, building up the network, laying the groundwork for future operations.

Then, in June 1974, he returned to Paris to plan his first real operation there. It took place on the night of August 2nd when three car bombs exploded in the heart of the city, one at the offices of the Jewish *L'Arche* and the others at those of two French right-wing newspapers, *L'Aurore*, a daily, and *Minute*, a weekly publication. Both papers generally support the Israelis. Although the bombs caused a good deal of damage only two passers-by were injured, both slightly. Responsibility for the bombing was claimed by the "Mohamed Boudia Commando", but there is no doubt that it was organised by Boudia's successor, for detailed diagrams of all three offices, as carefully annotated as military maps, were later found among his papers.

In Paris, Carlos lived as he had done in London, using girls to provide him with bed, board, pleasure and protective camouflage. He became the lover of Nancy Sanchez, another Venezuelan, who was studying anthropology at the Sorbonne. She had a flat in the rue Toullier on the Left Bank, close to the university. It is a student quarter of shared flats, full of young people from all nations and elderly buildings from many periods of Parisian history. In this cosmopolitan atmosphere young students, ageing students, and the numerous hangers-on of the arts mingle and move round in ever-changing groups. It is ideal territory for those who wish to live unnoticed by the authorities.

We have an insight into Carlos's behaviour at the flat from Angela Armstrong, a lissom twenty-two-year-old British girl born in South Africa, who lives and works in Paris. In an interview with Don North of Canadian Television she said: "Nancy's a friend of mine. I've known her for four years. We studied sociology together at the faculty. She lived in this flat very near my work and I used to pop over at lunchtime and there were crowds of Latin Americans there. One day there was a person called Carlos, who I was told was a Peruvian. That's the first time I met him."

Nancy, who at that stage did not seem to know a great deal about Carlos, told Angela that he worked for some international company and was a commercial correspondent who travelled a good deal and had plenty of money. The fact that he was a Peruvian did not specially endear him to Angela, for she had been married to a Peruvian. As her French lawyers later told us, she feared that because the Peruvian community in Paris is a small one, Carlos might be connected with her estranged husband with whom she wanted no contact. Nancy reassured her by saying that he was not often in Paris.

Even so, Angela was not particularly impressed by Carlos:

"I came into the room, and they'd got only one big chair and he was sitting in it. He's fairly sort of well built and – I don't know how you say it – they called him El Gordo, which means the fat one. He seemed very much at home, very sure of himself, better dressed than most of the students, you know, classic clothes, not blue jeans, not long hair. And I thought he was oversure of himself. But I didn't pay him much attention at first ... He seemed sort of just to be there and he spoke to everybody as if it was his flat."

There were half-a-dozen people in the flat and when Angela, who is a great Francophile, made some conversational remark to Carlos in

French, Nancy said, "Oh, Carlos doesn't speak French." Then to prove that he could speak English, Carlos said something to Nancy in that language. "I can't remember what – 'I've been to London' – or something like that, and he spoke very good English."

Describing what life was like in the rue Toullier flat, Angela gave this impression of its atmosphere: "There were always a lot of people there. Students that lived in 8th floor rooms with no water came to have a shower, some came to do their washing, others to borrow books, or just to sit down and spend half an hour before their classes. There was a constant flow of people, you'd meet someone once and you'd never see them again. I wasn't surprised, it was the very casual relationships that you have with people."

From a terrorist's point of view, this must have been an ideal milieu. Carlos could flit in and out of such apartments which abound in Paris with no questions asked, and if anybody did show any casual interest in his movements he would only need to say that he had been on a trip, and conversation would shift to something else. He lived anonymously under cover in this way for months among people who are quite friendly with people whose second names they do not even know.

About a month after Angela's original encounter with Carlos her friend Nancy confided that he was her lover. "She told me she was rather depressed and said that he had been away for two weeks and was in Geneva. Then she said it was very serious and that in September she was thinking of permanently sharing the room with him. From then on every time I met her she talked to me about Carlos and how fantastic he was."

The fact that Nancy had fallen in love with the stout Venezuelan, and was serious about it, surprised Angela, who knew that she had many boyfriends and had always said that she believed in being free. Now she was ready to give up a lot of things for Carlos and "was very obviously dominated by him". When she spoke about him she did not talk in the same way as before, and somehow this did not fit Angela's picture of her.

A complicating factor in the rue Toullier situation was that Nancy was sharing the flat with another Venezuelan, Maria-Teresa Lara, who had introduced Carlos to Nancy. Maria-Teresa resented the fact that Carlos began to take an increasing interest in her flatmate Nancy. "Sometimes when I went there they were not talking to each other because of Carlos," reported Angela. "There was just one bedroom with a bed on each side of it with just a curtain to divide them and when Carlos spent a night there it was awkward – according to Nancy. And I thought perhaps Maria-Teresa was interested in that way in Carlos because they both liked him."

Maria-Teresa was something more than just an ordinary student. According to Angela Armstrong: "She was withdrawn and very sure of what she was doing. You felt that she had tremendous control over herself and that unlike most Latin-Americans who were here to have a good time and drink and play the guitar, she had plans. She followed her plans, she went to the library. She did certain things and had tremendous determination. She was the complete opposite of Nancy, who was very happy-go-lucky."

French lawyers acting for some of the girls after their subsequent arrest and questioning by the police are convinced that most of them were more interested in Carlos the Latin lover than in Carlos the terrorist. But in the case of Maria-Teresa they make an exception. Maître Jacques Perrot, the Paris barrister acting for Angela Armstrong, told Payne he believed Maria-Teresa was the only one of Carlos's feminine network who really understood what he was about. She was a journalist active among Cubans and other Latin-Americans and, according to Angela, she had caused trouble within the set. Maître Perrot said: "Of course, none of the girls who circulated around Carlos knew very much about the other mistresses. But it is perfectly normal for a man not to talk to one mistress about another that he enjoys simultaneously. With Carlos it was the same except that discretion about his sexual activities coincided with his desire to remain secure from prying intelligence officers. His love life also served another practical purpose, for each girl provided an additional refuge."

One of these refuges was provided by Amparo Silva Masmela, a Colombian girl who at one time worked in the head office of Lloyds Bank in Paris, near the Opéra. Carlos met her, as he had met Angela Otaola in London, by chance in a restaurant. Her flat, which was to prove vital to Carlos, was in what the estate agents call a desirable neighbourhood on the Left Bank near Les Invalides in the rue Amélie, only two blocks away from the headquarters of the SDECE, the French counter-intelligence organisation. It was in this flat that the French police were to find the treasure trove of Carlos's weapons and documents and Moukharbel's diary of revelations.

By the autumn of 1974, the Carlos complex was in full operation in Paris and we now know that he and Moukharbel were responsible for the planning, equipping and financing of the Japanese Red Army seizure of the French Embassy at The Hague. We shall describe this operation fully in a later chapter on the activities of the Japanese Red Army. All we need to note here is that the raid was mounted to secure the release of a member of the Red Army imprisoned by the French, that it was successful and that details of its organisation were faithfully recorded by Moukharbel.

He also recorded that at the planning meeting held in Zürich with the Japanese raiding force, he and Carlos had decided on a support operation if the French and Dutch governments did not give in quickly enough. On September 15th Carlos went into action. He hurled a grenade into the crowded Drugstore, a popular meeting place in St. Germain-des-Prés for Left Bank nightlifers. It killed two people, wounded a score of others and created such panic that no one saw the grenade-thrower disappear. At first it was thought the attack had been made because the establishment belonged to a rich and prominent Parisian Jew, M. Bleustein-Blanchet. But later a man telephoned the news agencies and told them that it had been a warning to the Dutch and French governments to agree to the Red Army's terms.

In the débris of the Drugstore, the police found part of the grenade's detonator and traced it. It had been fitted to an American M26 grenade of a type identical to three which were left behind by the Japanese terrorists at Schipol airport when the French and Dutch gave in to their demands and they were flown out. These grenades were traced to the same batch of seventy-five stolen in June 1972 when members of the Baader-Meinhof gang raided a US army base at Niesau, near Kaiserslautern, in West Germany. Other grenades from the batch were left behind in Carlos's Paris hideout, and this may be taken as hard evidence of the collaboration between Carlos, the Japanese Red Army and the German anarchists.

By such pieces of material evidence the counter-intelligence men in Paris were later able to build up proof of the involvement of Carlos in the organisation and execution of numerous terrorist enterprises. They believe that after the Drugstore attack his next operation in France was one to please his Latin-American friends – the assassination of Colonel Ramon Trabal, military attaché of the Uruguay Embassy in Paris at his home near the Arc de Triomphe. The Colonel had busied himself before his foreign posting with tracking down the Tupamaros terrorists in Uruguay, and South American militants argued that he was still an intelligence man. Responsibility for his murder was claimed by an international brigade and it is suspected that Carlos had a hand in it. The police report simply said: "So far enquiries have not made it possible to arrest the assassin."

Carlos was also under suspicion of being involved in the shooting, a few months later, of the Yugoslav Consul in Lyons. Of course, once the world had heard so much about the Carlos complex, and so much evidence had been produced about some events, a tendency developed to blame him for every political-seeming crime in France.

The reputation was partly of his own making, for both his Paris and London hideouts contained long death lists with names of a variety of French and British public figures marked down for execution by himself and Moukharbel. The London list consisted of no fewer than five hundred names ranging in scope from John Osborne, the playwright, and his wife Jill Bennett, by way of the impresario Bernard Delfont and the violinist Yehudi Menuhin, to the former Prime Minister Edward Heath. Teddy Sieff also appeared on the list and the attempt to murder him helped to give credence to the other threats. Sheikh Yamani of Saudi Arabia was another "listed" victim. He came close to fulfilling his role when he was captured and threatened with death during the raid on the OPEC headquarters in Vienna.

Surveying the list, those who understood little of the aims of terrorists asked why on earth such-and-such a person should appear on it. Wives of those mentioned dutifully recorded in several cases that their husbands took no interest in politics – "Why pick on him?" was the cry.

What they forgot was that the principal aim of terrorism is to terrify. The one thing that people on the death list had in common was that their names were well known. Therefore if they were assassinated the act would become part of the street theatre of violence, it would be extensively reported on television and in the newspapers. Then the terrorist organisation could claim its share of publicity, and add to the belief that terrorists will strike wherever they wish in order to achieve their political aims.

The French list was similar to the British, though perhaps with a higher political content. What gave point to it was the fact that Moukharbel, with his customary thoroughness, had noted down by many of the names the fruits of careful observation of the person concerned. To take two examples: Mr. Ben Nathan, the Israeli ambassador to Paris, and M. Jacques Soustelle, the well-known right-wing French politician, had been carefully observed – for not only were their home addresses and telephone numbers noted down, but also the network had spied out details of their habits and routine movements.

Among the overseas names of people listed for assassination the most fascinating one was that of Gihane Sadat, the half-British wife of President Sadat of Egypt. The reason for her inclusion was without doubt the fact that she had clashed in argument with President Gaddafi of Libya. A few years ago he paid a visit to Cairo pleading for Egypt to unite with Libya. In the course of debates he had rather a rough time from the sophisticated Egyptians, and in particular the ladies of the Egyptian women's liberation lobby with which Mrs. Sadat is associated. They bluntly told the fanatically Moslem President of Libya that they had no wish to be consigned to the harem just to satisfy his old-fashioned ideas. After his return home Moammer Gaddafi was so furious that he attacked Mrs. Sadat several times in public, and ludicrously put it about that she had tried to seduce him. Now in order to please his master in Libya, Carlos included her on the death list. The group also left behind precise plans for placing a time-bomb in a ship passing through the newly re-opened Suez Canal.

But these were all future targets and were not revealed until after Carlos had fled Paris. In January 1975 he was concerned with a more immediate task: the destruction of an El Al airliner at Orly airport. It is likely that this target was chosen for him by President Gaddafi as one of his attempts to avenge the loss of the Libyan airliner ruthlessly shot down by the Israelis into the Sinai Desert.

On January 13th, two men drove their Peugeot 504 onto the apron at Orly airport. A French passenger waiting for his flight saw them take out a rocket launcher wrapped in an orange cloth. They set it up and fired at a Boeing 707 of El Al as it taxied towards the runway. It was about to take off for New York with 136 passengers on board.

The Israeli pilot took evasive action as the rocket crashed into and through the fuselage of a Jugoslav DC9 waiting nearby to embark passengers for Zagreb. It failed to explode and a policeman and a steward were the only people slightly injured. Disappointed, the terrorists fired again and this time hit an administration building and caused a good deal of damage. They raced off towards Paris in their car, later found abandoned in a nearby suburb at Thiais. They left it in such a hurry that they had no time to remove the Russian-built rocket launcher with its Cyrillic markings from the back seat. The police also found a Russian-made 9mm automatic on the runway.

The attack had failed miserably and the abandoned car provided valuable clues. It also provoked a quarrel between Carlos and Moukharbel, who argued that the raid had not been well enough planned and was badly executed. Even so he had made a reconnaissance to Orly, for carefully preserved among his accounts was a two-franc ticket to the public viewing terraces at the airport. He was now in favour of abandoning the airport attack plan. But Carlos, anxious to please his patron, did not hold the same view.

It was Carlos who had his way, and six days later a man of North African appearance set up another rocket launcher on the terrace overlooking Orly-South ready to open fire on another El Al flight ready to leave for Tel Aviv. This time the Air Police who guard Orly were more alert and a police officer who saw him fired off a burst from his submachine gun. Unhurt, the terrorist fled and was joined by an accomplice, and as they ran into the main hall one threw a grenade and the other fired into the crowd. To cover their retreat into the toilets, the terrorists threw more grenades and in the confusion grabbed twenty hostages. After bargaining with the French authorities, the terrorists were allowed to leave two days later aboard an Air France flight in return for releasing their hostages.

They were never identified. But they left behind clues which at last began to set the police onto Carlos's trail. Once again a grenade was left which was later found to tally with those discovered at Carlos's flat. Two cars – a Simca 1100 and a Citröen – were found abandoned a few days later. Both of them were hire cars. In the Simca were two more grenades and a Russian automatic. The Citröen had no weapons in it, but the gang had left in it a parking ticket dated January 19th and the Hertz hire contracts for these two cars as well as for the one used in the earlier raid six days before. The DST think that the Citröen had been used by Carlos, who had gone along to superintend the raid, and hastily left when things showed signs of going wrong. It was through his carelessness in leaving the hire contracts behind that the police were able to identify the German anarchist who had hired them and so establish another link between Carlos and the Baader-Meinhof gang – although the police at that stage were still thinking in terms of the "Mohamed Boudia Commando" and not Carlos. The German had given the name of Klaus Müller and produced a driving licence to match. But when the DST checked this licence with the West German branch of Interpol they found it was among a batch stolen in West Berlin in November 1970 by Baader-Meinhof members. The West German police were later able to prove that the man who had used the licence and hired the cars was Johannes Weinrich, a twenty-eight-year-old lawyer who ran a left-wing publishing house in Frankfurt called "Red Star".

Weinrich was arrested there late in March 1975 and Carlos must have been aware of this, for he had made a clandestine trip, using a false passport, to Frankfurt in May of that year. A mutual friend and collaborator in the terrorist network named Wilfried Böse had a flat in Paris in the seedy 10th arrondissement, at 26 avenue Claude Villefaux, which Carlos and Moukharbel often used. And when Carlos returned from Frankfurt, fearing that Böse, who was a Baader-Meinhof activist, had also been "blown" by the West German security people, he brought new identity papers for him in the name of Klaudius Axel.

Böse survived his Paris experiences and later achieved a desperate notoriety by leading the terrorists who carried out the Entebbe hijacking. That was his last operation. The Israeli commandos who rescued the hostages riddled him with bullets.

It was at this time, early in 1975, that Angela Armstrong became increasingly worried about the effect Carlos was having on her friend, Nancy. Angela was too busy looking after her six-year-old daughter and working as a secretary at the Collège de France to have much time to take part in the hectic social life of the quarter. She lived out in the suburbs and could only meet friends at lunchtime or in the evenings, if she managed to make baby-sitting arrangements. But on her visits to the flat she noticed changes there. Maria-Teresa had moved out and had been replaced by another Venezuelan girl, Albaida Salazar. Angela recalls: "In retrospect some things stick out. It had been a very open studio, you just walked in and said 'Bonjour'. But about January [1975] they put in one of those peepholes. You knocked, somebody came up and looked at you and very often there was a pause ... There was a change of atmosphere and it was no longer a question of just walking in."

Made curious by these developments, Angela invited Carlos and Nancy to supper. They did not turn up. So Angela went to the rue Toullier to find out what had happened. "They were in the studio. Nancy was upset. She said she would explain, but she never did and somehow I didn't press her. But it always intrigued me why she didn't come when she obviously had not gone anywhere else and it was a Saturday night."

The truth is that things had started to go badly wrong for Carlos. The Orly rocket attacks had been fiascos and he knew that he had left incriminating clues behind. His cover had begun to crack. For the first time he began to fear the knock on the door. Then he received devastating news. Moukharbel had been arrested by Lebanese security agents at Beirut airport on June 7th.

Various reports have attributed the arrest of Moukharbel to the activities in the Middle East of French Intelligence and to the American Central Intelligence Agency, which was especially vigilant at that time because of the various plots being made to murder Secretary of State Henry Kissinger, then commuting round the Middle East. The truth is more complicated.

Moukharbel, who was born in Tripoli in the Lebanon, became involved in left-wing politics while studying art in Paris in the 1960s and gravitated to the Palestinian extremists. On his return to the Middle East he joined the Syrian People's Party and then the PFLP. But even this body was not sufficiently violent for him and after a doctrinal dispute with George Habash in 1974 he became involved, while remaining a member of PFLP, with an even more extreme Palestinian group, the Arab Communist Organisation, which believes in perpetual war against Israel. It is an organisation which exists precariously in a state of continual conflict, and whenever less vociferous groups want to try to prove that they are men of peace they tend to take it out on members of ACO. Six of its members were executed in Damascus in the summer of 1975. In Beirut at about the same time the apartments of members were searched and Kalashnikov automatic weapons seized. In these circumstances it is more than possible that Moukharbel had been denounced to the Beirut security men by political enemies in a rival terrorist group; for inter-terrorist gang warfare became common as the state of Lebanon began to disintegrate into anarchy. For all that, he remained an important link in PFLP's chain of terror.

After his arrest in Beirut, Lebanese security men carried out a prolonged interrogation of him which lasted for five days. Arab sources claim that he was tortured and that CIA and French Intelligence men also questioned him. In any case, he was released and then flew to Paris on June 13th, carrying money and operational orders for Carlos.

The terror masters wanted the Paris group to assassinate Asher Ben Natan, the Israeli ambassador to France. They also ordered the kidnapping of a Lebanese politician then staying in Switzerland. This seemed to be a fairly full programme for the Moukharbel-Carlos group, already busy organising for the month of July a conference (never in fact held) of international terrorists with representatives from a number of European groups including Germans and Spaniards, as well as Japanese.

The French security services made no attempt to prevent Moukharbel from entering France, though from the moment of his arrival they kept him under close surveillance and photographed everyone he met. The Brigade de Surveillance followed him to the flat at 26 avenue Claude Villefaux, took photographs of the arrival of Carlos and noted that Wilfried Böse, the German terrorist, also went there. As a result they prepared an order to expel Böse and send him back to Germany. Carlos was still an unknown figure to the French authorities but it was useful to establish his connection with Moukharbel.

By now Carlos was in a state of high anxiety. Moukharbel was the man he had travelled and planned operations with over the previous two years, his closest collaborator and an experienced terrorist. Yet his arrest and interrogation in Beirut cannot but have been deeply worrying, for the leader of any undercover operation must assume that if one of his people has been interrogated there is a grave danger that he has either given something away or been "turned", so that after his release he can betray other members of the group by acting as a double agent. French Intelligence men have some evidence that the meeting between Carlos and Moukharbel was a stormy one. Already they had clashed over the impulsive conduct of the two failures at Orly airport. Carlos was always difficult to discipline. And when he was worried he became tetchy and lost his temper.

The DST continued their cat-and-mouse game with Moukharbel and a few days later he flew to Geneva, partly to complete his banking arrangements, for he had a numbered account in Switzerland, and partly to contact a local group and prepare it for the kidnapping attempt. On June 21st he arrived at Heathrow airport, London, but Special Branch officers, who had been alerted by their French opposite numbers, turned him away. He circulated freely for two days until the DST tired of their game and "lifted", that is to say arrested, him.

At the same time, the DST was working methodically through the links provided by the Police Judiciare investigation after the rocket attacks at Orly. This is the kind of task at which the DST excels. Its main work is dealing with big power espionage in France and its men have long experience in the field of intelligence analysis. Through Weinrich, who had hired the Orly cars, they had probed a connection with Böse. They put their mark on the German when he met Moukharbel, and then, on June 25th, arrested him when he arrived at No. 26 avenue Claude Villefaux not knowing that Moukharbel had already been arrested. They did not hold Böse but simply, as was their practice in these matters, deported him to Germany where a mild charge was made against him and he was released. They really did him no favour. If they had put him in prison for a couple of years he would not have ended his life in a pool of blood at Entebbe airport.

By now it was obvious to Carlos that the DST were closing in on him. What should he do? If Moukharbel had "sung" to the police then they would have details of his passports. The airports would be watched. He decided to go to ground and it was at this stage that he persuaded Maria-Teresa Lara, the coolest and most reliable of his women, to help him transport his documents, weapons and belongings to the flat in the rue Amélie which Silva Masmela had recently rented. Another reason for the move was that Nancy Sanchez had decided to go back to Venezuela to study a little-known tribe of Indians.

She was due to catch the evening plane to Bogota on the first leg of her journey on June 27th and she had arranged a farewell party which would carry on after she had left. Carlos was going to be there and had planned to spend the night at the rue Toullier before seeing what the next day would bring.

We know something about Carlos's movements on that day because by chance Angela Armstrong met Carlos and Nancy at the post office near the Sorbonne. Angela was shocked by Nancy's appearance.

"She was completely demoralised, and physically, her face was chalk white and she looked awful. I wanted to say something but Carlos was there and I disliked him even more then. His attitude towards her was bad. While we were talking he pinched her cheek and said 'Eh, Negrita' [Little Nigger], you know, very derogatory. I didn't like that at all and I was surprised she put up with that kind of treatment. Although I couldn't ask her, I thought there was something wrong."

In retrospect Angela Armstrong thinks that Nancy must have learned the truth about the Carlos she loved. "Now I think that the Friday she left, I'm sure, she knew then. But before there was no indication that she knew." There is no means of knowing what would have precipitated the discovery by Nancy Sanchez of Carlos's secret life. She may have overheard a conversation, or he may have boasted about his activities, or there may simply have been a quarrel because Nancy had found out about his network of other mistresses in Paris, all playing a role similar to her own.

Nancy went off to the Sorbonne to make arrangements about her studies while Carlos sat beside Angela on a bench and complained that he could not get through to England. This is interesting, for Scotland Yard learned later that Carlos had telephoned Angela Otaola that day. Saturday, the following day, was the Basque girl's birthday and apart from wishing her a happy one, Carlos told her he intended to come to London.

Was he hoping to lie low in London? Or was he laying a false trail? Whatever the reason, it would appear that he took a gamble in making the call when it was likely that the police were on his trail.

He was in a bad mood. The weather was hot and French post offices are crowded and frustrating places. Angela Armstrong says that Carlos, looking at the young people crowding the place, made some disobliging remarks about students and universities in general which led her to suppose that he himself had university experience. "I was still waiting for my call and, okay, we were sitting on this bench in front of the telephone booth. I sat there not knowing what to say and I didn't really want to say anything. I looked at his reflection in the glass and I really couldn't see what Nancy saw in him."

After a while Nancy Sanchez came back to the post office and casually said to Angela: "I'm leaving tonight. We're having a few drinks at about five or six, and you can come along if you want."

"I don't think I can," said Angela, "because I've got no one to look after my daughter." Later she was to realise that, as she puts it, "If I had gone, I wouldn't be here today."

Chapter Five
Drama in the rue Toullier

IN CONTRAST TO CARLOS, ILL-NATURED AND ILL AT EASE, CHIEF Commissioner Jean Herranz, the fifty-two-year-old "patron" of Division B 2, the international anti-terrorist squad of the DST, faced the morning of June 27th 1975 in a sunny mood. He specialised in the nefarious activities of Palestinians in France, and over the last two weeks he had made a good deal of progress towards breaking up the "Mohamed Boudia Commando". The watch that his men had set on Moukharbel, about whose activities he now had solid information from Beirut, was proving fruitful. Wilfried Böse had already been sent home to West Germany.

And although Moukharbel did not yet know it, the Chief Commissioner had in his pocket a signed deportation order to expel him from France. To help persuade him to talk, the DST inspectors had asked the Lebanese where he would like to be sent, supposing they decided to turn him out of France rather than to charge him. Slightly to their surprise he had chosen Tunisia, which is one of the moderate Arab states and not sympathetic to terrorists. But Moukharbel had good reasons of his own for not wanting to return to the Lebanon. Chief Commissioner Herranz had in any case decided to accompany Moukharbel to Orly airport the following day and put him aboard a plane to Tunis. But before that could be done there was one point that remained to be checked.

During his interrogation Moukharbel had been forced to agree that he knew the plump young man with whom he had been photographed, though he insisted that this person was of no importance, a small fish.

But having admitted that he knew Carlos he was also forced to reveal that he knew where he might be found – at a flat on the Left Bank.

Herranz decided that it would be worth paying a visit to this flat and possibly talking to the small fish. Information is what all policemen seek and there was a smell of it around. But first there was a pleasant social occasion planned for eight o'clock in the evening, when a number of senior DST officers would be gathering for drinks to celebrate the retirement of one of their *confrères* in the service. After the jokes and the drinks and the farewell speeches Herranz picked up two other officers still on duty, Divisional Inspector Raymond Doubs, a fifty-five-year-old veteran on the verge of retirement himself, and a newcomer to the service, Inspector Jean Donatini, aged thirty-four. As the visit to the flat was to be their last job that night they checked in their automatics at headquarters as regulations required, to avoid having to go back to the office after the visit. Then they collected Moukharbel and a car to drive across the Seine and along the Boulevard St. Germain into the heart of the Left Bank.

The car left them near the Sorbonne and the chauffeur, who was going off duty, drove away promising to send another car to pick them up later. It was a particularly hot and heavy night in Paris, café terraces were crowded and television noises could be heard through open windows in the shabby street, a short one leading down from the rue Soufflot. The polyglot natives of the district were busy trying to keep cool and quietly entertaining themselves.

Curiously enough the street had been prophetically described much earlier by Rilke in Les Cahiers du Malte. "Do people really come here to live?" he wrote. "I am tempted to believe it more likely that people come here to die ... So far as I could smell, it reeked of iodine, the greasy odour of fried potatoes, and fear."

No such philosophical thoughts occurred to the three DST agents as they went through the "porte cochère" of No. 9. They were mildly surprised to find there was no concierge, just cards and bells to mark the apartments. The one they wanted was second floor right, labelled "Sanchez-Salazar", the names of the two girls who shared it. They went through the courtyard and up to the first floor and then over a little cast-iron bridge which hangs above the fusty courtyard. A dark passage lay ahead and Herranz pressed a button, believing it to be one of those "minuterie" devices which switch on the lights in French corridors for a few minutes only.

He was mistaken, for it was the doorbell of an apartment occupied by a Spanish domestic, Incarnaçion Carrasso. She shuffled to the door and was told who the visitors were. They had come to the wrong address. But Incarnacion took advantage of the visit to complain, as she frequently did to other occupants of the building, about the behaviour of her upstairs neighbours who made so much noise at night with their parties, their singing and their guitar playing that sometimes went on until dawn.

As if to make the point for her a burst of guitar music came to Herranz's ears. Although he did not know it, it was Carlos's signature tune.

When there were parties at Nancy's place there was always Latin-American music played on a "coto codos", a kind of small guitar which produces its own special, haunting sound. Carlos sometimes played it himself, and his favourite number was a Mexican song called "Give thanks for life". Angela Armstrong remembers going to parties and always hearing this song, written by a Mexican woman who committed suicide. It could be heard by anyone approaching the flat as they came across the little bridge.

By the time Herranz arrived at the party Nancy Sanchez had already left to catch her plane, but the festivities were continuing. The two junior inspectors of the DST stayed down the corridor with Michel Moukharbel while Herranz rang the bell. The singing stopped as the door opened. He declared himself to be from the DST.

They invited him in. There were four men and a girl in the shabby studio with its flaking paint and dark green curtains. The DST officer began talking to the guitar player, a stocky young man in shirt sleeves wearing sunglasses. Herranz recognised Carlos from his photograph. He produced a copy of the picture and Carlos and his friends laughed about it.

For perhaps a quarter of an hour Herranz and Carlos talked. Some of the others, still in a party mood, made a joke or two. One offered Herranz a drink. But the Commissioner had decided it would be worthwhile to take Carlos back to headquarters for more serious questioning. First, he planned the trick always used by French police whenever an opportunity presents itself – the confrontation. Moving to the door he called his two inspectors to bring in Moukharbel. Herranz felt sure of himself and was convinced that Carlos could not escape, for a police officer had made a reconnaissance of the apartment earlier, and had reported that there was no back way out.

As Herranz went to the door to call in Moukharbel, Carlos moved into the bathroom to grab the gun he had brought to the party. His weapon, a .38 Czech automatic, was concealed in his toilet bag and Carlos, convinced by the tone of his questions that the DST man intended to take him to headquarters, was determined to resist.

As Moukharbel entered the room Carlos instinctively believed that the Arab had betrayed him. He took no chances and at point-blank range, as Moukharbel began to speak, his comrade in terror fired two bullets into his body. Two more shots killed the DST inspectors and a fifth hit Chief Commissioner Herranz in the neck. As he moved towards the door Carlos put a final shot into the dying comrade still scrabbling on the bloodstained floor.

Carlos jumped over the bodies and ran down the corridor. No doubt fearing there were more officers on the staircase, he vaulted over the balcony on to a scaffolding in the courtyard of number 11 rue Toullier and, still in shirt-sleeves, disappeared into the twilight of the Latin Quarter.

Back in the apartment the bewildered Latin-Americans tried to help the badly wounded Herranz and took him by taxi to the Cochin Hospital. With prompt treatment he survived his wound and lived to answer a number of embarrassing questions about how it had come about that three DST men and a terrorist under their arrest should have been shot in just a few minutes.

Undoubtedly it was the flexibility and speed of decision shown by Carlos which saved him and the remains of his network. It is this quick thinking and straight shooting which makes him, despite his many weaknesses and his ineffable vanity, into a formidable terrorist leader.

"What happened in the rue Toullier was a blunder, even the CRS riot squad could have done better," commented Roger Wybot, the distinguished former director of the DST, a French secret service chief comparable to Allen Dulles in the USA. And indeed, so it appeared to the French press and public opinion when news of the shooting broke. But it could equally be argued that the fault lay as much with the structure of the anti-terrorist squad as with the comportment of the officers concerned.

The Direction de la Surveillance du Territoire, to which it belongs, comes under the direction of the Minister of the Interior, and the main task of this agency, 1,500 strong though one of the least publicised of the French police forces, is to combat the activities of foreign agents within the country. It was set up after the Liberation at the end of the Second World War and re-organised twenty years later. Details of the decree defining its functions together with those of the sister body known as the Service de Documentation et du Contre Espionage (SDECE) were never even published in the Journal Officiel. In recent years there have been constant rumours that the whole espionage service would be reformed after numerous scandals and that the DST would be dissolved. But nothing has been done.

For years the DST has been mostly concerned with detecting, following and building up copious documentation on Soviet and Iron Curtain agents operating in France, many of them in the field of industrial espionage. Its experienced officers know the form perfectly well. Spies linked to embassies are discovered, and in many cases quietly expelled. The DST is heavily engaged in the expulsion business. In the case of bigger and more flagrant offences, agents are brought to trial and imprisoned for a few years before being exchanged for Western intelligence men similarly detected in East Europe and the Soviet Union.

As an experienced officer from the Police Judiciaire put it more vulgarly: "*Ces mecs* [these guys] are used to dealing with gentleman spies. They don't know about violence like we do. The big powers play it quietly and there is no nasty business these days. They've forgotten the rough stuff because it's all pussy-footing in their business. Very often they don't bother to carry their revolvers – it spoils the cut of their suits."

This seems to be the only explanation for the casual way in which Chief Commissioner Herranz and his men, unarmed, went about tackling Carlos. They had failed to adapt their tactics to the ruthless ways of international terrorists.

Other police officers insist that the DST men ought not to have tried questioning a wanted man in a strange apartment. The operation should have been carried out with a police cover round the rue Toullier and with cars waiting nearby. Carlos ought to have been frisked, arrested and taken off to Fort de l'Est, where the DST has a headquarters, before thorough questioning began.

The fact that such methods were not adopted raises the question as to whether the French really wanted to capture and imprison a terrorist leader. Might not this have led to more Air France hijackings to obtain the freeing of Carlos and his friends? Such calculations always weigh upon ministerial minds in the West and they often settle for questioning and quietly slipping some wanted, or rather unwanted, man across the border to pass the problem to someone else. The French did not want to get unnecessarily involved in the Middle East mêlée. What is more likely is that these political considerations did not arise because they did not have the slightest idea that Carlos was such an important terrorist leader.

The key to assessing the behaviour of the DST agents that June night is to know how much information they had managed to extract from Michel Moukharbel. Did he betray Carlos? The answer is no. He could not deny knowing the Venezuelan because they had been photographed together. But Moukharbel would admit no more than that they were supporters of the Palestinian cause. A suave and cultivated man, he was used to dealing with interrogators. The irony of his death is that when Carlos shot him, he was trying to reassure his executioner that his secret was safe.

Since his death, Moukharbel has emerged as a much more important figure than he was thought to be when alive; and indeed he has been translated into a hero and martyr by the Palestinian terrorists. A communiqué published in Beirut declared:

Our fighting comrade Michel Moukharbel took part in the planning and execution of numerous, heroic and audacious actions within the ranks of the PFLP or the Organisation of Armed Arab Struggle. Here are some of them:

The attempt on the life of the British Zionist billionaire Joseph Sieff, who every year gives millions of pounds to the Zionist usurpers and their war machine.

The two operations at Orly airport.

The sabotage of the Israeli exhibition in Frankfurt.

The blowing up of a munition factory in West Berlin working for the Israeli army.

The blasting of the offices of Jewish newspapers in Paris.

The explosion at the Jewish Agency in Paris.

> The operation at The Hague which stressed the international character of the revolutionary action, and forced the French services to liberate the fighters of the Japanese Red Army.

The list of targets discovered on the body of Moukharbel was just a small portion of a wider plan against Zionism, its agents and those who cooperate with it. The death of Comrade Moukharbel is not the end but just a new incentive to future struggle.

The importance of this bombastic communiqué is to demonstrate the stature of Moukharbel, something which at that stage was not fully comprehended by the DST.

Because of his many terrorist successes, Michel Moukharbel must have felt great alarm when he was arrested in Paris after being held in Beirut. He was also scared at the prospect of being sent back to Beirut. He had enemies there, even among those who later edited his eulogy, and they might well use the fact that he had been for several days with French counter-espionage as an excuse to settle old scores and liquidate him. So, in order to ward off the threat of being returned to the Lebanon, he no doubt did supply some information to the DST, though it is highly unlikely that they succeeded in persuading him to work for them as a double agent. The risks were too great and that is why Herranz went along himself.

But when Herranz played his confrontation card, Carlos gave Moukharbel no time to complete his explanation. It may even be that because Carlos's Arabic is not very good he did not understand what Moukharbel was trying to say. Even if he did, however, he would probably have killed him, and probably, too, he was right to do so, for Moukharbel was ruthless enough to have sacrificed his partner so that he himself could save his life and fight another day on the terrorist battlefields. It was Herranz, who, through lack of information about the people he was dealing with, misjudged the situation. Of course, it is simpler to form judgements after the event than to decide correctly on the spot what the right decision should be.

"On joue sur toutes les cordes dans l'interrogation," as another DST man commented. In the event it was Carlos who, in this tight corner, made his decision without hesitation and acted.

Chapter Six
Escape to Algiers

When the alarm was raised a dragnet was put out by the Paris police and the DST. Their first move was to interrogate the people who had attended Nancy Sanchez's farewell party, then to haul in a score of others who had been in contact with Carlos. They trawled the streets. They came close to trapping him in an oriental bar in the rue du Buci, just off the Boulevard St. Germain, centre of Left Bank night life.

But they still had no knowledge of Silva Masmela's flat in the rue Amélie and it was there that Carlos spent the night before waking up to find himself notorious. He was "blown", but he was still free. And he set about organising his disappearance from France with such effect that he was safely in Algeria before the police picked up the trail.

Their first real break came from London on the Monday three days after the rue Toullier affair. A number of developments enabled Scotland Yard to identify Carlos and begin the process of revealing details of his contacts and activities.

That evening Barry Woodhams, a twenty-seven-year-old biologist, read a newspaper description of Carlos which confirmed for him the frightening suspicion that the man he knew as Carlos Martinez, a Chilean businessman, was Ilich Ramirez Sanchez, the killer. Woodhams figured in Angela Otaola's somewhat complicated lovelife. He had known Angela for some time in the free and easy ambience of Bayswater bed-sitter land and had moved in with her, while maintaining his own flat, when Carlos started to spend more and more time abroad.

Later Woodhams was to recall: "He thought he was a bit of a

Romeo, that he was God's gift to women. He used to boast about drinking Napoleon brandy. He went to the best clubs and his life was getting up at two or three in the afternoon and going on until two or three in the morning. Martinez used to talk about women a lot. He used to say he loved all women. He described himself as a Chilean. All I knew was that he was in business and had rich parents. We used to sit and talk about politics quite a lot. He mentioned terrorism during our discussions but always as if we were talking about someone else, not about himself.

"We discussed firearms, but for a man calling himself a City gent he knew too much about them. I remember commenting on the most stable position for shooting being a crouch. I knew because I had done some game-hunting abroad. Martinez replied, 'If you shoot like that, you will make a profile and people will shoot back.' I was talking about game-hunting. He seemed to be talking about people."

On one of the occasions when the talk got round to terrorism, said Woodhams, "he argued that it was very easy to smuggle arms through existing security precautions. I said I thought it must be impossible because I had seen a television programme on the increased security measures. He said no, it wasn't impossible for someone who knew what he was doing."

The two men, who met on some thirty occasions, had a rather barbed relationship, with Angela acting as the catalyst. She came to favour Woodhams – one of Carlos's problems with women is that he has thick lips which tend to slobber and more than once women who came in contact with him, while appreciating the charms he could turn on, could not bear his constant drooling.

However, while Angela came to view his infrequent appearances with distaste, she allowed him to make use of the bed-sitter and keep his locked black holdall tucked away behind a bookcase.

Woodhams's suspicions that Carlos was something other than he claimed to be were roused when Angela asked him to see if the boarded-up fireplace in her sitting room still worked. To get at the fireplace Woodhams had to move a chest of drawers and while doing this he found two envelopes, one containing an Iranian passport and the other a Kuwaiti driving licence. Both carried Carlos's photograph, but both were in different names. There were also newspaper cuttings, mainly from the *Jewish Chronicle*, and an address book with a list of names, mainly Jewish, but also those of show business personalities along with their nicknames and ex-directory numbers. Woodhams had stumbled on Carlos's English death list.

His curiosity stirred, Woodhams picked the lock of the holdall – which he had tripped over and kicked several times. In it he saw a Czech automatic with a silencer and ammunition. Woodhams shut up the case and put it away, determined that the next time he saw "Martinez" he would tell him to take the holdall away.

But the next time he saw him was in a newspaper photograph with a description of the killings in the rue Toullier. Woodhams, by now a frightened young man, re-opened the holdall to make a complete inspection. What he saw panicked him. Too frightened to get in touch with the police, he rang the *Guardian* newspaper. In the newsroom they were not inclined to take his information too seriously – it is in the nature of newsrooms to be pestered by readers with all kinds of strange obsessions. However, good news-sense prevailed and they asked him to call at their Gray's Inn Road office. He packed some of Carlos's armoury into a bag and took it by tube to the newspaper. What he had to show sent two reporters and a photographer back with him to Angela's flat. They then rang the police – having first made sure their paper had a full story and photographs. In the holdall were sticks of sweating dynamite, three pistols, hand grenades, plastic explosives, cords of wire fuse, two coshes and a gas gun disguised as a pen. One of the reporters went to the restaurant where Angela was working and told her what had happened. "Oh, dear, what have I done?" she said, badly shaken. She had recovered sufficiently to clown with the police when they arrived at her flat and even had her photograph taken wearing a policeman's helmet. But the clowning ended when Angela and Woodhams were taken off for intensive questioning at Harrow Road police station. Woodhams was released after two days but was not too sure if he wanted to be set free – not with the killer he had once twitted for being too fat on the loose. Angela was held in custody and charged with possessing guns and ammunition without a firearms certificate. She told the police that Carlos had left the holdall with her in about April 1975 telling her it contained guns he needed for self-protection.

She also told the police about the astonishing letter she had received from Carlos after the rue Toullier killings. It read:

Dear Angela,

    As you already know things were very serious over here.

I have just managed to save myself. I did not phone you because I had to tear up the card. I am sending this letter in duplicate, one to the bistro and the other to your home in case my memory fails and I get the wrong address.

Carlos went on to explain that he was going away on a trip and did not know when he would return. He then referred to Moukharbel, the colleague he had killed: "I sent Chiquitin to a better life for being a traitor."

The letter also gave her strict instructions: "Do not call my friend." Who was the friend? Angela, by this time very frightened indeed, said that Carlos had given her the telephone number of someone to contact in order to get rid of the case if he was unable to re-enter the country. The police found this number on a scrap of paper in a jar of marbles by Angela's bed. It led to Nydia Tobon.

Her home was searched and she was charged with possessing a stolen blank Italian identity card given to her by Carlos. Another charge of possessing a forged Ecuadorian passport was not proceeded with. At her trial, the prosecution said that she had acted as banker for Carlos. She also helped Antonio Bouvier to find a house and posed as his wife to convince the estate agents. She also met Angela Otaola once, collecting a package from her for Carlos. He made her regular monthly payments of 500 French francs and once gave her £1,000 which she banked for him. Later she returned £900 to him. She looked after documents for him, and for Bouvier, continued the prosecution, and sent some to her friend Mrs. Anna Pugsley, another South American married to an Englishman, so that they would not be found if the police searched her.

Nydia told the police that when she first met Carlos she was on the verge of a nervous breakdown. Alphonse, her eldest child, and the only one living with her, had had three clashes with the British police over drugs and dishonesty. Carlos had given her the false Italian identity card – one of twenty-three stolen from an office in Brindisi in May 1973 – and told her to get her son out of the country and to never see him again. She took it, she said, because she was grateful, "because he was thinking of my son", but was determined not to use it. She acted stupidly, she agreed, but "I was thinking as a mother not as a lawyer".

The false passport had been left with her by Bouvier. It began to worry her when she realised he had gone abroad without it. She sent both documents to her friend for hiding because she wanted to talk to her about them. Two other identity documents found in her flat, she said, belonged to former boyfriends. One had been left accidentally and the other she kept for sentimental reasons. She had thought Carlos was working for political exiles and that was the reason for the secrecy and use of false names. Bouvier, she had been told, was being followed and that was why he needed a secluded house.

With this sort of evidence both women may be thought lucky to have been prosecuted on only minor charges. Both pleaded guilty and were sentenced to a year's imprisonment to be followed by deportation.

The deportation orders seemed to worry both of them more than the year in jail. There was some reason for Angela Otaola's concern, for she is a Basque and Carlos's name had been linked with the Basque nationalists. Angela's fear was that she would be arrested by the Spanish police, who have harsh ways of dealing with Basque nationalists, as soon as she was returned to Spain. She was eventually reassured by an official letter from the Spanish Consul-General, Sr. Fernando Moran, to her lawyer, which said:

We are satisfied that your client is not considered by the Spanish authorities as a member of any international or terrorist organisation and should she return to Spain she will be able to do so and enter the country in the same way as any other Spanish citizen.

That is precisely what she did and the part she played in the Carlos complex ended with her deportation. Her Counsel, Mr. John Hazan, QC, probably got it right when he described her as a "naive young girl presumed on by an international terrorist with great charm and skill and persuasion to do something which was entirely out of character for her".

Nydia Tobon appealed against her deportation order. When most people thought that she had got off lightly she said that she had been stunned by the severity of her sentence and argued:

If Ilich Ramirez committed his crime in Paris, not in London, I want to ask you if before your law, before human rights, it is fair to punish me with twelve months' imprisonment and deportation as well.

When I chose Britain as the country I wanted to live in the first thing which moved me to take this decision was the respect you have for human freedom, the way that, in an international context, you defend human rights. This belief was confirmed with four years living in your country, but now I have the feeling that I was living in a dream.

Unsurprisingly, this appeal was rejected. She was sent back to Colombia at the end of her sentence. It remains to be seen if she, like Angela Otaola, has severed her links with Carlos.

By the time Angela and Nydia were arrested, information about Carlos and his connexion in France was beginning to flow in Paris as well. The trail began with a discovery in the wallet of the dead Moukharbel. There, the police found a cheque for 2,500 francs made out to Amparo Silva Masmela and endorsed to Moukharbel. By the Monday evening following the shootings, the same evening that Woodhams made his deadly discovery, the French police, through the bank, tracked down the man who had signed the cheque, M. Pierre Regnier, who worked in a jewellery shop in Paris.

He was able to tell them something about Silva Masmela. "I met her a few months ago when she had a job at 'Silver Bijou' where I am a salesman. Then a couple of weeks ago she came to see me and asked me to lend her 2,500 francs. She told me: 'For me it's a question of life or death' and she seemed in such a state that I let her have the money."

Moukharbel had several accounts with different banks in Paris though none of them contained really large sums. Payments into them were regular and each account usually contained between 20,000 and 30,000 francs. This may also be the reason why Moukharbel was so careful in keeping his accounts. Even in a terrorist organisation the accountants keep a strict eye on expenses and there is a spirit of bureaucracy even in this branch of human endeavour. In general the financial float of the Carlos-Moukharbel network in Paris was kept at around 150,000 francs and only the two men were allowed to draw on it. Heavy expenditure earlier in the year had reduced their funds and after Moukharbel's arrest in Beirut and their justified fears that he was being watched neither of them dared go near their joint accounts. This is the reason why Silva Masmela urgently needed to borrow from the jeweller. As she worked in Lloyds bank she probably thought that some friendly employee might help her to cash the cheque on behalf of Moukharbel.

Through the jeweller, the DST made an even more important discovery. He was able to give them the address of Silva Masmela's flat – 11 rue Amélie in the 7th arrondissement, the place where, with the aid of Maria-Teresa Lara, Carlos had so recently hidden away his papers and weapons. It was a comfortable second-floor studio flat. It contained a complete terrorists' arsenal.

Before investigating further, the counter-intelligence men set a trap to catch Carlos who might still, they thought, be in Paris. However, because of an indiscreet radio news bulletin announcing that they had discovered his hideout, all chance of this vanished, but they did arrest Silva Masmela. This attractive Venezuelan in her twenties had come to France in 1974 with her sister Martha. Describing themselves as students of political economy, they both signed on at the Alliance Française language school and lived for a while in a convent. Silva was already full of revolutionary ideas and in search of a cause to serve when she first met Carlos and fell easy prey to his charms.

She worked for a while as a domestic servant, like many other Latin-American girls who come to Paris in search of glamour and excitement. About the time that she met Carlos, Silva changed jobs and went to work for the jewellers, Silver Bijou. Meanwhile, her sister had taken up with a mysterious Basque and gone to work for a car-hire firm. By this time they were both swimming in terrorist waters. Carlos diligently pursued Silva Masmela and was always telephoning her at the shop and picking her up there. Finally he persuaded her to change jobs again and go to work in the mail department of the British Lloyds Bank in Paris. At Lloyds they said that her job was not an important one and that she was only there for three months. Nevertheless she may have been able to pick up information of use to the Carlos network.

She had hired the flat in the rue Amélie only a month before the shooting and she simultaneously hired another apartment in a different part of the city. It looks as though, like Nydia Tobon, she was used by Carlos to provide a number of safe houses which he could use in time of danger.

When the DST swooped on the flat, they found Moukharbel's green notebook, written in Arabic, as well as Carlos's arsenal. He had left there two machine pistols, two automatic pistols, thirty-three clips of ammunition, twenty-eight grenades and enough explosives to blow up the whole *quartier* – fifteen sticks of dynamite, thirteen pounds of plastic and three home-made bombs. Examination of the papers and material stored there made it possible for the first time to build up a complete picture of the terrorist activities of Carlos and Moukharbel.

It took weeks of patient research for the DST and French police departments to correlate and assess the information about them and their relationships with various terror groups. On the night of June 27th when he left the dead and wounded behind in rue Toullier little was known. Yet, as he fled in search of a safe refuge where he could plan the next stage of his escape, Carlos must have felt that everyone in Paris was looking for him. He probably assumed that Moukharbel had told everything to the police.

On the Saturday morning, the day after the shooting, Carlos suddenly appeared at Les Invalides air station in central Paris. Situated by the Seine on the Quai d'Orsay, it is only ten minutes' walk from the hideout flat in rue Amélie By that unfortunate chance that seemed to haunt her connexion with Carlos, Angela Armstrong was also at the air station to make arrangements for her young daughter to fly to England to stay with her grandmother when the school holidays started. There was a queue at the desk and because a long wait seemed certain she was almost pleased to see a familiar face in the crowd – that of Carlos. She had already been there for half an hour when she saw him casually sauntering into the main hall.

"He came over, not quickly but, well, cool. It all happened so quickly. He put his arm on my shoulder, but in a friendly way, and we walked towards the exit. I said 'This is my young daughter', and he said 'No problems'."

Only a few hours before, this cool young man had shot down four people. As he had originally been introduced to her as a Peruvian, Angela thought he might be buying a ticket for Peru, but he said: "No, no I'm not Peruvian."

"Have you heard the news?" asked Carlos. Angela had heard nothing. He began talking in Spanish so fast that although she speaks the language Angela could not follow him.

"I've killed two men. The Arab bastard betrayed me. I kill all those who betray me. Write to Nancy [Sanchez] and tell her to stay in Venezuela," he said. Then he added: "It's a nuisance, we'll have to do the papers, we'll have to make the papers again. I'm going to the Middle East."

So saying he disappeared through the exit door. Clearly he was preoccupied with the business of being fitted out with a new false passport so that he could leave the country. But it seemed a fairly reckless act to appear at such a place as Les Invalides, where the police might have been expected to keep careful watch for him. Why had he gone there at all? Not to meet Angela, for so far as she knew he had no idea that she might be there. One possibility is that he hoped to fall in with other Latin-American friends who had been scared by news of the shooting and were buying tickets to leave the country. Or he may have been in search of more hard news about the results of his marksmanship, for he told Angela that he had killed only two men, and therefore still did not know that three were dead and one badly wounded.

He did mention two people who had been present in the flat the night before and said that they were okay. Though, as they were being questioned by the police, it was unlikely that he had been in touch with them. By "okay", it is possible that he simply meant they had not been injured in the shooting.

Poor Angela was baffled by this singular encounter. At first she thought that Carlos must be drunk, but when she bought the Paris papers, with the news of the shooting all over the front pages, she realised that his statement was sober and accurate. Panic set in and as she took the Métro she was already convinced that the police must be following her. She realised that she was one of the few people who could identify Carlos. For the same reason Carlos himself might have taken her hostage or even killed her.

Angela Armstrong had a desperate need to tell someone what she had heard, but did not dare go to the police. She tried to telephone her friend Nancy in Venezuela but only succeeded in talking to her mother. After consulting other Latin-American friends, Angela, still in a state of high emotion, flew home to England. Even there she did not feel at ease and returned to France to her job. It was in Paris on Monday, while she was still havering about whether or not to tell the authorities what she knew but dared not reveal, that the DST, who had traced her through the network of Carlos's friends, picked her up for interrogation. She was held for twenty-one days before being released.

Finally, Miss Armstrong was charged with being an accomplice and in contact with "X" (Carlos) and others, who as agents of a foreign power were acting in a manner likely to harm France diplomatically and militarily.

Conviction for such an offence can carry a sentence of up to twenty years' imprisonment. Maître Jacques Perrot, the lawyer appointed to look after her interests, told Payne that he considered that Miss Armstrong was entirely innocent, but had acted foolishly in her panicky fear after the terrifying encounter at Les Invalides. He expected that the case would not be heard and finally cleared up until two years after the events. At the time of writing Angela Armstrong still lives in France, free to do anything except leave, which she has no intention of doing.

On the weekend after the shooting, Latin-American mutual friends of Nancy Sanchez and Carlos, who themselves hastily left the country, reported that Maria-Teresa Lara, the girl who had helped Carlos to hide his papers and who had co-operated with him in other ways, was still in France. On the day of the shooting she had fled to Marseilles. The haste of her flight was shown by the fact that she asked the friends to send her money. She told them that she was trying to get to Algeria. And indeed it was in Algiers that she was next heard of, living with Carlos.

After the Vienna raid, French television men in Venezuela asked José Altagracia Ramirez Navas about the whereabouts of Carlos, his son. He replied: "The Algerians were extremely kind to my son. They provided a luxurious refuge for him and his Venezuelan friend, Maria-Teresa Lara, and President Boumedienne gave him 50 million dollars for the cause." Paternal pride – for he had just described Carlos as a veritable "professor of terrorism" – no doubt affected the old gentleman's grasp of economics, but he, of all people, must have noticed the postmarks on the letters he received from his son.

It was to Algiers also that two other Venezuelan girls from Paris made their way a few days after the events in the rue Toullier. Maria Eugenia Romero and Delfina Rosalia Rincon were both mentioned in a Telex from the Algerian consulate in Paris referring back to an earlier one from Algiers marked "Relative to Carlos affair". The message was reproduced in *Minute*, the right-wing Paris news magazine, whose offices had been damaged by one of Carlos's car-bombs.

Middle East sources in Paris agree with the theory put forward by *Minute* that President Boumedienne and his diplomats did indeed furnish a certain amount of aid to Carlos in his flight from France.

They claim that Carlos first made contact with DGI agents masquerading as Cuban diplomats. But it was the Algerians who gave practical help – there was one report of their driving him in a car with diplomatic plates. And the Algerians were well disposed to Carlos, not simply because of his aid to Palestinian extremists, but because of his role as a KGB correspondent and because he had, in his freelance capacity, done various bits of dirty work for President Boumedienne against the Algerian leader's many political enemies among the migrant Algerian workers in France.

Be that as it may, the escape trail for Carlos when he was hunted by the DST ended in Algiers. The route he took was an overland one, first to Lyons in southern France and then to the Mediterranean port of Marseilles. While the police kept watch over airports throughout the country, Carlos quietly boarded a fruit boat sailing from there and enjoyed a few days of seaborne repose after the violent dénouement of his drama as head of the Mohamed Boudia Commando in Paris.

He must have been glad to be in North Africa for a while rather than the Middle East, for he had some difficult explanations to make about the killing of Moukharbel who was, after all, one of the most accomplished of Wadi Hadad's foreign operators. It was easy for Carlos to say in Paris, "He betrayed me". But that might have been harder to justify at headquarters. There were therefore certain advantages in waiting for a while in Algiers. Carlos made use of the pause to convince his masters that he had acted properly and the proof of his success is that while they praised Moukharbel, they began building Carlos up in their publications as a hero figure, the "Chevalier" of Arab terrorism. It seems that his new-found notoriety outweighed his failures. Even the demise of Moukharbel was justified by the way in which Carlos had forced the Palestinian cause once again upon the attention of the world. Carlos was returned to favour and, with Wadi Hadad, set about planning the most audacious coup of all – the OPEC raid in Vienna.

Chapter Seven
Curiel and curiouser

THE FRENCH AUTHORITIES AND, IN PARTICULAR, THE DST WERE enraged by the shootings and by their inability to capture Carlos. Part of this rage was caused by their knowledge that they had bungled the Moukharbel business. But an equal part was because they felt they had been betrayed by a collection of foreigners, diplomats and political activists who had abused the traditional hospitality offered them in Paris.

In fact the shootings in the rue Toullier forced the French to acknowledge what the police forces of Europe and the Israelis had known for some years: that Paris has become the world capital of terrorism. It is ideally placed by geography and circumstances to fulfil this role. It has excellent rail, road and air communications with the rest of Europe and the Middle East; it connects with five land frontiers, which, because of the volume of traffic crossing them, are difficult to police, it is, moreover, traditionally a haven for political refugees and a magnet for young people, still full of romantic notions about its charms.

Since the 1968 student revolution which brought alive the older and more venerable tradition of the great eighteenth-century revolution, young men and women with left-wing aspirations have flocked to the city from abroad. Idealistic liberals and radicals in search of a cause are ready, like the Carlos girls, to give help and support to those they believe are fighting for a good revolutionary cause.

The Japanese Red Army found security there, hidden among the most numerous colony of Japanese students in Europe. From Germany, just across the open border, came members of the Baader-Meinhof gang, able to mix with ease among the young new Europeans who nowadays all seem to look and act alike. All roads lead to Paris for the terrorists and in the sleazier parts of the city there can be found members and supporters of almost every "liberation" group in the world, from Palestinians to Tupamaros.

During Carlos's time in France efforts were made to broaden the terrorist connexion even further by wooing ethnic separatist groups from all over Europe. Indeed they all met in a conference at Trieste – Croats, Bretons, Irish, Welsh, Corsicans and Basques. Carlos tried to establish links with them all and, as we have seen, succeeded with the Turks. For him Paris was a city full of recruits for his confused revolutionary dream.

But what really made Paris the world centre of terrorism was the arrival in the early 1970s of the Palestinians. When Black September was born, based on the Fatah intelligence unit, Razd, it was centred on Razd's own headquarters in Rome. But when, after a series of outrages, both the Italian police and the Israeli Wrath of God teams started to harry them in Rome where there was little natural cover, the terrorists headed for Paris. There they submerged themselves in an Arab population which had grown enormously since the end of the war in Algeria in the early 1960s. In one of those recurring political paradoxes, the very people who had fought so hard to kick the French out of Algeria flocked to Paris in search of money and jobs in a booming economy. There were also those, like Mohamed Boudia, who fell foul of their revolutionary comrades and had to flee for their lives. Today any Arab can pass unremarked in Paris with its Moslem population of half a million.

It is of course impossible for the security services of a democratic country to control the political activities of so many different communities with so many different languages and different grievances, and the terrorists based in Paris took full advantage of this situation. To give an idea of the scale of terrorist activity in Paris, police figures show that in the eighteen months up to June 1975 there were no fewer than five hundred bombings and five murders of senior diplomats. Such statistics make London, a city sporadically under attack by the Irish Republican Army, seem a peaceful place.

The French police seemed to adopt a somewhat casual attitude. When they caught someone being particularly obstreperous they showed him the door as they had with Wilfried Böse and as they had planned to do with Moukharbel. Then, after the affair in the rue Toullier, they started to tighten up. The first to get hurt were the girls who, wittingly or innocently, sexually or platonically, had become involved with Carlos. Angela Armstrong was arrested. Amparo Silva Masmela was given a short jail sentence and then deported. Maria-Teresa Lara fled to Algiers. Albaida Salazar, who shared the rue Toullier flat with Nancy Sanchez, was deported and so was another Venezuelan girl, Leyma Palomares Duque, who was in the flat when Carlos opened fire.

It was these three girls who led the DST to the Cuban Embassy in Paris. Albaida Salazar worked for Ernesto Herrera Reyes, a Second Secretary at the Embassy, and one of their jobs was to send parties of French students to Cuba where they were organised in international youth brigades to harvest sugar cane. Leyma Duque and Maria-Teresa Lara both had boyfriends at the Embassy who were later discovered to be Cuban intelligence agents posing as diplomats. With this lead the DST discovered that Carlos himself had been in frequent contact with the Cuban agents in Paris and other places in Europe. This persuaded the French that the Cubans were involved up to their necks in Carlos's activities.

They also became convinced that the Cubans had helped him to escape, and ten days after the shootings the French Foreign Affairs Ministry announced that three Cubans, all described as "cultural attachés", Raul Sainz Rodriguez, a First Secretary, Ernesto Herrera Reyes, and Pedro Zamora Larra, had been declared *persona non grata* and would be expelled from France.

It was the first time that the French Republic had expelled diplomats, not for espionage but for collusion with terrorists. In a strong statement Michel Poniatowski, the Minister of the Interior and himself on Carlos's death list, said: "Certain foreign intelligence services are giving aid to international terrorist organisations." He would like to have named the Soviet Union, but was restrained on the orders of President Giscard d'Estaing, who was about to make a visit to Moscow and had no wish to embarrass the Russians on the eve of it. Even this tactful gesture did not prevent the Russians from making their customary complaints. They showed their sensitivity by attacking Poniatowski, saying that the expulsions were an attempt to exploit the Carlos affair in order to spoil the process of détente.

M. Poniatowski went hot and strong for the terrorists themselves. Although he did not believe in "the black hand of international terror" there was no doubt in his mind that "a group of international anarchists and leftists from Latin America and from the Middle East" were responsible for what had happened in the rue Toullier. The Minister's spokesman, André Mousset, declared:

The Carlos case, which until now constituted a striking demonstration of the unity of action among terrorist groups, has been enriched with important elements showing the assistance given to international terrorism by certain states.

Developments in the case confirm the close links between terrorist networks and the espionage services of certain states. There are clear signs of collusion between DGI and other foreign states. This was clear interference in French affairs within the framework of terrorist attacks which caused several deaths.

It is disquieting to find that Cuban agents of espionage and counter-espionage services together with those of certain East European countries are interfering in the activities of this international of violence.

In their attacks on the Cubans the French went a stage further by implicating in the affair a Cuban diplomat based in London. They denounced Second Secretary Angel Dalmau as a DGI agent and claimed that he had been in regular contact with Carlos's London banker, Nydia Tobon.

The French government spokesman added: "It has been noticed in Paris that there have been a number of unusual and recent departures from London of several members of the DGI, the Cuban Secret Service." This was clearly intended as a hint to the British government that it, too, should take action against the Cubans, a hint which was not acted upon. The British Foreign Office was furious with the French for implicating the Cubans and denied that there was any truth in it. Nevertheless it is true that Nydia Tobon did know Angel Dalmau.

The French also turned their attention to the activities of some of the radical groups which seem to hover on the blurred dividing line between left-wing politics, support for the Third World and espionage and terrorism. And in this connexion they looked hungrily – and not for the first time – at an extraordinary man called Henri Curiel. They would dearly love to arrest him and he is a subject of great interest to a number of Western intelligence agencies, but except for a short period during the Algerian war the French have never been able to prove anything illegal about his activities which centre round a network of interlocking groups. Not itself a terrorist organisation by any stretch of the imagination, this network, as its original name "Solidarity" and the one later adopted, "Aid and Friendship", both imply, is a collection of do-gooders devoted to the welfare of the Third World countries. But beneath this level of activity is another at which militant idealists recruited for the first purpose stretch their activities to provide safe houses, money and false papers for terrorist groups, on the gounds that they are acting in the cause of putting things right in, for example, South Africa and Latin America.

The organisation was examined in detail by Georges Souffert, one of France's most respected political journalists, in the Paris news-weekly *Le Point*. After a three-month investigation he wrote a thoughtful article accusing Curiel, a sixty-two-year-old Jew born in Cairo, of running Solidarity as a support group for terrorists. Curiel at once denied this, saying that he despised both terrorism and the terrorists themselves. And this, comments Souffert, is indeed the point about him. "Curiel is not a terrorist; for him terrorism does not amount to much and does not fit his political views or personality."

Curiel, in fact, is a Communist, and, as he said himself, a Communist of the Stalinist persuasion; and the importance of Souffert's article was that it showed how he had penetrated the terrorist movements. He had done so by supplying them with helpful services. Then, from the inside, he proceeded to find out about their finances, aims and targets and so kept the KGB informed on activities viewed with suspicion by Soviet leadership. For the Russians were in the beginning as ignorant as the Western intelligence services about the new terrorism.

More details of the activities of Curiel and his Solidarity movement came to light through the revelations of Breyten Breytenbach, the South African poet, who was sentenced to nine years' imprisonment under anti-terrorist laws in his home country, which he entered illegally with a false passport. He told his brother that he then began pondering on his actions in Paris in recent years, and started to realise that under cover of opposing apartheid he had been manipulated by Curiel, and recruited for other activities at meetings devoted to studying the ways and means of helping under-developed countries and oppressed nations of the under-developed world. And it was in this way that he came into contact with Curiel.

His poetry was so good that he won an important poetry prize in South Africa and was given a visa to go and receive it. While on this visit he made a number of speeches before university bodies and cultural gatherings denouncing the evils of South African policies. By so doing he became the idol of left-wing and Communist bodies.

In August 1975 Breytenbach again returned to South Africa, this time bearing false papers. He was arrested and put on trial for trying to organise a revolutionary movement there, and although the prosecution asked only for a five-year prison sentence, the judge sentenced him to nine years. A South African friend of his told us about his strange behaviour during that period in South Africa.

"He behaved as though he almost wanted to be caught. He made absolutely no attempt to cover his traces during this clandestine stay. It seemed as though he was trying to get away from the people who had persuaded him to work for them." And, once arrested, he admitted his guilt. By so doing, of course, he forestalled attempts in London and Paris to organise a campaign for his release based on appeals that he had been unjustly charged by the South African government. Breytenbach had been persuaded to take part in plotting activities against his will, even though he believed in the cause, and it seemed almost a relief to him not to have to go further into the world of subversion.

Curiel himself, known simply as "Raymond", travels frequently and has a whole collection of passports. To the South African poet he declared: "My dossier is the biggest one the DST has. But they can do nothing against me." Curiel was not boasting, his dossiers are among the bulkiest in virtually any Western country's intelligence file.

After the appearance of Georges Souffert's article in Paris, the Ministry of the Interior took the unusual step of declaring that it was true that a number of people mentioned in it were under surveillance. The spokesman added that in France people might only be brought to justice if formal proof existed justifying charges against them. This led to speculation that the French security services had leaked information in order to expose Curiel and to persuade his supporters to think twice about his network's activities and those of similar groups.

Curiel is a curious man. His father was a Cairo banker of Jewish descent, and his mother ran a smart bookshop in Cairo. A brilliant man, speaking at least four languages, he travelled widely during the 1930s. Just before the Second World War he emerged on the Egyptian political scene, and during it formed an Egyptian political party, the Democratic Union, which grouped together Communists and fringe left-wing groups. After being imprisoned by King Farouk he made his way back to Europe, to Athens, Paris and Prague.

Later expelled from Egypt by Nasser, he went to Italy and was in touch with many Russians and Czechoslovaks there before installing himself in Paris in 1951. It was at this stage that intelligence services began to suspect that he had become a professional and was working for the KGB. In the 1950s he became an active anti-colonialist and tried to take over the French intellectual group led by the philosopher Francis Jeanson which was helping the Algerians in their fight against the French. Curiel and a number of others were arrested. In the course of their searches the police were checking on a friend of Curiel when he, in a panic, began throwing papers from the window. When they were collected it was revealed that they were photocopies of official reports on discussions between the French and German governments.

These had nothing to do with the war in Algeria, and the DST took renewed interest in Curiel. They were convinced that he belonged to something more important than an anti-colonialist group, and came to the conclusion that he was a real spy using the Algerian movement to obtain diplomatic espionage material. However, they could not prove anything and Curiel could only be imprisoned on charges of aiding the Algerians. When General de Gaulle made peace in Algeria by granting independence Curiel benefited from a general amnesty. By now a hero of the anti-colonial struggle among the Parisian intellectuals, he had no difficulty in establishing himself as a fashionable figure of the left among those people in France who were obsessed with the hardships suffered by the developing countries. Among the notable members of the Solidarity organisation are Maurice Barth, a well-known Dominican priest, and René Rognon, a Protestant pastor, who worked devotedly for the Soviet-inspired Peace Movement. Both denied any involvement in clandestine activities after the revelations made by Georges Souffert.

Nonetheless, it is known that eight-day courses are provided for Solidarity members, during which small groups are given lectures on such helpful subjects as police methods in various countries, and on the activities of anti-government groups both in Europe and other parts of the world. They then progress to more technical instruction in how to make false papers, the rules of clandestine activity, and what to do after arrest. As Georges Souffert says: "It is at this point that the young militant crosses the ill-defined line beyond which he is transformed from a naif into an accomplice." And when idealists of the kind he mentions do, in fact, give their aid to experienced terrorists by acting as messengers, taking money and false papers across frontiers, the amateurs, simply because they are amateurs, are very useful and safe because in the nature of things they have no police records and are protected by their innocence to date. The idealists find themselves being exploited on the fringes of illegality, as Breytenbach was, while other and more experienced supporters make deeper penetration into the terrorist cells, seeking information for the benefit of the KGB even as they provide help and succour.

What is even more remarkable about Curiel is another of his astonishing connexions with the world of espionage, which we discovered in the course of investigating his activities. He is the cousin of George Blake, the notorious British double agent who betrayed members of the Secret Intelligence Service to the Russians, and who is now an exiled pensionary of the KGB in Moscow.

Although himself born of a Dutch mother in Rotterdam, George Blake was the son of Albert William Behar, a member of the Sephardic Jewish family that lived in Cairo. Mr. Behar became a British citizen after serving in both the French Foreign Legion and the British army. The family did not approve of his marriage to a Dutch Christian and cut him off without money. When he died in 1936, he left his widow and George Behar (later George Blake) in reduced circumstances.

One of the Behar sisters had married a wealthy banker in Cairo and this man, Curiel's uncle, also called Henri, offered to educate his nephew provided that he went to live with the family in Egypt. After much heart-searching in the family, George, then aged thirteen, was packed off on the long sea voyage to Egypt aboard a freighter from Rotterdam. It was during his time in Cairo that he learned to speak

English, attending the English School in Cairo, and became closely involved with the life of the Middle East.

When the Second World War broke out, George Blake was staying for the school holidays with his mother in Holland and was trapped there by the invading German armies. His mother made her way to England, and so eventually did George after service with the Dutch Resistance. When the war ended he read modern languages at Cambridge and after changing his name for convenience from Behar to Blake he was recruited into the British intelligence service.

While serving as Vice-Consul in Seoul, he was captured during the Korean war and spent some time in Chinese captivity. After his release he went to the Foreign Office Arabic language school at Shemlan in the Lebanon. But by this time he had been turned and was working for the Russians and revealing to them many secrets of the British Middle East networks he had helped to organise. From 1953 until his unmasking in 1961 he was a senior Soviet spy working within the British secret service and did great damage to it. It has been estimated that he was responsible for the death or capture of forty British agents.

When he was caught and put in the dock at the Old Bailey his trial was one of the shortest in British history. It lasted just fifteen minutes, enough time for him to plead guilty and the Lord Chief Justice to sentence him to forty-two years' imprisonment, the longest term imposed in a British court this century. "Your case," said Lord Parker, "is akin to treason."

But he served only five years before making a daring escape, planned by the KGB, from Wormwood Scrubs Prison in London and fleeing to Moscow, where he was awarded the Order of Lenin and the Order of the Red Banner and where he still lives. Although it was not until after the war, when he was serving at Hamburg, that he was suborned by the Russians, there is little doubt that his youthful experiences in Cairo and contacts with Communist sympathisers like his cousin Henri Curiel affected his subsequent career.

If all this seems far removed from the activities of Carlos and his complex in the late 1970s, it must be remembered that old spies never die, and seldom completely fade away. In order to keep his network in action, to evade arrest and the break-up of his cells, Carlos needs help from inconspicuous and apparently harmless helpers. Much of his support for his most desperate acts comes from "committed" people, especially women, who themselves would never dream of bombing and machine-gunning. As the DST tracked through the list of Carlos's contacts left abandoned in the Paris apartment, they came across evidence that his friends were connected with members of the Curiel network.

The first link between Carlos and Curiel was established – in the convoluted manner typical of international terrorism – through the Japanese and through the all-revealing notebook of Michel Moukharbel. In the wake of the Japanese Red Army's successful attack on the French Embassy in The Hague, the French police picked up Taketomo Takahashi, a former assistant professor at Tokyo's Rikkyo (St. Paul's) University, who had moved to Paris to become one of the leaders of the JRA cell there. When he was arrested he tried in true spy fiction style to swallow a piece of paper. The police pulled it out of his mouth and found written on it two code-names: "Acheme" and "Jean Baptiste".

"Jean Baptiste" was identified as André Haberman, a specialist in photography and microfilm already listed in DST records as the producer of false documents for members of Curiel's network. He was arrested, charged with forgery and then released. "Acheme" was even more interesting. After some difficulty he was identified as a Brazilian named Antonio Perera Carvalho who acted as a "letter box" for the Japanese and is thought to have supplied them with the arms used in The Hague affair. It is there that he appears in Moukharbel's notebook, under yet another name, as Felipe Fereira. Carlos himself had travelled to Amsterdam on the day before the attack on the Embassy and changed a substantial amount of money – a transaction later verified from bank records – which he handed over as an emergency fund to the man he left behind to watch over the raid. That man was Antonio Carvalho alias Felipe Fereira alias Acheme.

The police theory is that Acheme and Jean Baptiste, both with lines to the Curiel network, were used by the Japanese and by Carlos in setting up The Hague raid. Following up, the DST found a number of connexions between members of the Carlos complex and members of Solidarity. This is not surprising because the same type of young radical would tend to gravitate towards both organisations and there would inevitably be some dual membership on the fringes. It becomes more interesting when high-powered operators like Acheme and Jean Baptiste are involved and what is really fascinating is the possibility that Henri Curiel could have provided Carlos with a direct link to Moscow. The link would have run from Carlos, the Moscow-educated killer, through Curiel, the Stalinist Communist, to the Kremlin, where possibly his cousin George Blake, earning his keep, could have handled the material.

Speculation? Certainly. Far-fetched? Perhaps. But when one studies Carlos's next operation, the attack on the OPEC headquarters in Vienna, the far-fetched is shown to be the norm.

Chapter Eight
Sheikh Yamani's tale

"YOU WILL HAVE HEARD OF ME ALREADY; I AM THE FAMOUS CARLOS. You can tell that to the others." This arrogant announcement, calculated to frighten, was made by Carlos to Al-Azzawi, the Iraqi chargé d'affaires, who acted as go-between for the quivering Austrian government and the multi-national terror squad which had just killed three men and seized the eleven OPEC oil ministers in their own headquarters in the Hapsburg heart of Vienna just before Christmas 1975.

At this stage in the operation Carlos was acting like a rather grand spokesman; he assumed a quasi-diplomatic status. Yet he could not resist employing the melodramatic language of the cinema, or rather the cinematic language of a Mexican bandit. And this reveals a good deal about his personality. With such remarks he expressed his dream-hero personality. He was dressed for the part in a long trenchcoat, he wore a Basque beret, tilted menacingly forward, his face was decorated with the thin fringe of beard which so effectively hides a double chin. His vainglorious and boastful words suited his plump face, with its aquiline nose and full lips from which proceeds a soft, almost caressing voice.

By building himself into a kidnapping "hero", he had finally taken revenge on all those boys at school in Caracas who mocked him for being the fat, rich boy. From the cocoon of podginess, El Gordo had emerged as a bully with a gun. And there he was in Vienna carrying out his greatest raid in the cause of a vague revolution and at the same time making himself rich, richer than all those bandit chiefs from Latin America he was subconsciously emulating, full of swagger and braggadocio. For when the raid was over he pocketed a million pounds from Colonel Gaddafi by way of President Boumedienne of Algeria. "You will have heard of me already . . ."

In Vienna, and on the aircraft which carried Carlos and his victims to Algiers, Carlos was in the open, speaking to intelligent witnesses for the first time in his career as a terrorist. Their assessments build up a picture of his character and of his behaviour under stress. The best account comes from the man who was his prime target, and who spent most time alone with him, Sheikh Zaki Yamani, the Saudi Arabian Minister of Petroleum. Yamani is a sophisticated, American-educated Arab, a skilled executive and negotiator in oil politics who has a fine eye for important detail. He knows how to read the small print in the Carlos contract. In the devout Koranic style favoured by Saudi Arabians which, in a curious way resembles the Biblical narratives of seventeenth-century English writers, Yamani described the Vienna saga in a lengthy broadcast on Saudi television:

TO TELL OR NOT?

"A believer, in his lifetime, encounters many tragic events which leave painful marks upon him, and he continues to mull them over as though the hour of tragedy would never depart from him.

"But a patient believer learns from his experience and allows it to be a guide for his actions, and a lantern to shine upon the remaining days of his life. Reason tells him to refrain from talking about such tragedy and attempts to remove from his memory the spectre of it, so that by trying to pretend it is forgotten, it might actually be forgotten.

"I made a personal vow after escaping from the hands of the criminals and returning to my homeland, people and relations, not to speak in detail about the crime and criminals. I thought that in this way I could recover my breath which had almost been stopped by terrorist hands. But the fears of my people, and their love, both apparent and concealed, forced me to respond to their enquiries and explain to them what happened in Vienna. That in itself brought back the sufferings which I was trying to forget. But I am forced to go back over those memories and to live with them. I consulted a friend who said to me, either you must refrain from talking about it altogether, or you must sit down and write about the things which happened to you and your colleagues. By writing your account you can, at the same time, bring out what is now locked in your heart, satisfy those who love you, and record the facts which may then be read later by anyone who desires to do so. I replied that, God willing, I should take this second course, because I could not at this moment publish all the facts which I had known and every word which I had heard. My freedom of speech is restricted by my feelings of responsibility, but there will come a day when the facts will be fully known, God willing, and the light of truth will unveil those who work in the dark.

"That which happened to me and my friends was not the first, nor the last, such happening. For the criminals and those who use them as tools have to their account a series of ugly crimes perpetrated against true believers in God and against those who fight against the forces of evil, atheism and all kinds of imperialism.

"If I seem to avoid some important facts for the present, this is not because I wish to sacrifice the truth, but as a step towards disclosure. A deep and precise reader will find what he wants by reading between the lines. And the day will come when we can hit the nail upon the head."

AT OPEC HEADQUARTERS

"The Minister's Conference of OPEC was in session [on Sunday, December 21st 1975]. Discussion was heated and strong differences of opinion were apparent. I was just listening at that moment and not taking any part in the discussions. Suddenly we heard shots fired inside the Conference Hall. I turned my face towards the door and I saw two gunmen with veiled faces. Like the other conference members I at once threw myself under the conference table hoping it would provide protection from the bullets of the attackers. My first thought was that those attacking must be Europeans protesting against the rise in the price of oil, who had come to avenge themselves upon those responsible for that rise. I felt certain that I was going to die and began to repeat from the Koran the following verse: 'To the righteous soul will be said: O thou soul, in complete rest and satisfaction! Come back to thy Lord, well content thyself and well-pleasing unto Him! Enter thou, then, among thy devotees! Yea, enter thou my Heaven!'

"I was still repeating this verse when firing stopped in the Hall. It continued outside and I heard the explosion of a bomb. Then there was silence for a short time before it was broken by a voice in Arabic with a foreign accent crying: 'Yusef, put down the explosives.' Another foreigner asked in English: 'Have you found Yamani?' The Oil Minister from Gabon looked towards me with pity when the terrorist with the foreign accent began examining the faces of those of us taking refuge under the table. When his eyes met mine he made an ironic salute and went to tell his colleagues that he had found me.

"After they had checked to see whether we were armed and searched us one at a time, they divided us into three groups: the 'criminal group', which included the Iranians and the Saudis and members of the delegations of Qatar and the United Arab Emirates; the 'liberals and semi-liberals', which included Iraq, Libya, Algeria and Kuwait; and the 'neutrals', which comprised the non-Arab members of OPEC. Officials of OPEC were brought together and assembled in another corner, after the release of those among them who were British because the gang leader said there was no enmity between the terrorists and the British.

"Two of the terrorists left the room and were replaced by two others, including a girl in her twenties. She said to her boss with a slight smile: 'I killed two,' and he replied, also smiling, 'Quite right, I killed one myself.' She asked about me and he pointed at me.

"Then the leader, speaking Arabic with a foreign accent, declared that they were Palestinian commandos and they had demands to make, and that their operation was basically directed against Iran and the Kingdom of Saudi Arabia. They asked everyone to co-operate and then no one would be killed. The leader wrote a message, gave it to one of the girl staff and set her free to pass it on to the Austrian authorities. We heard later that he had demanded that the Austrians should broadcast a previously prepared political statement and provide a getaway aircraft for him and the gang. If the Austrian government refused, then he would kill a member of the United Arab Emirates' delegation, then an hour later a man from the Kingdom of Saudi Arabia's delegation, and then an Iranian delegate. If that failed to win the gang's demands, then other steps would be taken. After a short time he asked, 'Who is the number two in the Saudi delegation?' Mr. Abdul Aziz Al Turki, the Deputy Minister, stood up. The leader ordered him to go and sit by himself, then he wrote another message to the Austrian authorities and had it delivered by another female employee of OPEC. We learned later that he had given them the name of the first victim chosen to be killed.

"In order to give a complete picture of the beginning of the story of terror, I must describe things which happened in the first stages of the assault on the building, which I did not see myself but heard about from colleagues who were outside the conference hall. When the two gunmen began shooting in the hall, two others entered side rooms to search them and detain people not taking part in the conference. The girl terrorist destroyed the telephone exchange with a bomb. At that moment the elevator door opened and a policeman in his sixties appeared. He had heard the explosion and the shots and had come to investigate. The girl shot him dead with her pistol. An Iraqi officer grabbed her gun hand, but as he bent over her she reached for another pistol with her left hand with remarkable speed and shot him in the stomach, killing him.

"The head of the gang moved with the speed of lightning between the hall and the main entrance, supervising the operation. A young Libyan who works for OPEC, known for his calm and excellent character, engaged in a hand-to-hand fight with him, threw him to the ground and seized his machine-gun. Perhaps the Libyan did not know how to use it and the head of the gang was fast and killed him with six shots from his pistol.

"The gang had no difficulty in entering the building for, despite the fact that OPEC had often been the target for threats and terrorism, there were no security guards there. On many occasions we have had to evacuate the building because of bomb threats. One bomb did explode on the first floor of the building where the Canadian Embassy is located. It killed and wounded a number of people.

"From the time that the terrorists attacked at 11.30 a.m. on the Sunday until 2.00 p.m. we constantly asked them about their identity and true aims. It was difficult to believe that they were Palestinian commandos, for their leader was a non-Arab, his native language was Spanish and his nickname Salem. One of the others was a foreigner speaking German, and the girl spoke little Arabic, though she was good in English and German, and her pseudonym was Nada. The second in command of the gang was Lebanese and was known as Khalid. They had with them one Palestinian, called Yusef, who was clumsy in his movements and had worked as a farmer in Kuwait. The sixth person looked like a Hadrami (from South Yemen), though his accent did not confirm either that or his pretence to be a Palestinian.

"Once the terrorists had everything under control and had sorted out their hostages and felt convinced that there would be no further resistance, they began talking to us. The leader, when he had finished talking to Arab ministers, sought out the Venezuelan minister and began talking to him in kindly fashion. That convinced us that the leader was the well-known terrorist, Carlos. This came as an unpleasant shock to me, for when the French government raided his apartment last summer and he escaped, papers and documents were found there – and among them was a plan to assassinate me. The plan revealed that he and his gang knew all the details of my movements and way of life, and had a list of places I visit in the town in which they had decided to carry it out.

"I kept quiet, reciting suitable Koranic verses which I remembered. At three o'clock Carlos asked me to go to one of the smaller rooms with him so that he could talk to me. I thought then that he intended to kill me, for when they kill a hostage they take him to an isolated place away from the others. The fact that some of my colleagues had the same thought showed clearly by the expressions on their faces.

"I sat with Carlos in the dark room waiting to know what he intended to do. He began by talking pleasantly and soothingly. He even praised me. I listened in disbelief. But soon he revealed the bitter truth. He said that despite the respect in which they held me, they would have to kill me as an expression of protest against the policy of my government. Unless the Austrian government agreed to broadcast their communiqué and provide an aircraft by 5.00 p.m. they had fixed 6.00 p.m. as the time for my assassination. Carlos then said that he hoped I would not feel bitterness against them because they intended to kill me, and that he expected a man of my intelligence and mind to understand their noble aims and intentions. At first I thought that he was manoeuvring with this strange talk and trying to put pressure on me by frightening me in order to get something. I replied: 'How can it be that you tell me that you will kill me and then ask me not to feel bitterness towards you? You must be trying to force me to do something.'

"He laughed sardonically and said: 'You! Why should I put pressure on you? I am putting pressure on the Austrian government to get out of this place. This is what I did when I sent the two messages', and he told me the contents of the two notes. 'So far as you are concerned I am just making you aware of the facts. If the Austrians do as we say, then we will all go from here to Tripoli, Libya, and there the non-Arab ministers will be released, excepting the Iranian ones, and so will the

Libyan and Algerian ministers and some of the delegation members. Then we shall go to Baghdad to release the Iraqi minister, and perhaps the Kuwaiti one if we decide not to stop at Kuwait. You and the Iranian will remain with us and we shall go to our last stop, Aden.'

"There my talk with Carlos ended, though here I have mentioned only part of it. Then I returned to my place and my colleagues were happy to see me back after the twenty minutes I had spent with the criminal in the dark room listening to his astonishing and frightening stories. The frankness of this talk as well as his lengthy later conversations surprised me. Yet I understood that the terrorist plan was aimed at killing me together with Dr. Amuzegar, the Iranian Minister of the Interior, when we arrived in Aden and I therefore believed that his confidences would go with me to the grave."

WRITING A WILL

"I cannot deny that waiting for death is a frightening and painful thing. But the human soul is strange. When the hour was five and the Austrian government had not broadcast the communiqué, Carlos, with a smile on his face, came to remind me what would happen. My feelings had changed and there was less terror in my heart. I began to think, not of myself, but of my family, children and relatives, and of those for whom I had responsibility. I began to write a farewell letter to them, explaining what I wanted to be done, and I asked my colleague Khader Harazallah to deliver it for me. Even so, how happy I felt when Vienna Radio began to broadcast the statement at 5.20 p.m. and when we heard that the Austrians had placed an aircraft at the disposal of the terrorists to take them wherever they wanted to go. Originally Carlos had asked for the Libyan ambassador to act as liaison officer between him and the Austrians. But he was absent and the Iraqi chargé d'affaires came instead and, with great energy and without rest, negotiated up to the time of our departure.

"The plan, as we were told by Carlos, provided for our departure from Vienna to Tripoli, Libya. But this was changed because the Algerians insisted that we should go there. Carlos agreed to accept the Algerian invitation and decided to release in Algiers the Algerian minister as well as the other non-Arab ministers, except the Iranian. Otherwise the plan would be as he had outlined already.

"At nightfall things were calm. They brought us food, but as there was pork and ham most of the Moslems refrained from eating. Then they brought the food prepared for a banquet which the Secretary General of OPEC had planned to offer us that night, but which the incident had prevented from taking place. Everyone ate and we stayed in our chairs all night without sleep.

"At 7.00 a.m. on Monday, Carlos began moving around issuing orders to his colleagues. Once they were convinced that their conditions had been accepted they led us, one delegation after another, to the waiting bus. They released all staff members of OPEC and then some delegation members because there was not enough room for everybody on the bus. We set out towards the airport preceded by an ambulance and two police cars.

"Careful precautions were taken by the terrorists as they brought us from the bus and into the aircraft. They had already made a search of the aircraft, which was empty except for the German terrorist, who had accidentally shot himself in the stomach with a bullet from his pistol . . ."

ON THE WAY TO ALGERIA

"As soon as we were airborne from Vienna, Carlos appeared much more at ease. I had noticed that, from the beginning of the raid until this moment, he seemed beset with worries which he tried to conceal by keeping a perpetual smile on his face. The flight from Vienna confirmed his success and he now felt sure that the rest of his plan could be carried through without hindrance. He began to talk and discuss things with us much more freely. I said to him: 'Why have you chosen Algiers as your first destination instead of Tripoli where you had originally decided to go?'

"And he said: 'Algeria is a revolutionary country, and I could not refuse its invitation. Despite the fact that I do not co-operate with the Algerians, they cannot obstruct my plan.'

"I said: 'Will our stay in Algiers be for long?' And he replied: 'Not more than two hours during which time I shall release some of the ministers I had previously decided to set free in Libya. Then I shall ask them to broadcast the statement, and I do not think they will refuse.'

"I said: 'Where will we stay tonight?' And he answered with his usual smile: 'Do not ask too many questions.' I said: 'Then you expect difficulties in Libya?' He looked at me strangely astonished and said: 'On the contrary, the Prime Minister will be there to receive us, and a Boeing plane will be ready to take us to Baghdad.' I said: 'Will it stop in Damascus?' And he replied: 'I gave you my opinion respecting the Syrians. They have become deviationists and dangerous, and I will not set foot on their soil.'

"The plane began to land in Algiers airport and the terrorists went about their preparations in a brisk and businesslike manner. They carried guns and other weapons and had the alert air of men about to go into battle. When the plane came to a standstill the blinds were pulled down so that we could see nothing and they warned us not to raise them. As the rear door opened, Carlos stood by it pointing his machine-guns outwards, while the other four in various parts of the aircraft trained their weapons on us. As one of the Algerians, and I found out later that this was the Foreign Minister, began climbing the stairway into the plane, Carlos shouted in a loud voice, 'Go out.' Then the Algerian Minister for Energy, who had been with us all the time, left the plane before returning to take Carlos with him. The aircraft door was shut again. Inside there was an atmosphere of silent horror among the hostages, caused by the alertness and anxiety of the terrorists. We kept silent for a long time during which Carlos was negotiating with the Algerians who tried to persuade him to release us all in return for complying with his demands. But he refused and insisted on sticking to his plan. They tried to make him give an agreement not to harm me and the Iranian minister, but he refused to give such a guarantee, although he did promise to do his best not to harm us. The Algerians also made an attempt to persuade Carlos to promise that after going to Baghdad he would return to Algiers and make that his final stop. He agreed to do this, unless he received orders while in Baghdad to continue his trip to Aden. Carlos returned to the aircraft with the Algerian Foreign Minister, who did his best to restore tranquillity and peace to our souls.

"Then the ministers and delegation members who were to be released left the aircraft. The plane door shut again as Carlos left for yet another round of negotiations which, despite the amount of time spent, did not, it seemed to us, produce any result.

"Carlos returned in the company of the Algerian Minister of Energy, who although released had decided to accompany us to Libya."

ON THE WAY TO LIBYA

"Once the plane had taken off from Algiers bound for Tripoli, the blinds were pulled up and the terrorists became calmer, and this was reflected in their behaviour towards us. They brought food, which we were more than ready for, and began talking to us more freely. Carlos spoke about the endeavours of the Algerians to save my life and that of the Iranian minister. He said that he was surprised to see their deep concern about two reactionaries, and then he spoke again about the plane which the Libyans would place at our disposal. He also spoke about our trip to Baghdad and the return to Algiers, unless he received orders to go to Aden. He was interrupted by the voice of his co-partner in crime, Khalid the Lebanese, who announced over the plane's loud-speaker that the Libyan Prime Minister, Abdul Salam Jalloud, would be there to receive us at Tripoli airport. At 7.00 p.m. after two hours' flight, the plane landed at the airport there. The terrorists were calm and their automatic weapons were not held at the ready, although some of them had their pistols out. No one ordered us to pull down the blinds. The Libyan Prime Minister was an hour and a half late arriving at the airport and during that time we had to stay inside the aircraft. When he did arrive at 8.30 p.m. the door of the plane was opened and the Libyan Oil Minister left it together with Khalid, the second in command of the gang. He was away for more than an hour during which time the plane door remained open and we were free to move about inside and to go to the lavatory without asking permission. I asked Carlos why he did not go himself to negotiate as he had done in Algiers. He said it was because of the mentality of the Libyans who demanded that the negotiations should be conducted by an Arab. In any case, things in Libya were easy to arrange and without complication.

"After about an hour Khalid returned in the company of the Libyan Prime Minister and the Minister of Petroleum. The Prime Minister was received at the door by Carlos. First the Prime Minister went to the other Oil Ministers aboard and spoke to them in kindly fashion before finally returning to salute the Iranian minister and myself. He told us that our lives were not in danger. After that he went with Carlos to the front of the plane where they spent a long time talking with no one to hear except God. We could not hear what they were saying though we could see the movements of their hands. The Libyan talked more than he listened, while Carlos listened more than he talked, and quite often his head moved as he listened.

"Finally, the Prime Minister left, together with his Foreign Minister. Carlos told us there was some kind of misunderstanding which might

require us to stay at Tripoli airport for some time. The plane which
the Libyans were going to supply was at Tobruk airport. It was a
Boeing 737 and would not have the range to reach Baghdad non-stop
unless headwinds moderated. For this reason the Prime Minister was
trying to charter a Boeing 707 from an international company or from
another Arab airline.

"Outside the weather was wet and stormy. Inside it was calm
although Carlos began to show signs of anxiety, and exhaustion showed
on the faces of his colleagues who, because they had been standing
guard over us, had not slept the night before. The girl went forward and
burst into tears, while Khalid was ill and began to vomit. Carlos sat
beside me trying to hide his worries by talking about himself, telling
me of his childhood, his studies, his relations, his adventures and his
amours.

"When midnight came, Carlos could no longer contain his emotions
and began openly criticising the Libyans, saying: 'These people are not
disciplined. It is impossible to work with them.'

"Carlos, seeing that the morale of his colleagues was collapsing,
decided, when he heard that the Libyans had failed in their efforts to get
a Boeing 707, to take our Austrian Airlines plane to Tobruk. There he
could transfer us to the Libyan Boeing 737 and fly on from there to
Baghdad. He asked the Captain of the Austrian plane to fly us there,
but the Captain said that he did not know Tobruk and he did not have
the charts for that journey. The Libyans offered to provide one, but
he said he could not adapt it to his DC9 system. Carlos had no choice
but to return to Algiers, where he might be able to find a Boeing 707
which could take him to Baghdad. He seemed to take this decision
against his better judgment and ordered the Captain to fly to Algiers
again.

"Before we left, Carlos offered to release, among others, two of my
Saudi colleagues. They refused and had to be forced off the plane by
Carlos. As he was leaving, one of them said: 'For God's sake, do not
harm Zaki Yamani.' Carlos replied, almost laughing: 'I have received
instructions here in Libya from my bosses not to do any harm to him
or to the Iranian minister, and I can now promise you that they will be
safe. I could not make that promise to the Algerians.'

"As I scrutinised his face I found that his expression was full of
mockery and sarcasm. But then I tried to convince myself that he
really was being honest in his words and that because of my own fears

I was reading fanciful interpretations into what I read upon his face. My lips opened with prayers to God and recitations from the Koran."

TOWARDS AN UNKNOWN END

"Once we were airborne again Carlos had an idea which would prevent him falling into Algerian hands again. He went to the Captain and ordered him to land at Tunis airport, and after informing the airport control of his intentions he began to prepare for landing. But the Tunisian government refused authorisation to land. Carlos was not convinced and ordered the Captain to take the plane down, no matter what the authorities said. At this point the Tunisians blacked out the airport runway lights, which made it impossible for us to land. So we had to climb again and make for Algiers. When we arrived the same precautions were taken as before. Carlos was away from the plane for a long time and finally returned with the kind of smile on his face which made us feel that he was hiding something unpleasant.

"He came to us and said: 'I do not know what I should do. I am a democrat and you (meaning me and the Iranian minister) do not know the meaning of democracy. I shall have a meeting now with my colleagues and consult them on what to do about your case. I shall inform you later about the decision taken.'

"Then they all went forward, though one man who stood quite close to them faced in our direction and kept us covered with his machine gun. We could see them talking and see that the girl and Khalid were obviously furious. Their faces were contorted and their hand gestures showed how nervous they were. We sat there silently awaiting the results of this meeting which would decide our fate.

"When it ended, Carlos came back followed by his comrades. His smile seemed broader and his eyes shone with self-satisfaction. Addressing my Iranian colleague and myself he said: 'We have finally decided to release you by midday and with that decision your life is completely out of danger.' I said: 'Why wait till then. It is late at night and if you release us now both you and ourselves can have some rest which we badly need.' He replied that he wanted the excitement to be prolonged until noon. My colleague Abdul Aziz Al Turki said there was no objection to that, but it was impossible to sleep because the plane seats were old ones and very uncomfortable. Carlos replied: 'We shall turn off the lights and pull down the blinds. You will sleep peacefully knowing that your lives are no longer in danger.' At this point the girl, to express her wrath, cried out an obscene English word, which I cannot mention in print. My heart sank, for I knew that Carlos had told us lies.

"But the gang began to treat us more kindly. One served the Iranian minister and myself with coffee, another brought me some sweets, and a third gave me a pillow to help me sleep.

"The lights were dimmed, the blinds lowered and the Captain of the aircraft and his co-pilot left the plane. The atmosphere was one of choking silence. It seemed to me like the calm before the storm. The Algerian authorities called Carlos by radio and asked him to go and discuss some points with them. He left and was absent for some time while I sat in my seat waiting for evil things to happen.

"I do not know how the Algerian authorities learned of the decision taken at the terrorists' meeting when they exercised their 'democratic rights' and discussed our situation. But the decision they had taken was the opposite of what Carlos had told us, for they had planned to execute me and my Iranian colleague at 7.00 in the morning and to deliver our bodies to the Algerians. By so doing they would have carried out their original plan with only slight modifications. Originally the plan was to execute me in Vienna and my Iranian colleague in Aden, or if that was not possible, to kill us both in Aden.

"Our Algerian brothers handled the situation with skill and ability, and God granted them success in saving our lives. After a long absence Carlos returned to the plane. Both he and his comrades looked very nervous and angry. He certainly was not exercising his democracy now, nor asking the benefit of the gang's opinion. I could see him talking in a tense manner as though he was giving instructions. Then he came back and awakened those who were asleep. Standing in front of myself and the Iranian he spoke in a rough manner full of threats for the first time since we met. He said that he and his comrades had decided to kill the two of us and that their decision was final. If we escaped death this time, their hands in future would stretch to wherever we might be and faster than we might imagine, to implement the decision. Carlos then made violent attacks against us and against the policies of our two governments. He told us that they were about to leave the aircraft and that we were to leave after that and to surrender ourselves to the Algerian authorities.

"They went and we waited for a few minutes expecting someone to come. Then tired of waiting we began to leave. We could hardly believe that we were stepping as free men on to Algerian soil. Our Algerian brothers led by the Foreign Minister arrived to receive us and took us to a room in the airport next to the one where the terrorists were sitting.

"I sat with my Iranian colleague and brother Abdel Aziz Bouteflika, the Algerian Foreign Minister, and the other released hostages. At this point Khalid, the Lebanese terrorist, asked if he could come over and talk to us. After he had handed over his pistol the Algerian security men allowed him to do so. Standing in front of us he spoke in Arabic, repeating what Carlos had said in English when he threatened us in the aircraft. His eyes were dilated while he talked and they shifted constantly. His right hand moved nervously over his chest. This gesture aroused the suspicion of the plain clothes Algerian security men keeping watch. It was the Algerian Foreign Minister who acted smartly. He offered him a glass of fruit juice and said to him: 'Khalid, take this and drink it.' Khalid took the glass in his hand and silently drank. Then he put it down and walked back towards the other terrorists.

"As he moved Algerian security men surrounded him and he stopped. They swiftly searched him and discovered a pistol in a shoulder holster. When they questioned him, he replied: 'I went to carry out the death sentence against the criminals. You have prevented me from doing that.'

"When the Algerians told us what had happened, we praised God again and bowed down with thanks, beseeching Him to let our lives – whether long or short – be consecrated to the service of our religion and creed, and praying that at the end He might take us back, completely believing in Him and following the teachings of His Prophet."

Chapter Nine
Kidnap at Christmas

SHEIKH YAMANI'S ACCOUNT OF THE OPEC AFFAIR DIFFERS IN SOME details from other accounts, but this must be expected in the confusing and frightening circumstances in which the oil ministers found themselves, especially as Yamani believed that he was living his last few hours. There is also a certain reticence on the part of Yamani to tell all he knows because he is an Arab and to tell everything would reflect on the Arab cause, the ideal of Arab unity. "My freedom of speech," he explains, "is restricted by my feelings of responsibility . . ." And, while his account has the immediacy to be expected from a man caught up in the desperate process and whose life was in danger throughout, it is necessary to leaven it with the somewhat less Arab-slanted accounts of others who saw what was going on. Here then is the story of what happened that icy Sunday morning a few days before Christmas, 1975.

Carlos had arrived in Vienna on a circuitous route from North Africa by way of Switzerland where he stopped to leave a copy of his political communiqué, the broadcasting of which was one of his main demands once he had the oil ministers in his power. He left the communiqué with the local collaborators who later made anonymous phone calls to journalists at the United Nations press centre in Geneva telling them where to find it. The result of this piece of planning was that the newspapermen knew the contents of the communiqué several hours before it was broadcast from Vienna and it would have been made public even if the raid had been a failure.

The frontier crossing from Switzerland to Austria presented no difficulties to Carlos, for the Christmas traffic meant that there were thousands of cars taking skiers to winter sports resorts in Austria. Dr. Werner Liebhardt, head of the Austrian special branch, who commanded the police on the spot during the incident, expressed the difficulties of security men in action against terrorist infiltrators.

"I cannot say whether the group brought their weapons with them, or whether they collected them in Vienna from a friendly embassy. I cannot give a detailed description of their weapons because the hostages were unable to say what kind they were, and they obviously never saw their numbers and marks of origin.

"But it is not difficult to smuggle such things into Austria. Millions of tourists come here. At peak times, cars come across the border at the rate of 6,000 an hour, and if we checked them all there would be queues of cars at least 100 kilometres long. We cannot do it. We cannot say, on the one hand, come and visit our nice country, and then search their cars when they come and ask questions of them all. So it is obvious that some of them bring forbidden things."

He was the first senior officer to arrive at OPEC's headquarters in the Ringstrasse, Vienna's famous central ring boulevard. He found that the terrorists were already in control. After several months of investigation and consideration of detailed reports of what happened, he said: "There is no doubt that Carlos and his group had made very careful plans. We could tell at once that they knew every detail about the building. They knew exactly where to go, and each member of the gang knew precisely what to do.

"Carlos is a perfect terrorist leader; he is a professional and probably works only for money. But he leads from in front. He was the first man into OPEC and he gave the orders at every stage in the operation. He was responsible for everything that happened."

Not one subsequent arrest has been made in Vienna. But the police reports and the comments of senior officers demonstrate that the Carlos group had collaborators in Austria who prepared the ground for them before they arrived on the eve of the raid. Who were these people? Certainly a number of Arabs with regular access to the building who might have sympathised with the Palestinians could have informed them about dispositions within OPEC. But the group also had detailed information about Vienna airport and German sympathisers with Baader-Meinhof were the most likely agents in a German-speaking country to acquire such knowledge, to hire the necessary cars, and to provide safe accommodation for the gang. Both Hans-Joachim Klein, one of its members, and his girlfriend, Gabriele Kröcher-Tiedemann, had contacts in the Austrian capital.

Carlos and his five comrades first emerged into public view when they walked through the deserted streets of central Vienna to the OPEC headquarters. A few hundred yards away the *Christkindlmarkt* was in full voice and carols celebrating peace on earth rang out as they made their way towards the modest white-fronted building which OPEC shares with Texaco and the Canadian Embassy. A solitary policeman at the door paid no special attention to the trendily dressed group of five men and a girl carrying Adidas sports holdalls. They might have been anybody.

Inside, the ministers were disagreeing about oil price differentials and the thought of lunch was hovering about the tables, for it was 11.40 in the morning. Sidney Weiland, Vienna bureau chief of Reuters, was chatting with an Associated Press correspondent from Rome, who noticed the group. Because most had swarthy complexions he made a mild joke: "Here's the delegation from Angola," he said, for there had been talk of Angola joining OPEC.

The group, among them the German girl wearing a grey wool cap pulled down to her eyes, also passed Ron Taggiasco, the Milan correspondent of *Business Week*, there to cover the conference. Carlos showed no interest in the journalists. His initial target was on the first floor – the telephone switchboard where Edith Heller, the receptionist, sat politely saying, "Good morning, OPEC." And his immediate task was to prevent a telephone warning from going out.

Klein, the German terrorist, took care of that. He went up to the switchboard and asked: "Where's the conference room?" Miss Heller had a moment to observe Carlos in his Basque beret before Klein started firing. As she reached for the telephone he drilled a neat hole in it with his handgun and then blasted the switchboard.

Among those in the reception area were the two Austrian police guards, Inspector Janda and Inspector Tichler, both of Special Branch. Anton Tichler, an agile sixty-year-old, made a brave attempt to disarm Carlos by grabbing the barrel of his machine pistol, but he failed and Carlos wrenched it away from him and ran on towards the conference room, where he had other business to attend to.

Tichler had specialised in VIP protection duties and had security responsibilities for the Shah of Persia when he visited Vienna. He was fascinated by the Middle East and had taken Arabic lessons. He intended, after retirement, to make a long trip to that part of the world. Inspector Tichler was also aware of Carlos. His boss, Dr. Liebhardt, said: "Tichler knew a good deal about Carlos. He had certainly seen his dossier and was well informed about terrorist attacks."

But now he was alone, except for his colleague Janda, against a heavily armed gang – equipped only with a Walther PPK holstered under his plain-clothes jacket.

When the girl terrorist Gabriele asked in English: "Are you a policeman?" he declared that he was and she deliberately shot him dead with a bullet through the neck. This action, and the words, betray her Baader-Meinhof training – "Policemen are pigs; they must be shot." She shot Tichler from behind at a range of four feet, then pushed him, mortally wounded, into the lift, which she despatched to the ground floor.

A few seconds later Ali Hassan Khafali, a security member of the Iraqi delegation to OPEC, tried to rush Carlos and seize his carbine. Again it was the German girl Gabriele who acted decisively to save her leader by shooting the Iraqi dead. Her two quick and murderous interventions to get Carlos out of trouble explain the self-satisfied girlish smile of pleasure when she said to him later in the presence of Sheikh Yamani – "I killed two." Later she apologised to the Iraqi chargé d'affaires mediator and claimed that she had to kill his country-man because he had tried to disarm her, and as though to prove it displayed her torn coat.

The German girl was later identified through meticulous Austrian police work with the aid of Interpol. A twenty-eight-year-old sociology student and anarchist, she is a classic example of the middle-class urban revolutionary.

She had been sentenced to eight years' imprisonment in 1973, convicted of three attempted murders, blackmail and theft. She was in prison at Essen until the Baader-Meinhof operation in Berlin in March 1975 when they seized Peter Lorenz, the Social Democrat politician, and threatened to murder him unless five imprisoned members of the gang were released. The German government, faced by a threat which the terrorists would have carried out, capitulated and Gabriele was one of the five released in exchange for Lorenz's life. She was flown to freedom in Aden. It was there, busy complaining about the food, that she was contacted by the Carlos group and readied for service in Vienna.

Among the pictures of known terrorists shown to the hostages of the OPEC siege, hers was identified by several people. The Austrians then showed television films made of the release of the anarchist prisoners at the time of the Lorenz affair, and no less than eleven of those held prisoner during the OPEC affair recognised her.

After Gabriele had killed the first police officer, Carlos himself seized the second guard, Inspector Janda, by the arm. Firing wildly, he ran with him down the corridor towards the main conference room, then thrust him into a side office. Through the careful reconnaissance he is known to have made, Carlos was aware that apart from the two uniformed police officers at the door of the building, who were more concerned with parking than terrorism, the only security was provided by the two Special Branch men inside. One had now been killed and the other immobilised.

Resistance was offered by only one other man, and he paid for it with his life. As Carlos approached the conference room, Yousef Ismirli, an economist on the staff of the Libyan delegation, bravely attempted to seize the terrorist leader's machine pistol. Although, as his friends in Tripoli later said, he was a calm and peaceful man, Ismirli almost succeeded in wrenching Carlos's weapon away from him. Only the sling wound round his arm retained it and this gave him the chance to draw an automatic and shoot Ismirli in the shoulder as he turned. Two 9mm bullets struck him down and then Carlos pumped three more rounds into the dying man. It was the same reflex which had prompted him in the rue Toullier to blast away in fury at the dying Moukharbel. It is entirely in keeping with Carlos's strange personality that later he apologised to the Libyans for this shooting. He behaves like a child who wantonly destroys things and believes that he can make amends with an apology and a smile.

Meanwhile, in the side office where Carlos had pushed him, Inspector Janda prudently got rid of his weapon, reasoning that the odds against him were too great, and asked a terrified secretary crouching there how to get an outside line. At just after 11.44 he rang police headquarters to give the alarm. "Inspector Janda, Department One," he said, "OPEC attack. Shooting with machine pistols." And as if in confirmation, the shots which killed the Libyan punctuated his message on the tape recording made of the call at police headquarters.

His call arrived almost simultaneously with one from an OPEC staff member named Enis Attar. By the time that Carlos and his confederates had rounded up the eleven OPEC ministers, and the fifty-one other OPEC staff and forced them at gunpoint to lie on the floor, Kommandos of the Vienna riot squad, trained in anti-terrorist work, were reaching the spot.

As the eight-man group, helmeted, wearing bullet-proof jackets and armed with Israeli-made Uzi sub-machine guns, drove up at 11.50, the Carlos group opened fire on them from the windows. Already they were too late. Even Chancellor Kreisky, defending himself later against charges that the Austrian government had mishandled the affair, was forced to admit that the police guard on this important international building was inadequate.

The riot squad did its best when it arrived. Three of the Kommandos ran upstairs to the first floor under terrorist fire. One of them, Inspector Kurt Leopolder, managed to force the door leading towards the conference room. At this point, a terrorist, probably Klein, hurled a Russian-made hand grenade which detonated in the passage only twenty feet from him. Leopolder fired several bursts and hit Klein in the belly. The other police gave him covering fire and during the lull caused by the shooting of Klein he made more ground. However, while he was taking cover, a shot from the terrorists caught him in the backside and this, for all practical purposes, ended the counter-attack. It was also the end of the twenty-minute battle, and Inspector Leopolder was able to make his way out of the building as the negotiation phase started.

Once again the Venezuelan terrorist leader had won, and won unscathed. But twice he had been in danger of being disarmed. He was saved by the action of his girl supporter, Gabriele. Chief Feyide, the Nigerian Secretary General of OPEC, reported after the affair was all over that very soon after the shooting stopped Carlos, who a few minutes before had been brandishing his sub-machine gun and screaming orders, relaxed and switched into a talkative mood. "He even became friendly," he said. The female, terrorist, Gabriele, was the only one who behaved "in a bestial way". Whenever she was on guard at the conference hall door, he said, it was impossible for anyone to go out, even for a minute, to the toilet. She never spoke a word to her prisoners and used her automatic weapon more threateningly than any of the others.

As the last shots were fired, Carlos was already briefing a British girl named Griselda Carey, who was Chief Feyide's secretary. She was summoned by Carlos who gave her a hand-written note setting out the gang's demands. He asked her to type it out and take it to the Austrian authorities. This was a highly dangerous task, for to do so she had to go down the corridor in which both Klein and the Austrian policeman had been wounded only a few minutes before. Carlos told the young blonde that she must get the policeman out as well.

Nervously shouting "Nicht schiessen, bitte" ("Please don't shoot"), she made her way cautiously down the corridor. When she reached the wounded Kurt Leopolder she said: "Please come with me. We must leave the first floor."

Pale and trembling, Miss Carey said to reporters outside as the police led her away: "Just look at me, I'm shaking. I can't say anything so please don't ask."

But while still inside, she had seen Hans-Joachim Klein, the German terrorist, come into the conference room, sit heavily in a chair near the door and roll up his shirt. She saw what she described as a neat bullet hole in his stomach, and was amazed that there was no blood. The police survivor Inspector Janda, by then rounded up with the others, saw Carlos go over and pat Klein affectionately on the shoulder. If the Uzi bullet had not been deflected by hitting his own machine pistol it would certainly have killed him. But for the moment the terrorists were convinced that he was not badly hurt, and this led to misunderstandings later after he had been taken out for hospital treatment.

Klein had been involved in terrorist activities for a long time and had collaborated with Carlos on several occasions. A rather slight figure in blue jeans, he was part of the Frankfurt connexion, a keen Baader-Meinhof support man who worked as messenger in the offices of a lawyer who had defended anarchists in court.

Althought he was in fact badly wounded and doctors at the Krankenhaus hospital in Vienna feared for his life if he made the long air journey, Carlos and the terrorists who had seen him only as he sat on the chair, apparently not badly hurt, demanded that he should fly with them to Algiers. They insisted not so much because they disbelieved the doctors as because they feared a police trick to keep Klein in their hands for interrogation. Had he stayed in Vienna after the final release of the hostages the police could have discovered a good deal more about the planning of the raid, and the activities of Carlos himself.

Stage one of the negotiations between Carlos and the Austrian authorities was delayed and complicated by the fact that Chancellor

Bruno Kreisky was out at Lech in the Vorarlberg, taking a winter holiday. Although he had been in telephone contact with the Ministry of the Interior he was not able to get back to Vienna until 6.00 p.m. Politically he was in a bad position, for already he had given in rapidly to terrorist demands on another occasion. He had been strongly criticised for agreeing to close down the Schoenau transit camp in Austria, where Soviet Jews stayed on their way to Israel, to save the lives of hostages among them seized by a Palestinian terror squad. Nowhere was the criticism more bitter than in Israel where they look upon him as a backslider, for the ageing Socialist leader was born a Jew, but had renounced Judaism early in his career. His brother, who kept his faith, now lives in Israel.

Reports at an emergency cabinet meeting convinced Kreisky of the seriousness of this affair. "The terrorists' violence of action and their disregard for human life, as manifested already in the killing of three persons, left no doubt as to the serious intention of their threat to kill the hostages held by them in case their demands were not immediately agreed to," he declared later.

His actions were more to defend himself from home political trouble than anything else. He put three conditions to the terrorists before agreeing to their demands. The first was that the hostages should give written consent to be taken from Austria as the terrorists demanded. Eventually he received fifteen such letters in a variety of languages, but as they were produced by men directly threatened by terrorist guns, they were not worth the paper they were written on.

The further conditions were that before the outward flight all OPEC employees domiciled in Austria should be released, and that when the aircraft landed in Algiers the hostages should be set free. Carlos, by now completely in command of the situation, treated these proposals with the contempt which, under the circumstances, they deserved. With a great show of Latin temper he shouted at the Iraqi go-between: "I command Kreisky and everybody else here. I decide who shall go and who shall stay." More coolly, he added that he did not intend to take everyone held in the OPEC building with him, though: "I don't want people telling me who to take."

After going through a number of ritualistic moves, such as summoning the diplomatic representatives of the OPEC states who solemnly endorsed the idea of finding a solution aimed at the prevention of further bloodshed, namely by giving in to the terrorists' demands,

Chancellor Kreisky did just that. The Austrians began making arrangements to provide a bus to the airport and an aircraft to take Carlos and his prestigious hostages wherever he cared to land them. And as we know from the account of Sheikh Yamani, he was still threatening to shoot them.

Chancellor Kreisky set down his views on terrorism in a statement to the Austrian parliament: "The intense terrorist activity during the last few years is a kind of warfare. The combating of terror through absolute rejection of the terrorists' demands has rarely produced their capitulation. On the contrary, it has often brought additional and terrible sacrifices. Retaliatory strategy against terrorism has even brought escalation of its intensity. In any case unyielding policies have not diminished terrorist activities, though I would be prepared to admit that parleys with terrorists and attempts to avoid more casualties are no sovereign remedy either."

In a confrontation between a democratic political leader like Dr. Kreisky whose views haver so publicly, and a ruthless terrorist such as Carlos, who knew precisely what he wanted and had no worries about the means used, there could be no doubt about the outcome. Indeed, one is entitled to speculate about the possibility that Carlos and his masters chose to carry out the operation in Vienna, knowing in advance that the Austrians had given in easily on at least one similar occasion, and reassured by the knowledge that insufficient security precautions were taken there. The final insult from Carlos was his total refusal to negotiate on Austrian soil with any Austrian official, and his final warning when all seemed settled for the departure: "Tell Kreisky that I know all the tricks. He should not try any."

So Carlos and his band ruled over OPEC headquarters all day and all night, making constant demands for small services. The Austrians were told to send in ropes and scissors, for what purposes no one ever discovered; for fruit juice and food – it eventually arrived from the Hilton Hotel. Whenever a delay occurred Carlos threatened to shoot a hostage. Through the night the bodies of the dead Libyan and the dead Iraqi were left lying where they had fallen. The Libyan Ambassador told the Austrians that Yousef Ismirli, the Libyan, had been at school with him.

Despite an appeal for their release by the Libyan diplomat, the remaining secretaries and other women hostages were kept there all night too. Eddie Hinterecker, an Austrian driver for OPEC, also spoke to Carlos and asked him to release the women because they were afraid. Carlos placed an affectionate hand on Gabriele Kröcher-Tiedemann and asked: "Don't you think *she's* scared?"

Once Carlos had the situation tidied up and felt secure enough to negotiate, he presented his demands. He refused to accept an Austrian mediator and demanded instead that the Libyan ambassador to Vienna should act as go-between. But he was not immediately available and so the job fell to Riyadh Al-Azzawi, the Iraqi chargé d'affaires, who, according to his own account, just happened to be nearby when he heard about the raid and therefore offered his services.

Al-Azzawi was alarmed by his first meeting with the terrorists and appeared to be thoroughly bewildered. "I would like to know who I am dealing with," he said to Carlos.

"We are revolutionaries, not criminals," replied Carlos with a smile. "We are the Arm of the Arab Revolution."

"But you're not an Arab," said the Iraqi.

"We are working for revolution all over the world," answered Carlos.

The first of Carlos's demands was that his political testament should be broadcast over the Austrian radio. This was easily agreed to. It was a verbose and banal document couched in all the clichés of Arab extremism. The gang announced that they were "The Arm of the Arab Revolution". This name means nothing except that it places them in the left-wing of the Arab spectrum. Every operation is undertaken by groups which seem to choose their own names, either for the glorification of some martyr or to confuse their origins. Black September was itself chosen as a name to hide its Fatah parenthood.

The communiqué went on to claim that the Arab people were "threatened by a powerful plot", the aim of which was to force the Arabs to capitulate to Zionism. The plotters were accused of attempting to destroy the resistance of the Palestinians. Significantly, in the light of following political events, they were also accused of destroying Arab unity by encouraging religious conflict in the Lebanon.

Then the plotters were denounced by name. They turned out, predictably, to be American imperialism and Zionism. But other active participants were said to be certain Arab governments prepared to capitulate. President Sadat of Egypt was singled out for blame in this respect and the Iranian régime was bracketed with him. They were jointly accused of being "traitors" both to the Arab and to the Palestinian cause. "The most progressive Arab régimes" were named as Syria and Iraq, and praised for acting in support of the Arab peoples. It is interesting to note that Libya, which normally figures in the list of nations actively supporting the Palestinian cause, was not mentioned. Perhaps the revolutionaries, though happy to accept money and help from President Gaddafi, could not bring their leftward-orientated souls to name his non-Marxist state as a progressive régime. Or, more probable, Gaddafi was so deeply implicated it was thought better not to mention him at all.

Be that as it may, the Libyans must have agreed with the hard core principles for a "Programme of National Liberation" laid down in the Carlos statement. The first was strict observance of the three basic demands of the Arab summit conference held in Khartoum: "No negotiations, no treaty, and no recognition to be granted to the Zionist Aggressor State." This was followed by a demand for rejection of any agreement to achieve peaceful solution of the Middle East conflict by compromise. The statement denounced the Egyptian plan to open the Suez Canal to Israeli ships, and called instead for the renewal of "the triumphal advance of the heroic Egyptian army" within the framework of a "war for total liberation".

Carlos and his gunmen who had just stormed their way into the holy of holies of the oil world also called for the nationalisation of Arab oil resources, and insisted that economic support should be given to the "peoples of the Third World, allied in friendship", on condition that priority must be given to the Palestinian resistance.

The statement concluded with a flow of mysterious and threatening rhetoric: "All political elements and forces close to the people's efforts, as well as all governments, are invited to act speedily and honestly in taking a stand on these serious questions on which depend both the future destiny of the loyal camp and the fate of the camp of national treason."

"The Arm of the Arab Revolution" even apologised for the difficulties it had caused the "peace-loving Austrian people" and asked them to understand the earnest and noble motives of the action. This apology was similar to the one given to sportsmen of the world after the Munich massacre: "... But why should our place here be taken by the flag of the occupiers ... why should the whole world be having fun and entertainment while we suffer with all ears deaf to us?"

The Arm of the Arab Revolution described itself as follows:

A movement uniting the fighting elements in all Arab countries, which, expressing the rise of national consciousness and sustained by the deep understanding of the fate and future of the Arab people, has resolved to counteract the plot, striking down its supporters and applying sanctions of revolution to all parties and personalities involved in the plot.

Through the jargon what emerges clearly is that Carlos's men, bravely tricked out in their new colours, were claiming to act on behalf of the whole Rejection Front. Its avowed aims – refusal to negotiate with Israel at any price, the use of force to solve the problem – are comprehensible. But how can it have been imagined that the mass kidnap of the rich and powerful delegates, the holding of them for a few days, and the killing of an Austrian policeman and two staff members would really help to change the minds of other Arab countries as varied as Egypt and Saudi Arabia? The raid can only be seen as a murderous gesture designed to show to the outside world, guilty of occasionally forgetting the Palestine problem and concentrating on others, that its sympathisers have the fire power to punctuate discussion, and that they believe that the sword is more powerful than either the pen or the ploughshare in international affairs. It was a notable coup in what may be called the armed public relations industry.

Once Carlos's precious testament had been revealed to an unastonished world, he set about the real business of the negotiations, the removal of his gang and his hostages to safety in a sympathetic Arab country where a suitable ransom could be arranged. His procedure followed well-tried lines. He wanted a bus with curtained windows to take them to the airport. He wanted a DC9 with a full load of fuel to fly him to whatever destination he named. He got all he wanted – and an astonishing parting embrace from the Austrian Minister of the Interior, Otto Rösch. To the outside world this hug marked the complete submission of the Austrian authorities to the terrorists, but Herr Rösch later argued that he did it not in friendship or with any warmth, but because "the man held out his hand to me and said he wanted to apologise for troubling Austria on what was a political matter".

Carlos had his route and his plan well organised. They were as he described them to Yamani.

"I was surprised that he was so frank with me," Yamani said later.

"But I finally realised that his plan was directed inevitably to the killing of myself and Dr Amouzegar, the Iranian oil minister, upon the arrival of the plane in Aden, and that what he was saying to me was going to be buried by my death."

However, while the negotiations were going on the Algerians invited Carlos to fly his hostages to Algiers. Captain Manfred Pollak of Austrian Airlines had volunteered to fly the DC9 and when they lifted off from Vienna he had been given no firm destination. He did, however, have landing clearance for Algiers and when they had been flying for half an hour Carlos confirmed that Algiers was their destination.

Captain Pollak reported that it was a normal flight, normal that is if you count it normal to fly with a terrorist behind your seat armed with two handguns and pointing a sub-machine gun at you all the time. Interviewed by Don North of CTV (Canadian Television), the pilot said his ordeal was made even worse by the fact that he knew that just one bullet could blow up his pressurised plane.

Meanwhile, his passengers were chatting. Carlos had words in Spanish for his compatriot, Valentin Hernandez-Acosta, the oil minister of Venezuela, and gave him a letter to be sent later to his mother in Caracas. Before the plane reached Algiers, Carlos had found time to sign his autograph for Remi Marinho, the Nigerian delegate. In blue ink he wrote: "Flight Vienna – Algiers 22/XII/75 – Carlos."

Captain Pollak and his co-pilot had been told that they would be freed in Algiers. But once there, Carlos told them: "Now we have to go on to Tripoli and later on to Baghdad." Captain Pollak replied: "Okay, we can make Tripoli easily, but Baghdad is too long a leg for a DC9. I would have to make an intermediate landing for refuelling in Damascus or maybe in Beirut." Carlos was none too pleased with this information and gave the impression that he did not want to land at either city.

Nor was he pleased with the Libyans when his party arrived at Tripoli. Quite apart from the fact that the Libyan diplomat Al Ghadamsi had been missing when he was supposed to mediate in Vienna, turning up nearly twelve hours after the attack started, the Libyan Prime Minister, Major Abdul Jalloud, who had arranged to meet the aircraft at Tripoli, kept them waiting for an hour and then spent another half-hour with Khalid, Carlos's second in command, before coming on board to talk with Carlos.

Captain Pollak described what happened: "At first we had to hold for an hour over Tripoli and then I said I'm getting short of fuel, I have to land, and they said okay and gave me landing clearance. I had to stop the aircraft shortly after leaving the runway. Carlos was frustrated because he was not allowed to go further on to the apron or nearer to the airport buildings. I had the impression that he was not happy with the Libyan government because of their inefficient dealing with him.

"He was very frustrated and dismayed that he could not get the right honour from the Libyan government because the aircraft was stopped by the runway. As I recall, he said something like, he had spent a month preparing this attack and this commanding action, and now he was not getting proper consideration from the Libyan government and that was not right."

Carlos made great efforts to persuade the Libyans to give him an aircraft capable of flying to Baghdad without putting down to refuel. But the Libyans would not, or could not, produce such a plane. The long wait began to tell on the terrorists as well as the hostages. Gabriele broke first. She crept into a corner and wept. Khalid was sick, as Yamani mentions in his account.

Finally, according to Captain Pollak, at about two or three in the morning Carlos said that he had decided to go back to Algiers. "The Algerian government, the Algerian people, are friends, good friends and they will give us an aircraft to go to Baghdad."

The Captain went on to say: "So we landed back in Algiers, and I had the impression that the second time we arrived the welcome was not as enthusiastic as the first. There were more negotiations and Carlos came to me and apologised for holding my plane while he waited for a bigger one. He said it was okay for me to leave, so I took my bag and left the aircraft. They told me to wait in case Carlos wanted to take off again, but after an hour it was all over. The terrorists and the hostages also left the plane."

The role of the airline pilot was finished and his ordeal at an end. "I got from Carlos two big cigars which he said were a present to him from Fidel Castro. I have them at home. And from the Austrian government I later got a medal."

Chancellor Kreisky, who played such an inglorious role in the whole affair, was questioned much later by Don North in an interview for CTV, and asked about his attitudes and conclusions.

"The whole OPEC raid story was an internal Arab one. It was motivated by divergences of opinion between the Palestine Liberation Organisation on one side, and the more extreme and radical Palestine groups represented by the so-called Rejection Front. This action had nothing to do with Austria. It could have taken place anywhere."

When he was interviewed, the Austrian leader had already made a long trip through the Middle East countries, and had no doubt discussed the affair with Arab leaders. His view is that Carlos and his crew had two aims: to kill Sheikh Yamani and Dr. Amouzegar and also to get publicity for the cause of the Rejection Front. The Chancellor then asserted that they had failed to achieve their aims, but he believed that the terrorists themselves "are now more independent because they got a lot of money afterwards. For not killing the two ministers they got a lot of money."

Asked how they got the money he replied: "That isn't up to me to say . . . They haven't got a single schilling in Austria. They got the money outside Austria . . . There was a kind of compensation for not killing . . ."

The Chancellor remains convinced that he did the right thing in yielding to terrorist demands. This, to his way of thinking, saved the lives of the hostages. Carlos, he believes – and this is confirmed by Sheikh Yamani's account – had a great deal of trouble with his comrades. He had to persuade the German girl and "the Palestinians" in the group not to kill the Saudi Arabian and the Iranian minister once they arrived in North Africa.

"When he made up his mind not to kill them and to accept compensation for that, he had troubles with his own people," said the Chancellor. He then hinted again that the result of all this was that Carlos had now become more independent financially. This can only be taken to mean that Carlos became less reliant on the PFLP. As we know, he received a good deal of money from President Gaddafi, as well as from the other sources mentioned by the Austrian statesman. This may well be the explanation of the long pause in Carlos's terrorist activities which followed the climax in Vienna.

The last stage of Operation OPEC ended with a diplomatic defeat for the Austrians. Within a short time the Austrian police, aided by Interpol, had built up dossiers on the persons who had carried out the raid. They were not as detailed and precise as might have been wished, but they were sufficient to allow arrest warrants to be issued. Armed with these, the Austrian government asked for the extradition of six terrorists from Algiers, where they had taken refuge after finally liberating their distinguished prisoners. The Algerian government refused to consider the matter "for legal reasons". President Boumedienne argued that no extradition agreement existed between the two countries and it was not possible to make a special arrangement as proposed by Austria to give reciprocal aid outside such an agreement.

At this stage the Austrians were under the impression that the raiding party was held under arrest in Algiers. This was certainly not true, for they were not only set free as soon as they left the airport, but Carlos himself moved straight to Room 505 at the Albert I Hotel there and was soon joined there by Maria-Teresa Lara, his old girlfriend from Paris. In fact, the Algerians showed that they were on the side of the terrorists and intended to take no action against them, despite the fact that Carlos and his gang had murdered three people, including two Arab "brothers". The Algerian government somewhat cynically declared that it had already made its contribution to the prevention of further bloodshed by allowing the terrorists' aircraft to land at Algiers airport. The spokesman added darkly that they had also been compelled to make their own specific concessions, and said that the extradition request could not be taken further.

The warrant of arrest as issued by the Vienna Criminal Court on December 23rd 1975, remains in force and could still, at least theoretically, provide a legal basis for action against Carlos and his friends. The document names six people:

1. Salem, aged about 30, about 180cm tall, slender but sturdy figure, round face, bold shaped roman nose.
2. Khalid, aged about 30, about 175cm tall, slender figure, curly black hair combed back to the neck, moustache.
3. Joseph, aged about 30, about 175cm tall, slender figure, curly black hair combed back to the neck, moustache.
4. A woman, aged about 25, delicate, small figure.
5. A man at least 180cm tall, who was wounded during the incident in question.
6. Another man who, already detained in connection with the facts of the case in question and in custody in Algiers, has committed the undermentioned crimes in conjunction with the five persons

listed above (in that armed with sub-machine guns and pistols they killed three men, broke into OPEC, etc.).

Those were the meagre descriptions of Carlos – No. 6 on the list – and his gang immediately after the raid. Later, of course, the Austrian police produced a more detailed description list. Hans-Joachim Klein, the wounded German terrorist, was positively identified by fingerprints taken by the Austrian police and sent on to the Wiesbaden Interpol section in West Germany. But the Germans asked for this fact to be kept strictly secret as investigations were still continuing.

Carlos and some of the others were identified by the hostages with whom they had held long conversations. A photograph of Carlos in profile taken at Algiers airport, which appeared in the French magazine *L'Express*, corresponded exactly with one taken from a similar angle by the French DST the previous summer. Yet although at that time, early in 1976, newspapers were writing about Carlos as "the most wanted man in the world", no police force and no secret service seemed very anxious to track him down and some showed positive alarm at the idea that he might be apprehended by mistake. The general fear was that his arrest might lead to a new and terrible act of terrorist retribution. He was, in fact, the world's most un-wanted man. Even the Israelis, who have always been the most ruthless of the forces tracking down terrorists, showed no great interest at this time, for, after all, Carlos had done them no harm. He had attacked, not an Israeli target, but an Arab one. He had killed Arabs and thrown into confusion the Arab-dominated oil exporting organisation, controller of the "oil weapon" which, when employed against Israel in the October War, had almost succeeded in bringing that country to her knees.

Dr. Kreisky, the Austrian Chancellor, believes that the raid had little effect on OPEC. "OPEC is still one of the most powerful institutions in the world. It is still the organisation of the oil-producing countries and as such it is very important for all of us who have to buy oil." That, of course, is true, but nonetheless the organisation was considerably weakened by the fact that its most important ministers were kidnapped and held to political ransom by a terrorist gang enjoying the support of several of its member countries. There can be no doubt that the operation was directed against the more conservative members of the organisation and this in itself has created an atmosphere of suspicion and distrust. Immediately after the raid the more cautious oil countries began considering the idea of leaving Vienna altogether on the reasonable grounds that it had proved unsafe for their deliberations. How can ministers and economists concentrate on the important details of exporting oil and fixing prices when they are in danger of violence at the hands of those who happen to disagree with them?

The events of December 1975 certainly deepened the rift between moderates and extremists among the Arab members of OPEC. The moderates demanded a full enquiry into the raid, the organisation moved to other parts of the world to hold its subsequent meetings, and there is still a strong likelihood that its headquarters may be permanently transferred to some other place, probably on the Arabian Gulf. Since the raid, Saudi Arabia, the biggest single producer of oil, has expressed its views more strongly than before. The Saudis, through their minister, Sheikh Yamani, have insisted on holding the price of oil steady despite attempts by more radical oil governments to increase it in order to "soak the Western capitalists". Whatever the final result, it does look as though Carlos and his terrorists were deliberately attempting to weaken the organisation of oil-exporting states.

That is certainly an objective which would have appealed to the anarchist revolutionaries who fought under Carlos's orders. For them its success would be a blow against capitalism, for in their view OPEC appears closely related to the hated multi-national corporations.

The truth is that the Vienna raid was carried out to satisfy several different aims and to satisfy a number of different clients.

Who were these clients?

Sheikh Yamani refuses to name them, but says: 'A deep and precise reader will find what he wants by reading between the lines ..." So let us do that.

The first client was Carlos himself, and his aim on this occasion was principally the collection of money. Ideologically, as Sheikh Yamani noted, Carlos "is not a committed Communist ... [he] does not believe in the Palestinian cause or in Arab nationalism but ... [considers] them as factors which might be exploited to help spread the international revolutionary movement". His colleagues were Baader-Meinhof militants, willing to strike at any aspect of Western capitalism, and members of the PFLP who regard the monarchical régimes of Saudi Arabia and Iran as only one stage less evil than the Israelis.

Then consider the role of the PFLP who, for ideological reasons and in order to promote the political schemes of the Front of Rejection, provided the logistic framework and resources for the raid. It is obvious from Carlos's refusal to land at Damascus and the scorn with which he spoke of the Syrians that they played no part in the affair. Similarly the Egyptians are innocent. However, the urgency with which he wanted to get to Baghdad and the way in which he was welcomed in Tripoli and Algiers leave little doubt that Iraq, Libya and Algeria were, if not party to the plot, at least sympathetic towards it.

The collusion of the Libyans became apparent when Carlos told Yamani on the flight from Vienna that Prime Minister Jalloud would be at the airport to meet them. The sympathy of the Iraqis is easily understood because of their fervent support for the Front of Rejection and the PFLP. But the Algerian involvement was puzzling at first and despite detailed stories from France and Israel we were, to start with, inclined to believe that the Algerians had merely acted as honest brokers to get the hostages released in exchange for a large ransom. But then Carlos's father started to boast about the way the Algerians had honoured his son and had themselves paid him a large amount of money. At the same time, the Algerian government showed every sign of veering towards the Front of Rejection and had started to make friendly overtures towards Libya. This was because the Algerians needed support in their quarrel with the Moroccans over possession of the Spanish Sahara and its rich phosphate deposits.

We also learnt that there had been a series of top-level meetings involving Iraq, Algeria, Libya and leading terrorists. George Habash and Ahmed Jibril were in Libya and Naif Hawatmeh was in Algiers when the raid took place.

So the "clients" would seem to include Carlos and his revolutionary colleagues, the PFLP, Iraq, Libya and Algeria. But these are only the more obviously interested parties.

Because Carlos is so deeply involved with the Arabs, and because the conflict between the conservative Arab states and the Rejectionist powers stands out so clearly, super-power interests have been left out of account. This is a mistake, for the Soviet Union, too, is an oil power and an oil-exporting power. Ever since the formation of OPEC, the Kremlin leaders have kept a wary eye on its activities, in case decisions taken by the oil exporters might threaten Soviet interests and policies.

In December 1975 the so-called North-South Conference led to the creation of a special committee within OPEC with special responsibility for prices, currency, and aid funds for developing countries. The

USSR was particularly suspicious of the activities of this group because it feared that the committee might upset Russian interests. Although the Soviet Union is not a member of OPEC, its oil-exporting revenue is to some extent affected by decisions taken there on oil prices. When the moderate group of oil powers, led by Saudi Arabia, began talking of holding prices down or even reducing them so as not to upset the world economy their attitude caused no pleasure in Moscow. For one thing, it was in the Russian interest to get increased prices from the fifty million tons of oil a year she exports, and if that objective could be combined with financial pressure to upset things in the West then so much the better.

Soviet interests overlapped with those of the Rejectionist Arabs, in the sense that both desired that the oil weapon should go on being used to cause dissension between OPEC and the West. At the time of the raid, OPEC was considering a plan to provide up to two billion dollars in aid funds for the developing nations. Aid on such a scale, in various parts of the world, would make the poor countries less dependent on the USSR and would therefore undermine Soviet influence. In the détente stage of competition for influence between state Communism and Western capitalism any move which increases the influence of countries like Saudi Arabia and Iran, from which the funds for development would largely come, and thereby the international power of the pro-Western camp, is bad for the Russians.

From the Kremlin eye-view any move which upsets such developments is a useful one. For it is in the Soviet interest to produce crises and friction which might disturb the oil-based relationship between the West, the Arab world and the Third World. It can be argued that the OPEC raid was in the Soviet interest for these reasons, and especially because it was calculated to upset an organisation anxious to support the Western system and to do this by a programme of re-cycling petro-dollars.

For the modest price of three dead, two wounded, fifty rounds of 9mm Parabellum fired and one Russian grenade exploded, Carlos made a powerful point for his masters in North Africa and in the Soviet Union. It is not surprising that he was rewarded with a million-pound bonus.

But of course the aims were not identical with the results, and as it transpired the kidnap partly boomeranged, at least to the extent that the moderates in office became more outspoken and more powerful.

Sheikh Zaki Yamani, who had suffered greatly, summed up the whole thing in his inimitable style, when he told his compatriots: "If a criminal were to deserve the admiration of non-criminals, then Carlos would stand high in the list of those who deserve such admiration. For in addition to his intelligence and outstanding ability, which was displayed during the terrorist assault upon us, many of us believe that he was able to combine all sorts of contradictions by grouping enemies in one force, whatever their aims and intentions. In one operation he served them all, but it was the will of God that not all the prepared aims of his plan were carried out."

NOTE   List of OPEC ministers seized as hostages:

1.	Belaid Abdesselam	Algeria
2.	Jaime Duenas-Villavicencio	Ecuador
3.	Edouard Alexis M'Bouy-Boutzit	Gabon
4.	Lieut. General Dr. Ibnu Sutowo	Indonesia
5.	Dr. Jamshid Amouzegar	Iran
6.	Tayeh Abdul-Karim	Iraq
7.	Abdul Mutalib Al-Kazemi	Kuwait
8.	Ezzedin Ali Mabruk	Libya
9.	Dr. M. T. Akobo	Nigeria
10.	Ahmed Zaki Yamani	Saudi Arabia
11.	Dr. Valentin Hernandez-Acosta	Venezuela

Chapter Ten
The paymaster

WHEREVER ONE TURNS IN THE MAZE OF INTERNATIONAL TERRORISM one comes across the fire-eating figure of Colonel Moammer Gaddafi, President of Libya. He believes in terrorism as a legitimate weapon in his self-appointed role as saviour of Islam, as supporter of nationalistic revolutions and as the most zealous warrior in the battle against Israel. "The battle with Israel," he argued in 1973, "must be such that after it Israel will cease to exist."

President Numeiri of the Sudan, a fellow Moslem, has twice accused him of trying to overthrow the Sudanese government. Numeiri has also made explicit charges that Gaddafi was behind the Khartoum massacre in which three Western diplomats were murdered. President Sadat has accused him of trying to overthrow his régime and of instigating bombings and assassination attempts. The Tunisians have blamed him for sending terrorist teams across the border to bomb and to kill.

He has boasted of his assistance to the Provisional IRA and to the Moslem rebels fighting against President Marcos of the Philippines.

He has given arms, money and training areas to the terrorist organisations. He welcomed the Black September killers of Munich as conquering heroes. Referring to the Lod massacre by the Japanese Red Army, he demanded that the Palestinians "carry out operations similar to the operation carried out by the Japanese . . ." And he has embraced Carlos as an ally in the fight against Israel and those Arab nations that he regards in his fanaticism as renegades. Sadat is blunt about the Carlos-Gaddafi alliance: "It's no secret that Carlos is living in Libya."

This does not mean that Gaddafi likes Carlos. He has bought the

Venezuelan hit-man, just as he would buy any other weapon. He paid Carlos £1,000,000 for the OPEC raid and compensated the German, Hans-Joachim Klein, with £100,000 to ease the pain of his wounds.

Sheikh Yamani has no doubt that it was Gaddafi who financed the OPEC affair and, while he still refuses to blame the Libyan President publicly, he threatens that he will do so when the time is ripe.

And Gaddafi, while boasting about so much of his support for terror, becomes reticent to the point of obtuseness when asked about OPEC – and he is not an obtuse man.

When Ronald Payne interviewed him a few months after the raid, he refused to be drawn, resorting as he often does in private conversation to his technique of counter-questions and heavy silences while he fixes his interviewer with a deep stare. The conversation, conducted under a mimosa tree in a plum orchard behind the Tripoli Cavalry Club, went like this:

Payne: The next question is about the OPEC affair, the raid at Vienna. Do you favour more operations of that kind, and do you believe that they further the cause of Palestine?

Gaddafi: What is the relationship between the raid on the OPEC headquarters in Vienna and the Palestine cause?

Payne: That is what I would like to know, also.

Gaddafi: What is the relationship between the two?

Payne: The relationship, as I understand it, is that it was Palestinians who organised this raid.

Gaddafi: The information I have is that those who carried out the raid were not Arabs.

Payne: Three were non-Arabs, but the others were Arabs.

Gaddafi: How many were there?

Payne: Six.

Gaddafi [smiling]: You have more information than we have.

Payne: I doubt if I have, Colonel. What I understand is that Carlos was in charge of the thing but that there were also a German man, a German woman and three Arabs.

Gaddafi: What nationality is Carlos?

Payne: Venezuelan.

Gaddafi: What is his relationship with the others?

Payne: Perhaps he is a mercenary.

At this point in the conversation Colonel Gaddafi made a most mysterious remark which the interpreter seemed unable to clear up. "Of course, this is a kind of parasite if we interfere in such a subject because we have nothing to do with it," he said. After a pause while the original question was rephrased the Libyan leader declared: "It is not right just to connect hijacking and raids with the Palestinian cause, because such events take place in places like America and other countries without the Palestinian cause being involved ... I think the purpose of connecting the raids with Palestine is just to defame the legitimate struggle for their freedom." This is a fine example of Colonel Gaddafi's disingenuous technique in quiet conversation. A tape recorder had been set upon a chair in front of the Colonel and it could be noticed that whenever questions were broached which caused him worry or embarrassment his foot, as he sat cross-legged, began tapping on the chair. When the tape was played through later the tapping rose to a crescendo during the talk about Carlos and the OPEC raid.

Gaddafi, now in his mid-thirties, has spent nearly half his adult life in command of his country, and the stress of his frequent international adventures, as much as the cares of office, have left their mark on his handsome face. The worry lines make him look older than his years. The son of desert Bedouin people, he came to power by coup d'état in 1969 when, with the aid of eleven other like-minded revolutionaries, he unseated old King Idris and established the Republic.

He and his brother officers, for this was an all-army coup, had one enormous advantage, and that was that Libyan oil had just begun to flow in quantity at the time of their takeover. By 1976 this small state with a population of just over two million people was producing at a rate of 1,737,000 barrels a day. The year before, oil revenues produced a balance of payments surplus of 1,700 million dollars.

Libya, once an Italian colony whose tribal warriors were finally subdued as late as the 1930s, boasted three large coastal cities, Tripoli, Benghazi and Tobruk, and a great deal of desert when it became the sand-table battleground for the epic contest between the Afrika Korps of the "Desert Fox", Field-Marshal Erwin Rommel, and the Eighth Army of "Monty", Field-Marshal Viscount Montgomery of Alamein. After the war Tripolitania, Cyrenaica and Fezzan were welded together under British influence and with British subsidies into the Kingdom of Libya. It was an impoverished country, which had always been kicked about by stronger nations and had developed a national sense of inferiority.

However, by the mid-seventies, all that had changed. Now Colonel Gaddafi is firmly in charge of a state he likes to think is in continual revolution. Under the inspiration of his zealous Moslem desire to clean and purify the Arab world, Libya has the money not only to control its own destiny, but also to finance the thrusting of its President's beliefs abroad. On taking over, Gaddafi set out to exact revenge for the years of indignity and became the paymaster of international terrorism.

In the *Sunday Telegraph* in May 1976, describing his meeting with Gaddafi and the interview already referred to, Payne wrote:

I finally caught up with him in a club house beside the show jumping course and the stables. The Colonel strode in purposefully, rather smartly dressed in well-cut blazer, windcheater and slightly flared Italian-style grey trousers. He greeted me in English and moved straight on to inspect a large coloured photograph of himself in uniform and sunglasses, astride a prancing horse. He and his friends admired this newly hung work of art and the interpreter explained that the Colonel thought it would be nice to talk to me in the open air.

He led the way to a small orchard of blossoming plum trees, inhabited until then only by sheep and goats. Men brought mats and pillows for the followers and folding chairs for the Colonel, the interpreter and me. All were placed in the shade of a mimosa tree, and so it came about that, while Gaddafi discussed matters of state with me, pollen and yellow blossom descended on our heads and the sheep punctuated our conversation with their "baa-ing".

There is no doubt that the Colonel has a flair for the theatrical, for this bucolic interview was carefully stage-managed to present him as a thoughtful and calm man of peace. On other occasions he goes out of his way to impress people differently. Once, while returning to Tripoli at the head of a procession of diplomatic cars, he astonished the ambassadors by borrowing from a passing Bedouin a lively horse and galloping off into the desert. Another time he appeared out of the desert wearing a white robe to address a village crowd in his philosopher-president role.

Even before my interview started, I began to wonder if his policy was not revealed more by his actions than by his guarded words. In a political sense he gallops off madly in all directions: the next minute he behaves pastorally; and the next minute again he is plotting quietly under the trees to bring about some assassination or handing out a few million pounds to a terrorist fund.

This, then, was the strange head of state who provided a North African base for Carlos and the international band of terrorists. Major Omar Mehaishi, the former Libyan Minister of Economics and one of the original junta that came to power with Gaddafi and who later defected to Egypt from where he broadcast a stream of vituperation at the Gaddafi régime, said: "No one can supervise the Colonel, who controls single-handed the budget of Libya." He is answerable to nobody and only he is empowered to sign any cheque above half a million pounds.

Many allegations have been made about Gaddafi conspiracies against Arab rulers of whom he does not approve. There is evidence that in 1975 he spent five million dinars on what proved to be an abortive plot to overthrow President Numeiri of the Sudan. ("Where did the money come from, Brother Colonel?" asked Numeiri at the time.) And in July 1976, after Numeiri had put down another coup, he accused Gaddafi of mounting an invasion of his country. The Tunisians accused two Libyans of plotting to kill their Prime Minister after he had turned down a Gaddafi bribe of 1,000 million dollars to unite Tunisia with Libya.

The Egyptian radio also claimed that Colonel Gaddafi conspired against the late King Feisal of Saudi Arabia, supported an attack on the rest house at Mersa Matruh of President Sadat of Egypt, and tried to set up an air base in the African Republic of Mali against the Algerians and the Moroccans. In 1976 he began purchasing Soviet-made small arms and automatic weapons and despatched quantities of them to left-wing groups fighting in the Lebanese Civil War. It is estimated that £25 million of Libya's money went to Beirut's leftists. And Sadat further accused Gaddafi of being "an instrument in the big power game", an Arab way of accusing Gaddafi of working for the Soviet Union.

The long arm of Libyan aid for mischief has stretched out even beyond the Arab world. On at least one occasion he sent weapons – on board the freighter *Claudia* – to the Provisional IRA for its terrorist war against the British in Northern Ireland. He insisted to Payne that: "It is not practical for Libya to send weapons, but we support the independence of Ireland." In fact, the only hand-held rockets which have so far come into the Provos' possession came from his Russian-stocked armoury.

To a friendly biographer (Mirella Bianco, author of *Gaddafi, Voice from the Desert*) he spoke more fully on this subject.

> We see ourselves as one of the supporters of world revolution. If we assist the Irish people it is simply because here we see a small people still under the yoke of Great Britain, and fighting to free themselves from it. And it must be remembered that the revolutionaries of the IRA are striking, and striking hard, at a power which has humiliated the Arabs for centuries ... But to return to the question of aid to Ireland, this enables us to kill three birds with one stone. We still support liberation movements; we are showing the whole world that the Arab world is passing from the defensive to the attack; we pay Great Britain back in some way, even though minimally, for the harm she has done and continues to do in our countries.

Such words reveal how emotional is Gaddafi's thinking and the way in which he persuades himself to take violent action and spend his oil money on fomenting revolution abroad. Major Omar Mehaishi, from the safety of Cairo and obviously an extremely hostile witness being used by the Egyptian propaganda services, does not hesitate to accuse his former friend of wild plotting. Because until the summer of 1975 he was so close to the centre of power, Mehaishi's words must be taken seriously. During that summer he conspired with brother officers to overthrow Gaddafi. The conspiracy was foiled and Mehaishi, after narrowly avoiding arrest, fled to Tunisia before being granted asylum by Egypt. The Libyans have made several attempts to kidnap him since then.

Mehaishi did not spare his criticism: "Gaddafi is a criminally inclined person with an unstable personality who operates on the assumption that he must use evil means internally and abroad to realise illusory and destructive dreams filling his mind. His reign is characterised by criminal insanity. For he has premeditated intentions towards the Libyan people and the Arab people in general which he believes he can only carry through by conspiracy and crime.

He believes in crime and terrorism. He uses embassies and diplomatic privileges to help and is now dealing with professional criminals from all over the world. He is a deceiver.

Gaddafi tried to assassinate me eleven times in Tunisia and six times in Egypt. He even recruited the German Mafia to kill me. After the OPEC raid when Carlos wanted to land the Austrian plane at Tunis airport he intended to bargain the life of one of the oil ministers for mine. But the Tunisians blacked out the airport so that the plane could not land there.

It has been proved beyond a shadow of a doubt that Gaddafi participated in the attack on OPEC ministers and that Carlos is in contact with him. Gaddafi wants to be the sole leader of the Arabs. When Yasser Arafat turned down his plan to establish a Palestinian government in exile in Tripoli he gave his support instead to the Rejection Front and their supporters.

To understand Gaddafi and his role as a supporter of international terrorist groups, it is necessary to appreciate his romantic and fanatical ideas about Arab unity. He sees himself as a kind of Napoleon of the Arab world and at the same time he believes that the mantle of Gamal Abdul Nasser of Egypt has fallen upon him. Yet he does not have the capacity to sustain his efforts and by trying to do too many things at once he fails to achieve his aims. Only sporadically are his dreams translated into action, so that on the spur of the moment and in a fit of enthusiasm he decides on a course of action. The Libyan enthusiast has neither the time nor the intellectual tenacity to follow through the consequences of his decisions. This helps to explain his relationship with Carlos and the terrorists.

In 1971 he suffered a severe nervous breakdown. Mehaishi says that a British doctor found that he was mad because his brain had been damaged by a fall from a camel when he was still a child. This sounds like a tall story. Probably President Sadat was nearer the truth when he said: "There are two sides to Gaddafi's character, one is devilish and the other admirable." In fact, he is unpredictable and wild rather than clinically mad as his enemies claim, and this can be seen from the way he impulsively pays out substantial sums of money to satisfy an emotional whim. He is known to be financing an assorted group of liberation movements, some of them operating in areas far from the Middle East and linked to it only by a common belief in Islam. He has made no secret, for example, of his support on religious grounds of the Moslem insurgents in the Philippines.

In one of his many speeches about Arab politics he declared: "It is time to settle accounts with the Arab reactionary forces which counter the revolution. It is time to take care of counter-revolutionaries and consider them as hostile agents of colonialism." To back up these words, and to intimidate Egypt and Tunisia, as well as Saudi Arabia, the richest of Arab states, Gaddafi committed himself in 1976 to paying cash down for Soviet weapons, ordered in far greater quantity than his own armed forces can possibly absorb. His army of 25,000 men has some 1,500 modern Russian-built tanks.

This lavish military equipment is intended in a *bella figura* fashion to strengthen the Rejection Front which itself enjoys the support of the Kremlin, and to provide an armoury for any country or cause Gaddafi cares to support.

The help given by the Libyans to Black September is already well documented. Asked about the Munich massacre, Libya's Foreign Minister, Mansour Rashid Al Kikhya, told a *Stern* magazine interviewer in November 1972: "We are in a position to be able to radicalise the war. And naturally we Libyans will support in this phase every Palestinian commando operation. I stress: every operation."

Gaddafi's excursions into terrorism have not always been so spectacular or successful as Munich. In the early days of his rule when he had no proper secret service, he used to hire the Razd organisation to do his dirty work. Razd, literally "Observation", was a group of Palestinians, based in Rome and better educated than most of their compatriots, who carried out intelligence missions for Fatah and became the basis on which Black September was organised. They liked smart clothes and starlets and were always short of money. Gaddafi's missions were, therefore, welcome – although their performance did not always come up to his expectations. One task he gave them was to take back to Tripoli to face his revenge a Libyan accused of "crimes against the people", supposedly committed when the old king, Idris, was still on the throne. Razd ran him to earth, but he, being a rich man, made them a cash offer which, with their flashy life-style, they could not refuse. They reported back to Gaddafi that they had been unable to find his quarry.

Despite such setbacks Gaddafi did subsidise attacks by a series of organisations whose efforts were crowned with bloody success. It is estimated that Black September in the guise of Fatah received some £20 million of Libya's oil money, while a similar sum went to other organisations. Millions more were sent out to opposition groups in neighbouring countries, whenever Gaddafi disapproved of policies pursued by their governments. Precise figures are impossible to come by, for only Gaddafi knows the full truth. There are no official published figures on terrorist aid, but even so there can be no doubt that the expenditure is huge. Mehaishi even goes so far as to claim that the Chairman of the Revolutionary Command Council, as Gaddafi likes to be known, has exhausted his treasury by making such subventions abroad. That is an exaggeration, even though there have been times when the Libyans did seem to be suffering from lack of liquid resources to pay for Western goods and services.

In April 1973 Gaddafi, in a long and rambling speech over Tripoli Radio, expressed his disgust for the established Palestinian groups and the way in which they spent more time squabbling among themselves than fighting the Israelis: "Where is the Palestine Resistance today? The Palestine Resistance today does not exist. There exist radios without a Resistance. Where is the Resistance? The Resistance has been finished."

This speech followed on his organisation of his own terrorist squads under the name of the Arab National Youth Organisation for the Liberation of Palestine. He invited to Libya a number of renegades, refugees from the internal fighting in Fatah and the PFLP, and put them in training camps under his personal supervision. The largest of these camps, at Tocra, could take some 5,000 men and there were smaller establishments at Tarhuna, Misurate and Sirte. In training the renegades were joined by a number of young Libyans, but in reality the National Youth Organisation began life as an extreme branch of Black September whose members had become dissatisfied by the lack of activity of its parent organisation.

The men responsible for this group of terrorists in exile were two members of the Revolutionary Command Council, Major Muhammed Najim and Major Abdel Moneim el Huni. As chairman of a special committee set up to supervise planning they appointed Ahmed el Ghaffour, a Lebanese who had been one of Arafat's closest colleagues. Arafat, in fact, had sent him to Libya as Fatah's ambassador to Gaddafi. But el Ghaffour, disappointed by Fatah's new-found passivity. and wooed by Gaddafi, defected to the Libyans. Fatah sentenced him to death for treason, but el Ghaffour, confident in his new role as terrorist leader and certain that Gaddafi would take care of him, took no notice of this sentence. He travelled frequently to various Middle East countries using only a number of aliases to protect himself. He was so sure of himself that he even went back to the Lebanon. It was a fatal mistake. Arafat's security force – run by the fearsome Abu Iyad – seized him, and a Fatah firing squad carried out the sentence of death.

The Libyans remembered him in a later operation by naming a hijack team "The martyr Ahmed el Ghaffour group". This was a time of dissension when there were constant clashes between different terror bands which sometimes ended in the killing of rival leaders.

The first confirmed operation of National Youth "commandos" was the seizure of a Lufthansa airliner in 1972. It was a highly successful action because the hijackers were able to blackmail the West German government into releasing the three surviving assassins of the Munich massacre.

These wild men who had left PFLP to join the group "owned" by Colonel Gaddafi struck again the following year. Two teams tried to blow up the Israeli ambassador to Cyprus and to hijack an El Al plane at Nicosia airport. But this time things did not go well for them. Four guerrillas blew out the entrance to the apartment block where the Israeli ambassador lived. But they failed to kill him and were all arrested.

Half an hour later, two cars crashed through the gates of Nicosia airport. One was halted by police, but the second, with five guerrillas in it, raced towards an El Al plane about to leave for Tel Aviv. The Arabs hurled grenades and sticks of dynamite at the airliner. An Israeli security guard opened fire on them and so did the Cyprus airport police. The Arabs were routed. Three were wounded and one was killed. The fifth man escaped.

Later in the year the National Youth, which claimed responsibility for this attack, launched a rescue operation to release the captured men, and took over a KLM airliner in flight on the Amsterdam–Tokyo run. They finally surrendered peacefully at Dubai, but in the course of their promenade around Middle East airports they spent some time chatting to Cypriot officials at Nicosia during a stopover. Some time later, President-Archbishop Makarios quietly released the seven comrades who had meanwhile been sentenced to seven years' imprisonment. He tactfully said that he did not want the island of Cyprus to become a battleground for Middle East conflicts.

In August 1973 two Arabs armed with machine guns and hand grenades opened fire at Athens airport on passengers waiting to board a TWA flight to New York, killing three and wounding fifty-five. It was revealed after their capture and interrogation that they had meant to attack the same airline's eastbound flight to Tel Aviv, but had chosen the wrong plane. Confusion arose about identification of the attackers because, although they claimed to belong to Black September, that organisation's spokesman denied all knowledge of them. Responsibility was claimed by an unknown body called the Seventh Suicide Squad. It is customary among terror groups for the same body of men to invent many grand names for themselves, and only by tracing through the rescue attempts was it possible in this case to track responsibility back to Libya.

The following December other hijackers at Rome airport linked to the Libyan connexion demanded in vain the release of the two assailants, a Palestinian and a Libyan, who by then had been sentenced to death by the Greeks. But in February of the following year three gunmen seized a Greek freighter in the port of Karachi and threatened to blow it up unless the Athens guerrillas were released. The Greeks were only too pleased to be rid of their embarrassment. The killers were released and put aboard an airliner to Libya. They made their way back to where the hijacking plots were hatched – to Tripoli. For they were all Gaddafi men.

The Libyan fingerprints on terrorism were seen again in 1973 when the Italian police arrested five Arabs in a flat underneath the approach flightpath to Rome's Leonardo da Vinci airport and then made an alarming discovery. In the flat were two SAM 7s. These Russian-made hand-held anti-aircraft missiles were to be used to shoot down an El Al airliner coming in to land at Rome. It would have been an easy target for the missiles.

The discovery of the SAM 7s was a considerable embarrassment to President Sadat, for they were traced back to a batch supplied to him by the Russians. What had happened was that Gaddafi, who was then urging the unification of Egypt and Libya, had put pressure on Sadat in the name of that unity to send him some of these then new weapons so that his army could learn how to use them. But the army never saw them. They went directly to the terrorists. Sadat was embarrassed and the Russians furious, for the rockets were turned over to the Americans and their secrets revealed.

This preoccupation of Gaddafi with Israeli aircraft and his almost pathological determination to have one shot down stems from the appalling incident of February 21st 1973 when a blinding sandstorm whirled over the Egyptian desert and a Libyan Boeing 727, flown by a French crew, lost its way on its regular run from Benghazi to Cairo, overshot the Egyptian capital and wandered over the Israeli-held Sinai on course for Tel Aviv. The Israelis, fearing that it had been hijacked and was destined to be crashed in a kamikaze dive on Tel Aviv, shot it down into the desert where it crashed and burned. One hundred and six innocent people were killed. Gaddafi swore revenge. He urged the other Arab countries to send their warplanes against Israel's towns and to destroy Israeli airliners wherever they could be found. The Egyptians and the Syrians refused to indulge in actions which could only result in all-out war. But Gaddafi's rage has never subsided.

The bloodiest assault of 1973 was carried out at Rome airport on December 17th when the National Youth group attacked a Pan American World Airways airliner. Thirty-two people were killed and eighteen wounded when five Arabs sprayed it with machine-gun fire. They hurled bombs and grenades into the crowded cabin where the passengers were strapped in, helpless, waiting to take off, and set it ablaze. They then commandeered a Lufthansa aircraft to fly them out. The five eventually surrendered at Kuwait before revealing their links with other guerrillas by demanding the release of the Athens hijackers.

Under interrogation they also produced a good deal of interesting information, saying that it was Gaddafi himself who had ordered them to carry out the Rome raid. Their instructions had been to seize hostages and hold them until a promise could be extracted to call off the Arab-Israeli conference due to open in Geneva on the following day, December 18th. This was the first conference convened after the Yom Kippur war and the first attempt, bitterly opposed by Gaddafi, to get the two sides talking under Great Power auspices, with the idea of making a Middle East settlement.

The Rome attack was in fact a secondary target, according to the arrested terrorists who "sang" under Kuwaiti questioning. Gaddafi had originally selected an even more dramatic mission for his killer squads: the assassination of Secretary of State Henry Kissinger with machine guns and grenades. For he believed that Kissinger's sudden disappearance from the scene would prevent the talks he had organised from taking place. On a pre-conference tour of the Middle East capitals,

Kissinger was to have landed at Beirut airport. Lebanese security men, who were then among the best in the Arab countries, discovered the plot and Dr. Kissinger's aircraft was diverted from Beirut International to a military airfield at Rayak, forty-five miles east of the city.

According to the captured assassins their weapons had been sent to them in the Libyan diplomatic bag and it was a Libyan diplomat at Madrid, their start line, who had given final orders that they were to seize hostages at Rome airport. Gaddafi, they said, was also controlling other groups in Western Europe. This information raises the possibility that Carlos himself was working with the Libyans at that point. There were various security alarms at London airport after the discovery by the Italians of SAM missiles in the vicinity of Rome airport. And Carlos himself later masterminded a rocket attack on an El Al airliner at Paris Orly airport. The objectives were the same and the methods similar.

Another fascinating piece of information vouchsafed by the captured terrorists in Kuwait was that Gaddafi had promised, before they were sent into action, to pay a bonus of £250,000 to their families if they were killed. His other terrorist insurance offer was that should they be taken prisoner he would guarantee to mount more hijack operations in order to secure their release. We have been unable to trace what happened to these terrorists after they left Kuwait. Perhaps they had given away too much embarrassing information.

What is known is that in the spring of 1974 the five talkative terrorists were flown to Cairo, "under the responsibility" of the Palestine Liberation Organisation. That organisation announced that the five men would be tried by a revolutionary court for carrying out an "unauthorised operation" considered detrimental to the Palestinian cause. Presumably this trial was carried out secretly for no more was heard of the matter. Who then had authorised the operation if not the Libyans?

The airport attacks of that terrorist season (1973) were the armed expression of Gaddafi's thirst for revenge and of a fight for power within the rival terrorist movements, as opposed to the earlier assaults designed to direct world opinion to the Palestine problem. The Gaddafi campaign was also designed to display his "more-ruthless-than-thou" capability and to prove that his words about the Palestinians not being sufficiently aggressive were in fact true. Innocent people who had nothing to do with Palestine, or even with the Middle East, were slaughtered and expensive airliners destroyed so that he could not only have his revenge, but also show that he was capable of mounting a terror campaign and of doing it more brutally than Yasser Arafat under the Black September trademark.

Gaddafi had been a hardliner in the war against Israel. He was, however, considered to be too unreliable to be consulted, or even informed, about the planning by Sadat and Assad for the Yom Kippur war of October 1973. He knew nothing of its timing and this greatly piqued him. For although the former colonel has never heard a shot fired in anger, he would like to have given the Egyptian and Syrian professionals the benefit of his advice. Neither he nor his 25,000-strong army played any part in the war, though he did lend some Mirage French-built jet fighters to the Egyptians.

He was therefore furious when the Egyptians and the Syrians agreed to a cease-fire. "A cease-fire imposed by the Americans and Russians – never!" he cried, when he heard the news in the presence of Eric Rouleau, Middle East correspondent of *Le Monde*. "It's a time bomb they're setting for us."

On another occasion he angrily declared that he wanted to keep the war going – "for a thousand years if necessary" – to get the Israelis out of Palestine. If he disapproved of an end to the war at that time, he execrated the idea of the front-line powers negotiating with the Israelis, and the possibility of a compromise state of Palestine emerging from those talks.

How could he prevent this happening?

He was already the paymaster of terrorism. He had set up his own groups to match the established Palestinian terror squads as well as to do his own dirty work. Now he decided that the best way to combat "moderate" arrangements in the Middle East was to throw his financial resources behind a new and bolder form of terrorism which, by generating fear and hatred, would create an atmosphere in which negotiations would become impossible. These were the dragon's teeth from which grew the Carlos raid on Vienna. Gaddafi was ready to spend money in the rejectionist cause on grandiose actions planned to terrorise the world until, in a weariness with killing, it would tolerate the destruction of Israel.

A training camp for hard-line resistance fighters was already in being at Tocra in Libya. Smaller camps were established as terror training centres, and luxurious rest villas stood ready in Tripoli to receive terrorists back from missions in the field. Through their Palestinian friends, the Libyans made contact with Carlos, the man with the experience and skill to undertake a major operation planned for Europe. In a pamphlet attack on Gaddafi a clandestine Libyan group which opposes his régime declared: "Freedom has become his alone, to play with the wealth of the people, using it for plotting world terrorism and dealings with Mafia gangs like that of Carlos and other international criminals."

Arab leaders' techniques for dealing with awkward questions are interesting. Here, for example, is Yasser Arafat, interviewed in NBC's "Meet the Press" television programme:

Question: Considering this record of assassinations in recent years, you don't consider that it is . . .
Arafat: We are against it; you know we are against it.
Question: You are against what?
Arafat: All what this operation you are speaking about.
Question: You are against terrorism?
Arafat: Definitely I am against it . . . I declared it, I am against all this operation which has been done in Munich or Vienna or Khartoum . . . It is not a Palestine operation.

These answers do not bear even the slightest comparison with other Arafat pronouncements on terrorism. An official statement by the PLO after Munich said: "Let us go back to the Munich operation which is great because of its heroism and sacrifices . . . we say that the importance of this operation lies in the fact that it has stunned all, including the enemy, and made them retreat from the round table of capitulation . . ."

In an equally brazen manner, when asked by Payne about the Vienna raid and Carlos's connexion with it, Gaddafi replied: "From what nationality is Carlos?" The idea that Arafat disapproves of terrorism is as absurd as the suggestion that Gaddafi did not know Carlos's nationality.

For the Libyan leader, the advantage of the Vienna raid was that it would strike a blow not only at the Arab-Israeli peace talks, but also at the Saudi Arabians and other oil monarchies and make them realise they were not beyond reach of the long arm of terrorism. In Gaddafi's mind the only real aim of these states was to prolong the life of their royalist system of government: "They are afraid of their people," he once said, "they are afraid of the revolution which is rumbling at their palace gates."

In his dreams the Libyan Colonel could see visions of his own brand of revolution sweeping aside the ancient monarchies, purifying as it went. And what better way of sparking this revolution than by capturing the oil ministers, and threatening their lives? Then surely the brother Arabs would see that Gaddafi, who had turned out his own King and was supporting all-out action against the hated Israelis, was the true leader, the revolutionary Caliph of the Arab world.

Early in 1976 Gaddafi made his fourth move in building his empire of terrorism. He had started by hiring Razd to do his undercover work, then established the Arab National Youth with renegade PFLP and Black September members, and moved on to hiring Carlos and his band of international terrorists. Now he decided to form his own Libyan unit, the so-called Special Intelligence Service. It turned out to be neither special nor intelligent.

Carlos was in Libya at the time when these units were being organised and Payne, who visited Tripoli in April, believes that he caught a glimpse of him dining in the restaurant at the Tripoli Palace Hotel. His bulky figure was concealed throughout the meal in a raincoat and beneath that he wore a colourful sports shirt with a pronounced bulge under the left shoulder. In Libya it is widely believed that Carlos lives in a villa in the smart Tripoli suburb of Gargoura, not far from one of Colonel Gaddafi's houses. This villa has its grounds floodlit by night and is heavily guarded to keep out curious strangers. This lends credibility to reports that after the Vienna raid the Venezuelan terrorist spent some time helping to train Libyan groups for action in the field.

The first public appearance of the Gaddafi squads was in the spring of 1976, when teams from the new strike force were arrested in Rome, Cairo and Tunis. The terrorist apprentices were taught their trade at a special camp in the desert 175 kilometres south of Tobruk in an area called Al Shoba. They were not very successful. The Egyptian secret police got wind of their plan to hijack a plane from Rome to Paris and discovered that the passenger they were after was Major Abdel Moneim el Huni, the selfsame member of the Revolutionary Command Council who had helped to organise the Arab National Youth Organisation but who had fallen out with Gaddafi and had fled from Tripoli into exile in Cairo. He had planned to go to Paris for medical treatment.

The Egyptian government, anxious to make international political capital out of the discovery, first warned Major el Huni not to board the aircraft and then alerted the Italian authorities to be on the watch for hijackers on the Alitalia flight to Paris. The three Libyan terrorists were searched when they arrived from Cairo although one of them was equipped with a diplomatic passport. A metal detector revealed three Browning automatic pistols, ammunition and hand grenades in their brief cases. The Libyan squad admitted that they had orders to hijack the flight and force it to land in Libya so that the truant minister might be seized there.

Shortly after the Rome arrests Egyptian security men in Cairo moved in to seize seven other Libyans described by them as "an assassination squad composed of Libyan soldiers". Their mission was partly to seize or kill the talkative Omar Mehaishi, who was threatening to publish everything he knew about Gaddafi, and partly to organise a terror bombing campaign in Egypt. General Hassan Abu Basha, the Deputy Minister of the Interior, said that their aim was to spread terror among the population and that plans had been made to plant bombs at a wide variety of targets in the capital and in Alexandria on the coast.

It was an operation which verged on the farcical, for when the Libyans were picked up, all carried standard issue suitcases, all had rolls of two thousand dollars and all wore identical army issue underpants. The Egyptians, who have a professional, well-respected secret service, gleefully spread the story of the Libyans' lack of expertise. Soon the fledglings of the Special Intelligence Service were in full song. They confessed that they had been given special training with Russian-made bombs. They identified Mohammed Idriss el Sherif el Shoheibi, head of Libyan Intelligence, as their training and control officer. General Basha further asserted that the men had been helped by Libyan diplomats in Egypt and that the aim of the operation was to justify Libyan propaganda claims that Egypt was seething with discontent.

Later in the month Tunisian police arrested a similar three-man terror squad in their territory and put them on trial for planning to assassinate the Prime Minister, Hedi Nouira, the man who had earlier refused to be bribed by Gaddafi to unite his country with Libya. The arrested men confessed that they had all undergone special training and that they had collected weapons and explosives from the Libyan Embassy in Tunis with the aim of carrying out their murder plan during the celebrations for the 20th anniversary of Tunisian independence.

Libyan diplomatic missions gave full support to these abortive operations. They provided communications and furnished weapons and explosives carried in the diplomatic bag. Libyan embassies have long experience of gun-running and it is known that they provided the same facilities for a number of Palestinian enterprises over a period of years.

The Libyans recruited for these operations were a mixture of young soldiers and university drop-outs. Mohammed Ali Nayel, an army intelligence officer unconvincingly disguised as a businessman, led the group which arrived in Tunisia. He told his captors that similar units to his own had been sent on missions to Egypt, Italy, Lebanon, Syria and Somalia.

The alarming thing about Gaddafi is the extent of his ambition to create trouble in so many parts of the world. Egged on by the schemes of terrorists constantly in touch with him, he formulates megalomaniac plans. For example, in 1973 he ordered two Egyptian submarines on secondment to his navy to torpedo the British liner *Queen Elizabeth II* as it sailed towards Israel taking five hundred American and British Jews to Haifa to celebrate the 25th anniversary of the founding of Israel. However, the submarine commanders, somewhat surprised by their orders, signalled their bases and asked for further instructions. President Sadat, horrified, ordered them to return to harbour. Nothing was said about this incident at the time, but later, when relations between Sadat and Gaddafi had become strained to near-fighting point, Sadat himself told the story of Gaddafi's machinations.

The fact that the Libyan ever contemplated such a monstrous idea demonstrates that he cannot be trusted to refrain from the maddest of projects. He is like a desert chameleon, darting about, his tongue flickering, changing his colours as he moves from one position to another.

In opposing by all means at his disposal a Middle East accommodation by which the Arab powers would tolerate the state of Israel, Gaddafi remains constant. But since the celebration in September 1976 of the anniversary of his seven years in power, there have been signs of a growing maturity in the Libyan leader.

During the summer, Egypt had threatened to invade her neighbour. It was Gaddafi who made the first gestures to take the heat out of that situation, saying that this was a quarrel between Gaddafi and Sadat, and not an occasion for Egypt to make war on Libya. His efforts in the Lebanon in support of the Palestinians and the private armies of the left brought him nothing but disappointment. Despite all his help and encouragement for the Palestinians, their backs were once again to the wall.

The first signs of growing world-weariness in Colonel Gaddafi appeared in his public statements at that time. He began to give the impression that in future he might not be so willing to furnish money and weapons of war for the indiscriminate support of guerrilla movements throughout the world, and that he was no longer so confident that terrorism paid.

Gaddafi himself has never been a bloodthirsty man in person. Opponents of his régime have been imprisoned rather than executed. He was prepared to use Carlos and his revolutionaries in support of the Palestinian cause, which to him is a holy one. He, like Carlos, took pleasure in the high drama of the Vienna raid. He did not want to kill Yamani and the other hostages, but simply to demonstrate that they could be threatened and held to political ransom.

It is to be hoped that Gaddafi may come to realise that terrorism is not the best way to achieve political aims, even though Carlos does soldier on beneath its banner.

Chapter Eleven
The German connexion

IN THE REVOLUTIONARY SPRING OF 1968, WHEN PARIS STUDENTS BEGAN throwing up barricades on the boulevards and occupying the Sorbonne, others from Germany, Britain and the United States rushed there to join in the endless street fights and street debates.

Among them was Rudi Dutschke, the German revolutionary student leader, known as "Red Rudi", who preached the abolition of "the power of people over people". It was a convenient formula for joining both Communists and anarchists in one, if only temporarily one, band of brothers. In any case, the dogma appealed to the discontented and usually well-to-do middle-class students of France and Germany who were already responding to the theory of Marcuse that acts of violence were justified for oppressed minorities. From this movement, deeply opposed to authoritarianism, arose the Baader-Meinhof group, which adopted as its title, the Red Army Fraction, implying that it was a part of a world-wide revolutionary movement.

Andreas Baader, then aged twenty-five, was formed in the ideas of the flourishing German New Left and early in his career turned away from the traditional paths of education open to him to become an art student drop-out. He even failed to win his school leaving certificate. His father, who was killed in the war, had been a state archives official in Munich, where Andreas was born in 1943. At the age of eighteen the boy gravitated to the revolutionary circles of West Berlin and began writing and planning action to destroy the German capitalism he hated.

In 1968 he teamed up with a girl terrorist, Gudrun Ensslin, then thirty-four, who has been described as his ideal "revolutionary bride". The daughter of a Protestant pastor, she had already produced an illegitimate child by the son of a famous Nazi writer. Baader and Ensslin met in Berlin and soon went into action with their first operation, in which they set fire to a Frankfurt department store. This was in April 1968. Baader announced that the purpose of the operation was to give the comfortable burghers of Germany "a taste of Vietnam". What it mainly did was to bring together members of the future band.

The fire caused damage estimated at £200,000. Gudrun Ensslin said: "We didn't care about burnt mattresses, we were worried about burnt children in Vietnam."

What caused an even greater sensation than the act itself was the approval of it promptly expressed by Ulrike Meinhof, then the radically chic heroine of the New Left, who wrote a weekly column in *Konkret*, its most fashionable magazine. She endorsed its criminality and wrote that what was "progressive" about it was not the destruction of shoddy goods of the consumer society, but the bold breaking of the law.

Like many of the other talented and resourceful intellectuals who were to join or support the movement, this rather handsome, shy woman seemed an unlikely candidate for service as a bloodthirsty terrorist leader. When her youthful brother-in-law had unexpectedly fired a pistol during a walk in the woods she was so upset by the noise that she burst into tears. Yet only a few years later she openly boasted of her skill with automatic weapons on the range at one of Arafat's Middle East training camps.

Born in 1934, she was brought up after the death of her art historian parents by a foster-mother, Dr. Renate Riemeck, co-founder of a socialist pacifist group, in the manner of a Hampstead intellectual. As a young student cradled in Christian pacifism she became a nuclear disarmer and then graduated to protest politics against the comfortable life at the time of the West German economic miracle.

At the age of twenty-eight, she suffered from a brain tumour which was eventually operated on in 1962. But she recovered and developed into a well-educated student with a philosophical turn of mind. She had begun writing for the magazine *Konkret* and, in 1961, married its publisher and editor Klaus Rohl. She displayed real talent as a writer and became what the Germans call a "Star Kolumnist". The magazine was a clever concoction of political articles and more popular trendy material, *Playboy*-type pictures and articles on sex and drugs and the developing sub-cultures. Under Rohl's skilful editorship it built up a circulation of around a quarter of a million. *Konkret* has been described by Melvin Lasky in *Encounter* (June 1975) as "a mixture of sex and politics. Rohl was a kind of ideological Hugh Hefner, alternating nude pin-ups (lightly disguised as a method of 'sexual enlightenment for the young') with militant left-wing propaganda (zippily spiced with a marijuanised modishness)."

During her time on the magazine Ulrike Meinhof moved happily around the cocktail circuits of West Germany and Europe, well paid, boutique dressed and jewelled, loved by German liberals for her outspoken articles and for her domestic role as the loving mother of her twin daughters, Bettine and Regine.

Yet even at this time, as Klaus Rohl has recently revealed, both he and his wife were secret Communist supporters and both had been members of the CP from 1956 to 1961. An even more surprising revelation was that *Konkret* had been subsidised from Communist funds. Ulrike and her husband had made clandestine visits to East Berlin and something like a million marks were channelled into their publication by way of Prague. In this way the Soviets had succeeded in influencing German opinion by way of trendiness and pin-ups.

But by 1968 Ulrike felt the need for stronger meat. She left her husband, taking her twin daughters with her, denounced the magazine, wrote a savage article attacking its editorial line, and went to live in Berlin. There she plunged into the revolutionary life of the Free University and immersed herself in the sub-culture of that city. As soon as she had approved the original Baader raid she joined the movement and devoted all her vigour to recruiting and plotting, for she was now convinced that the system she disliked so much could only be challenged by the use of force.

The original activists, Baader and Ensslin, were also joined by Horst Mahler, the lawyer who defended Baader in court, and soon, with the help of Ulrike Meinhof, they were ready for bolder actions, bomb and fire raids on a wide variety of targets. However, Baader was arrested by the police in West Berlin during a car check and was sentenced to three years in jail. In May 1970 his comrades in terrorism planned an armed raid to "spring" him.

Because of the amazing tolerance of the German legal and penal systems devised after the end of the Third Reich deliberately to prevent any revival of the old ways, this proved to be very much easier than might have been expected. In spite of repeated warnings that the terrorists might try to escape, Baader was authorised during his prison term to continue with "sociological research" and even permitted to pursue his studies outside prison in various West Berlin libraries. He had told the authorities that he was commissioned to write a book on youth problems, a subject on which he might well have been considered an expert. And on May 14th his guards took him to the Sociology Institute at Dahlem.

Ulrike Meinhof was already in the library when they brought him in and shortly afterwards four other members of the band, suitably disguised in wigs, shot their way in under cover of tear gas. In the exchange of fire between guards and attackers a librarian was badly wounded by a Beretta automatic bullet, and several other guards and people in the library were also hit. Baader and his friends escaped unhurt and in melodramatic fashion he and Ulrike raced away in a stolen silver-grey Alfa Romeo. Before going underground the pair had time to collect Ulrike's twin daughters.

Having done that, they devoted themselves to preparing their new offensive in the violent campaign against bourgeois society by first robbing a bank to provide funds and then, a month later (in June) taking off for the Middle East for the main part of their training. Contact had already been made with Fatah and other Palestinian organisations through the Arab students who attend West German universities and take a keen interest in left-wing politics.

The group flew to Damascus, probably by way of East Berlin, then on to Lebanon and Jordan. Their stay in the Middle East, which lasted until August, could not have been more badly timed, for King Hussein was at that moment busily driving the Palestinian commandos out of his country and the whole Arab revolutionary movement was in turmoil. Nevertheless, they lived in an Al Fatah camp and managed to get in some training with explosives and small arms – though Baader was rebuked by his Arab instructor and called "coward" because he refused to crawl under barbed wire. What was even more important for the group was that they were able to meet men and women from other international terrorist organisations sympathetic to their urban guerrilla cause. A Swiss group encountered there later supplied them with arms.

Although the Berlin gang were promising enough pupils in the art of guerrilla warfare, their conduct in other respects left a great deal to be desired so far as the Arabs were concerned. The Palestinians are abstemious by nature and they were shocked by these people who behaved like German tourists in a holiday camp and gave the impression that they were as devoted to the sunshine pleasures of sex, drinking and pot smoking as to the gratifications of guerrilla warfare. Because of their behaviour they were expelled, and this disrupted Ulrike Meinhof's plan to bring her daughters to live in a Palestinian orphanage near the training camp. The children in fact were lucky, for the building was soon afterwards partially destroyed in a Jordanian air raid. They were, instead, spirited away along revolutionary underground channels and eventually recovered in Rome by their father Klaus Rohl who had obtained a court order for their custody.

There is no doubt that the Baader-Meinhof gang benefited from their indoctrination into the ways of international terror as propounded by the Palestinians. Horst Mahler wrote in *Urban Guerrilla Concepts*, his work on armed conflict: "A fighting group can only come into being through conflict. All attempts to organise, educate and train a group without the existence of such conflict lead to the most ludicrous results – often with a tragic outcome." They had all experienced the feeling of togetherness with other international bands and thought of themselves as a part of a world revolutionary movement. Their new expertise with the weapons of terrorism encouraged them to plunge into a renewed campaign on home ground.

Still a small and relatively new underground organisation, the gang now concentrated on actions to create infrastructure. They needed safe houses, garages, false identity papers and radio equipment to ensure their own communications as well as to listen in to the messages of the forces of law and order. They also needed cars and the means to disguise their cars, though here their love of BMW vehicles, for the sheer pleasure of the coincidence of initials, rather let them down. They favoured a small-calibre pistol named the Landmann-Preetz, and built up an arsenal of weapons and explosives.

To do all this they needed money. Their favourite method of acquiring it was to raid banks, which provided in addition the intellectual satisfaction of "striking a blow against the system". Three simultaneous bank robberies in West Berlin in September 1970 carried out by twelve people in six cars brought a haul of DM 220,000.

Willing support for the activists came from fellow travellers and sympathisers. Weapons came mostly from abroad, paid for sometimes by favours to the Palestinians in the form of later attacks on such suitable targets as El Al offices or the installations of Americans who supported Israel.

Like all revolutionary movements, the Red Army Fraction was profuse in words and statements. One point made emphatically was that "the revolutionary is armed", and must have his gun about him at all times, not just when in action. Members were told that they must use their weapons to resist arrest and that in the case of sudden attack police officers were to be fired at – a policeman was shot by one of them at Kaiserslautern in December 1971. Ulrike Meinhof told *Der Spiegel*: "We say the person in uniform is a pig, that is, not a human being, and thus we have to settle the matter with him. It is wrong to talk to these people at all, and shooting is taken for granted ..." The word "pig" was an American importation, for the German word "schwein" does not have the same degree of offensiveness.

The "RAF", as the Red Army Fraction was called in Germany, defended itself against accusations of favouring bank robberies rather than popular actions and declared that only this solution of logistic problems could secure the continuity of revolutionary organisation. The technical means could only be acquired in a collective process of working and learning together. This early Baader-Meinhof period was marked by constant and usually pompous public pronouncements full of home-made and borrowed revolutionary slogans.

An early paper published by the gang asked: "Does any pig truly believe we would talk about development of class conflicts, or reorganisation of the proletariat, without simultaneously arming ourselves?" Their war cry became: "Build up the Red Army!" That was something new, for in its guerrilla context the Red Army had only been vaguely heard of in Europe as the name of a small Japanese group. Now the name was adopted by the Baader-Meinhof gang and they began calling themselves the Red Army Group. It is not impossible that they had conceived the idea in the Middle East through contacts with the Japanese. "It is not itself a party," explained Ulrike, "but is organisationally, practically, conceptually a necessary component of a Communist party worthy of the name."

The German revolutionaries consciously drew inspiration from Third World revolutionary movements. They punctiliously used the mini-manual of the Brazilian urban guerrilla, Carlos Marighella. Their first actions in Berlin were aimed at Tshombe from the Congo and the

Shah of Persia, a well-known villain in the eyes of student militants. Ulrike Meinhof, always anxious to make use of newspapers to spread the good word, told a magazine that "guerrilla is going to spread, the development of the class struggle will carry through the idea . . . the idea of guerrilla developed by Mao, Fidel, Che, Giap, Marighella is a good idea and no one will ever be able to do away with it . . ." She peppered her papers of revolutionary philosophy with emotive quotations from the masters. On one occasion, in a pamphlet, she mentioned with approval Mao Tse-Tung's version of an old Chinese proverb on death: "Weightier than the Tai mountain is the death of a socialist fighter; the death of a capitalist weighs less than swansdown."

Tactically the group defended its bank robbing methods over and over again. To rob banks was logistically correct and it was also politically correct because it could be put down as an act of dispossession as well as being a proletarian action. It is not surprising that the group should make such play with phrases about the proletariat, for they were conscious of the fact that almost all of them were well-educated young people from respectable middle-class and professional families. Of the original seventeen hard-core members most were students. But included in the number were two lawyers, a medical assistant and two journalists, also a woman hairdresser and a woman photographer. Most of their supporters and sympathisers were also professional people. As might be expected, most of them continued to maintain that theoretically the revolutionary leadership should come from the working class. Only Horst Mahler, one of the lawyers and himself a dentist's son, boldly put forward the contention that revolutionary theory should be developed by those who, because they are not members of the working class, are able to stand aside and view both past and present struggles objectively.

"A capacity for abstract thought allows them to appreciate the modern class struggle within its historical context." This was an attitude of mind characteristic of the young, he said, because their own class was increasingly menaced.

Small wonder that one of their few working-class converts in the group, Karl Ruhland, complained later that they treated him as a second-class revolutionary and would not allow him to take part in intellectual political debate. The only task they allotted him was to maintain the getaway cars.

In May 1972 the Baader-Meinhof group began their urban guerrilla campaign in earnest and there was daily news of some fresh outrage. They placed a series of bombs at the headquarters of the US Fifth Army Corps in Frankfurt. This raid was ostensibly to retaliate against American action in Vietnam. It killed Colonel Paul Bloomquist and wounded thirteen others.

Only a couple of weeks later the same band claimed responsibility for exploding car bombs at the US Army's European headquarters in Heidelberg. Three people were killed and eight others injured. In the same month other bombs exploded at police headquarters in Augsburg and Munich. More bombs at the Axel Springer press building in Hamburg injured thirteen, some of them sustaining appalling wounds. A news editor there said that an explosion on the third floor buried a dozen people under a collapsed wall and reported that another bomb in a sixth floor women's lavatory injured more. "I met a colleague, half of whose lower jaw was hanging down, and another whose hand hung only by a thread of skin."

Axel Springer himself commented: "What has now begun is the Devil's harvest sown by leftist radicals. We have warned for years that this would happen."

It was not long before the Baader-Meinhof gang, after this wild orgy of terror, were themselves to reap the whirlwind. By the summer of 1972 every member of the original hard core had been arrested, though their followers survived to fight on. The West German security services, tightly controlled by legal limitations, at first faced an almost impossible task in tracking down a highly intelligent group of conspirators, supported by thousands of non-active sympathisers from the New Left. Dr. Alfred Stumper, chief of police at the Interior Ministry of Baden-Wurtemberg, said in Stuttgart that he believed at a later stage there were still one hundred persons ready, and potentially in a position, to engage in crimes of terror and violence. He estimated that they had behind them at least three hundred active helpers and up to three thousand others whom he classed as sympathisers.

Not for several years did the West Germans, who since the end of the war had lived in conditions of peace and prosperity, take in the full implications of the terrorists' campaign. An Israeli living in Germany said that people at large were reluctant to admit what was really happening in modern and comfortable German cities. Terror for them was something that might break out in Latin countries, but not in clean, well-ordered Germany where most citizens respected law and order. And if it was happening, how on earth had it come about that middle-class boys and girls with a university education should have turned before their eyes into a bunch of gun-slinging political gangsters?

Even greater distress was caused to traditionally-minded Germans when they realised how great a part in the terrorist campaigns was played by women. In the original Baader-Meinhof band there were no fewer than twelve women among the force of twenty-two. The girls carried and used guns as willingly as their menfolk. As Dr. Stumper put it: "There is a very high female content in the terrorist organisations. These ladies do not seem to me at all tender and loving; they are happy to take up the gun. In fact, we often find that they are the ones who ginger up the men and push them on to greater deeds of violence."

Even so the girls acted not only as fighters, they were very useful as the providers of flats, helpers, lovers, advisers and spies. They used the old-fashioned respect which German society has for women to avoid searches when smuggling arms or papers from those in prison. In one terror attack a girl employed what was known as a "baby bomb", concealed under her skirt so as to give the impression that she was pregnant. The other part of this ingenious device was an inflatable balloon, so that when the bomb was planted she was able to leave the premises still appearing to be pregnant. Symbolically the baby bomb was contrived by a young metal-worker from Frankfurt persuaded that he was making it for use in a film about terrorists; symbolically, because the act reveals how closely real-life actions are related to the phantasy inventions of the cinema in the minds of young people who have taken to terrorism.

All this was difficult for the citizens of West Germany to comprehend and cope with. Justly proud of the democratic and liberal institutions installed in their Republic after the fall of the Nazis, they were reluctant to increase police powers and take emergency actions to deal with the terrorist crisis. The West German liberal conscience remains guilt-ridden from the past and many scruples had to be overcome before anything could be done. Even when it was proved that lawyers sympathetic to the Baader-Meinhof gang were not simply defending them but actively supporting them by smuggling orders out of prison, the Bar Association took a long time to react, and only after lengthy public examinations of conscience were they expelled. When Diether Posser, the socialist Minister of Justice, proposed the granting of immunity from prosecution to "Crown" witnesses ready to testify against law-breakers (a practice long since established in English and American courts) there was a great public outcry that this would undermine justice. The Baader-Meinhof supporters' club mocked this as "Lex Baader". Nonetheless, the measure was finally adopted and has strengthened the hand of the state without damaging the cause of justice.

In spite of such difficulties, fresh techniques were at last evolved. Special anti-terrorist squads were set up in the state police forces. Bonn, the Federal capital, saw the establishment of Group Nine, an anti-terror section specially equipped and made mobile with helicopters for use in freeing hostages and to deal with emergencies. A Federal Terrorist Department got to work in Bonn to co-ordinate measures, and at Wiesbaden the Federal Criminal Bureau of plain-clothes police increased its strength to 2,500. Successful attempts were made to infiltrate the terrorist groups.

But the downfall of the original Baader-Meinhof gang came partly from within, and partly as a result of denunciations by disabused sympathisers shocked by the growing violence. A case in point was the arrest of Ulrike Meinhof on June 15th 1972. Moving through her network of safe houses provided by sympathisers, usually in respectable and anonymous areas, she came to stay in the apartment of a Hanover schoolteacher with left-wing views, named Fritz Rodewald. He had begun to fear that the anarchists and terrorists were creating a political atmosphere that might be exploited by the extreme right. When the guests sent there by mutual friends arrived in his apartment Rodewald began a debate of conscience with himself – should he call the police? In fear of reprisals if he did so, he passed a sleepless night considering the matter and finally decided it was his duty to inform. The bloody drama had to be ended bloodlessly and he telephoned the Hanover Baader-Meinhof Police Kommando.

The police made a swift raid and captured at a blow the most wanted woman in Germany. In the flat they discovered not only a hoard of papers and messages sent from gang members already in prison, but also ammunition and false identity papers. There was also a home-made ten-pound bomb carefully wrapped in a red leather case.

To take the official pictures at headquarters the police had to hold Ulrike by the hair and a detective said, "Her entire face is puffed and swollen because like some enraged trapped animal she has been struggling and screaming and weeping for hours . . ." When they X-rayed her for traces of the earlier brain surgery to get a positive identification she fought back, shouting "You want to kill me." Then she threatened – "You're all next on the list." But she seemed in mortal terror of being brain-washed.

The good Herr Rodeweld, though relieved to find that the deed was done, thought that he ought to donate the reward money to the Ulrike Meinhof defence fund.

The strange story of Ulrike Meinhof, the most enigmatic and interesting of the Red Army Fraction leaders, ended in May 1976 when she was found dead in her cell after she had been on trial for almost a year. She was already serving an eight-year prison sentence for her part in freeing Baader in West Berlin and had spent long months in Stammheim prison at Stuttgart refusing to take part in her trial on other charges.

The official account of her death states that she hanged herself with a towel. She had secured it to a crossbar above the cell window, stood on a chair and then kicked it away. Her body was not found until several hours later. Defence counsel at once raised hysterical protests that she had been murdered by the authorities, and with great clumsiness the court refused to suspend its hearings for a few days.

Anyone who has studied the career of Ulrike Meinhof would not feel surprise at the idea of her contemplating suicide. Indeed, in retrospect it looked as though a brilliant student and writer, deeply moved by the fate of people less fortunate than herself, who turned revolutionary and terrorist anarchist, was precisely the kind of anxious and unstable woman who, at the age of forty-one, might take her own life. No letter was found explaining her action, but the night before her death she had been busy typing in her cell and fragments of burned paper were found in the lavatory attached to it.

The strain of the long judicial process and prison life in conditions where she was still allowed to work and write until far into the night had taken its toll on an unstable personality. Prison psychiatrists who examined her during the trial expressed the view that she had undergone a personality change after her brain tumour operation in 1962. To ease the pressure on her brain a silver clamp was inserted.

As a child aged fourteen she had wanted to become a nun. As a student she turned to poetry and the pleasures of an intellectual life. She played the violin and recited long passages from the German poets. While she studied philosophy and sociology her greatest act of rebellion was to smoke a pipe. Then came the brilliant journalistic and television career which brought her a glittering social life; then, even more suddenly, the transformation into an extrovert revolutionary. Now she dressed like a man, in trousers, boots and sweater, and she fought like a man.

After her death friends recalled again the strange episodes in her life, how she had once broken down and wept in the woods because of a love affair and how they had feared that she intended to kill herself. The breakdown of her marriage coincided with the decision to throw in her lot with the Red Army Fraction and to try to send her seven-year-old twins to a Middle East camp as a kind of offering to the Palestinian cause.

Only a few days before her death the Baader-Meinhof trial reached one of its turning points. After months of silence Gudrun Ensslin, the other woman accused, suddenly issued a statement. "We have been organised in the Red Army Fraction and are thereby responsible for the attacks in Heidelberg and Frankfurt," she said, and this amounted to the first confession of responsibility. It may have been this development which brought on a final fit of depression for Ulrike Meinhof. For her the long-drawn-out show trial marked the end of her battle against the society she had come to hate and despise.

Ironically enough, the one lasting achievement of herself and her friends had been to create a situation in which their "left-wing fascism" had brought illiberal changes in the law and signs of repression in West Germany. As the London *Times* commented, "West German society was and still is sufficiently open to give dissident groups a hearing. If it is somewhat less so now than at the end of the 1960s Ulrike Meinhof must bear some of the responsibility."

Even in bad times the Baader-Meinhof network remained remarkably cohesive. Its members maintained their group loyalty and solidarity when all seemed lost. Two weeks before Ulrike Meinhof was taken in Hanover another tip-off to the police from a fringe sympathiser, not a full member of the gang, brought the definitive arrest of Andreas Baader. This was a more full-blooded affair and the police had to bring up an armoured car in support before they stormed the apartment firing carbines from the hip as Baader and four companions offered resistance. Baader and Holger Meins refused police orders to come out after a cordon had been thrown round the house and made a run for it, firing as they came. Police marksmen fired back and wounded both men.

Gudrun Ensslin was arrested quietly while shopping in a smart Hamburg boutique because a girl customer saw a 9mm automatic in her handbag. She had two such weapons but was unable to get to them after an assistant called the police, although she did struggle. The maxim that a good revolutionary should always be armed does not necessarily pay off.

Dr. Stumper was responsible for the security of the special prison built to accommodate the arrested members of the Baader-Meinhof gang. Interviewed in early 1976 he said: "I cannot exclude the possibility of a Carlos-type attack here, even though we have a massive guard on the place. What I can tell you is that we have other forms of protection than the uniformed guard that can be seen. What we have always feared is that they might try to take leading citizens as hostages so we have to watch over them as well as over sensitive buildings and the prison itself.

"It had always been recognised that the term of greatest danger would be at a moment when the court comes to its decision. Luckily we have reinforcements of the Federal Border Guard available as well as other police elements from outside Stuttgart and it is possible for us to identify suspicious people who come here and to identify them even without necessarily making arrests."

Construction of the brand new high-security prison and courtroom in the suburbs of Stuttgart, where the trial of the Baader-Meinhof gang took place, has been a heavy burden on the state of Baden-Wurtemberg. Because of the attack on the headquarters of the US Army at Heidelberg it was considered as the state most closely involved and this has cost it something like twelve million Deutschmarks. Because no city felt safe from the danger of fresh attacks to release the prisoners, the new prison and court were constructed at Stammheim, at the northern limits of the city of Stuttgart, best known until then as the home of Mercedes cars and of Count Graf von Zeppelin, creator of the Zeppelin airship. An elaborate system of electronics was installed to give warning of any attempt to release the twenty-one Baader-Meinhof captives and six hundred armed police kept guard.

Inside the court during the lengthy legal proceedings a curious atmosphere prevailed. The accused announced that they considered themselves to be soldiers in an army fighting against society and when the trial began in May 1975 they refused to reply to the charges made against them. The four principals were Meinhof, Baader, Gudrun Ensslin and Jan-Carl Raspe. They faced six charges of murder and fifty-nine of attempted murder; also charges of robbing banks and forming a criminal association. Not until January 1976 did any of the accused testify at all and even then they made no comment on the charges. They merely intervened to describe themselves as "urban guerrillas" using weapons to pursue political objectives.

After endless-seeming hunger strikes and legal complications, the accused settled down to a pattern of behaviour. They were not forced to appear in court and on the winter day that Ronald Payne visited Stammheim, proceedings continued for forty-five minutes before any of them made an appearance in the dock. Yet this was a most interesting day, for one of the rare prosecution witnesses, Dierk Hoff, gave evidence. Hoff admitted making bomb cases for the gang but, clearly hoping to benefit from the new law on witnesses for the prosecution, said he had been forced into doing so. When the group did consent to appear in the dock they wandered in one at a time, hands in pockets, and treated the court with high contempt. "Hi, judge," said one of them sarcastically. "I'm here now." They smoked, joked and sneered throughout the hearing.

Hoff, from Frankfurt, had made the "baby bomb" already described, having been told by Raspe and a lawyer called Holger Meins (who later died in prison on hunger strike) that it was for use in a film. He described to the court how he began to worry when his new friends asked him to modify a shot-gun they brought him. When he mentioned his suspicions and said he would tell the police they threatened him with a revolver saying: "We don't like traitors." His defence was that he had genuinely believed that the artefacts he was making were intended only for the film.

The most extraordinary feature of the long-drawn-out Baader-Meinhof trial was the extent to which the terrorists, at a time when no fewer than thirty were held in various German prisons, were able to carry on with their political activities while in jail or on trial. They contrived an excellent system of communications and Ulrike Meinhof continued to write and distribute her manifestos.

Andreas Baader, partly with the help of his lawyers (he had at one point no fewer than twenty-two), passed out regular instructions to supporters outside on how to continue the struggle and on how they might help to get him out of prison. Police searches on their cells un-earthed files of political manifestos, escape plans, propaganda and instructions to action groups. The prisoners used their lawyers as will-ing messengers and were allowed, thanks to their skilful exploitation of German prison rules, extra cells for their libraries of Marxist and revolutionary literature.

The arrest and detention of the principal leaders of the Red Army Fraction did not end terrorism in Western Germany. A new off-shoot speedily emerged to carry on the struggle and in some cases to come to the rescue. The 2nd of June Movement, so called in memory of Benno Ohnejorg, a student killed during a violent demonstration against the visit of the Shah of Persia to Berlin on that date, had common ancestry with the Baader-Meinhof crowd. Naturally in such movements there were various doctrinal differences, but the aims of the new movement were roughly the same. It inherited and exploited the same links with international terrorism through the Popular Front for the Liberation of Palestine and Black September, both of which have sections operating in West Germany. It also worked fairly closely with the Red Brigade in Italy.

Believed to consist of about fifty hard-core members backed up by 2,000 sympathisers and helpers, the 2nd of June Movement operated on Brazilian guerrilla principles in small groups of three to five anarchists. It concentrated, under the leadership of Ralf Reinders (known as "The Bear") on the spectacular kidnapping of prominent personalities rather than on bank raids and bomb and gun battles like the Red Army Fraction. Its most notable action was the kidnapping of Peter Lorenz, Chairman of the CDU in Berlin, on the eve of elections in the city in February 1975. Carried out with all the skill and panache of a raid by Mafia veterans, this new-style coup was a brilliant success. The organisers won all their points and within seventy-two hours the Bonn government gave way to their demands by releasing five of the major Baader-Meinhof terrorists.

Within a few hours Verena Becker, a twenty-two-year-old telephone operator serving six years for bomb attacks and bank robbery, and Ingrid Siepmann, thirty, technical pharmaceutical assistant, serving twelve years on similar terrorist charges, were released from their West Berlin prison and put on board a French military aircraft at Tegel airport to be flown to Frankfurt. All the details of this operation were carefully shown on German television to prove to the terrorists that their orders were being obeyed, and thus they obtained maximum publicity for their cause. On board the same aircraft, acting as an additional hostage, was pastor Heinrich Albertz, a former Mayor of Berlin.

At Frankfurt the party was joined by Rolf Pohl, a thirty-three-year-old lawyer, sentenced to six years for membership of Baader-Meinhof, and Rolf Heissler, twenty-six, a student doing eight years for armed robbery. They, too, had been released and brought from their prison in Bavaria. The last to arrive was Gabriele Kröcher-Tiedemann.

One other terrorist on the "liberation" list refused to make the trip. Horst Mahler, one of the original Baader-Meinhof four, was a lawyer terrorist, serving a prison sentence. Although he grandly declared that he had chosen to stay in prison so as to remain loyal to the revolution and not to desert the class struggle, it was strongly suspected that his political back-sliding down the slope to Maoism might have incurred the fury of old comrades even though they had demanded his liberation. It is not uncommon for terrorists to execute those suspected of political heresy.

From Frankfurt the five terrorists were flown to Aden, now the capital of South Yemen. They travelled first-class on a Lufthansa aircraft, each with pocket-money of 20,000 DM reluctantly provided by the West German government. At the airport a South Yemen minister greeted the group and officially offered them political asylum. "We shall conquer," they replied. Once again terrorism had been made to pay.

Any hopes in West Germany that soft-line dealings would buy off terrorist assault were soon dashed. Within a few months another squad which had connexions with the 2nd of June Movement, and with Baader-Meinhof, made another raid. This time it was the turn of the self-styled Holger Meins Commando, named after the anarchist lawyer. Meins had been a student at the Berlin Film Academy before throwing in his lot with the Red Army Fraction. He was arrested after the Frankfurt gun battle in 1972 which led to the capture of Baader, and as he was dragged from the building by police he let out a series of piercing screams (the "eight howls of Holger Meins", as they were called on television) and then collapsed. After two months of hunger strike he died. The following day, terrorists in Berlin performed a particularly brutal act of revenge when they killed the President of the Berlin Appeal Court, Gunther von Drenkmann. On his sixty-fourth birthday he went to the door of his home in Charlottenburg to find a group of young men standing there. One of them held a bouquet of flowers which he thought had been brought in honour of the occasion. They shot him four times and made off in two cars. This act provoked public outrage and destroyed the anarchist campaign to turn Meins into a martyr of the revolution.

The commando bearing his name launched an even more desperate affair in April 1975. Brushing aside the one guard on duty, the gang of five men and a woman burst into the West German Embassy in Stockholm, seized the building and held the Ambassador and his staff of twelve at gun point, demanding in exchange for their lives the release of all twenty-six Baader-Meinhof prisoners held in German jails. Their ultimatum – typed on a three-page document – was brought out of the Embassy by a woman hostage released for the purpose. In Bonn, Chancellor Schmidt, who dramatically pronounced the raid "the most serious challenge in the twenty-six-year history of our democracy", summoned a cabinet meeting. Both the cabinet and party leaders agreed with the government view that to give in this time would be to encourage a new wave of terror. For the twenty-six whose release was demanded were the dangerous hard core of the German terrorist movements. As a government spokesman said: "They have upon their consciences already the lives of nine people and the wounds of a hundred others."

In Stockholm, while Swedish police threw a cordon round the Embassy, the German government's refusal to accept their demands was passed by telephone. Inside, the terror group were busy mining the building with thirty-five pounds of TNT and after more threats they killed the military attaché, Lt. Col. Andreas Baron von Mirbach, and the economic councillor, Herr Heinz Hillegaart. The final act came when they sent out three more women hostages with another note saying that their demands were withdrawn. Then, just before midnight, loud explosions were heard and the whole Embassy burst into flames. As the remaining hostages made their way to deliverance five of their captors, who had thrown away their weapons, were discovered by Swedish police wandering about in the Embassy grounds. Only one of those arrested figured on any police wanted list.

One of the Stockholm raiders had blown himself up. Two of the remaining five, including the woman terrorist Hanna Krabe, were wounded by the explosions. Although two German diplomats had lost their lives, it was generally believed that the government had scored a qualified victory over the forces of terrorism by categorically refusing to give in on humanitarian grounds to outrageous demands. For it is precisely such humanitarian feelings which give determined terrorists their best chance of success. On this occasion Chancellor Schmidt promised energetic measures to pursue the criminals round the world, and stated his conviction that international co-operation was needed to combat "the horrible epidemic of international terrorism". The other moral drawn from this failed raid was that greater effort should be put into protecting vulnerable places like embassies.

All the evidence is that the Stockholm raid was carried out by apprentice terrorists of the new generation and this may explain their lack of success. Hausener, who led the group, came from a social medical collective in Heidelberg run by a Dr. Huber and his wife, who also used it as a psychiatric clinic. The theory of this "SPK" (socialist patients collective) was that mental illness in particular is caused by the present condition of society, and that society should be changed as part of the treatment. Both the doctor and his wife were sentenced to four years for their part in a criminal action in the course of which a policeman was shot.

Dr. Stumper believes that on the post-Baader-Meinhof scene lawyers, doctors and other professionals are deeply involved. "Frequently we find very intelligent leaders who pull the strings to control their puppets. There are many extreme left-wing lawyers in Germany who would themselves never dream of detonating bombs or firing automatics, but who nevertheless happily give orders and make plans for other people to take violent action. And there is no shortage of people with the necessary technical skills."

One of the terrorists on trial told a West German court that a professor of psychology in Hanover had rented a bungalow for his group. On another occasion a priest had given them the key to his apartment.

Among the people suspected by the security forces of helping to train the Stockholm gang is the lawyer Siegfried Haag from Heidelberg, who acted for the Baader-Meinhof defence but was arrested on suspicion of aiding a criminal conspiracy. After his release he went underground and announced that he was no longer a lawyer but had decided "to take part in battle against imperialism". He at once fell under suspicion of forming a new terrorist group.

He is suspected of having received automatic weapons from Swiss terrorists and two Suomis were found by Swedish police in the burnt ruins of the West German Embassy in Stockholm. They also discovered American made M26 grenades of the kind found in Carlos's Paris hideout.

In launching their attack, the terrorists had made a close study of methods used by Arab assault groups, who have long experience in the business of taking diplomats as hostages. The tactics of this raid provide yet another example of the fashion in which international groups not only work together, but are quick to imitate one another's methods, which all derive from the same urban guerrilla principles.

As things became more difficult for the German terrorists, with the arrests and break-up of cells through police action, a number of their members made their way to other European countries. As soon as arrangements had been made for the trial of the Baader-Meinhof leaders, a rash of attacks was reported from France, where the terrorist small fry had fled and made contact with French groups of sympa-thisers. In 1975 occurred a series of relatively minor attacks against premises belonging to German concerns in France: the Mercedes Branch in Paris, near the Étoile; the German television offices there; the West German consulate in Nice; and even a German coach in the South of France. Responsibility for these attacks was claimed by various bodies such as the Baader Solidarity Group, the Holger Meins Brigade and the Ulrike Meinhof Commando. Names of such gangs have little significance, the members switch easily from one to another, but the French police believe that Germans played some part in these operations together with native Frenchmen. In Common Market Europe it is easy to cross frontiers.

Some of the Germans who came to France also fell in with co-terrorists from outside, and as we have seen a number of Baader-Meinhof people gave help and support to Carlos's group in Paris.

In the words of Ulrike Meinhof, in a communiqué smuggled out of her prison cell: "Scorning both frontiers and the law, our forces are grouping together ..." After the attacks on German businesses in France another group threatened the life of M. Lecanuet, French Minister of Justice, and boasted: "In France our *international collectives* have avenged the death of Holger Meins by attacks on Mercedes." That message, sent to the French newspaper *Le Figaro*, came from a commando called "Puig-Antich – Ulrike Meinhof". Puig-Antich was a Spanish anarchist leader of the Iberian Liberation Movement executed by Franco in 1974.

Carlos himself floated easily between his European headquarters in Paris and Frankfurt, which seems to have been his favourite place for meetings with German members of his network. He is known to have stayed at the National Hotel there in May 1974 and again just before he shot the DST men in the Paris flat. It is believed that he had gone there to brief supporters for a new operation, and to bring a false passport for Wilfried Böse, the Frankfurt publisher and member of a commune who was almost certainly Carlos's most important contact man in Germany. He has cropped up in this story before and will enter it again. In the summer of 1975 Böse was questioned by the DST in Paris because they discovered his name after the rue Toullier shootings and had reason to believe that he was the man who had originally rented the flat where Silva Masmela lived in the French capital. Both he and his friend Weinrich (alias Klaus Muller) were expelled from France. It is known that they had been in contact with Michel Moukharbel, for the French police had a full record of his contacts in Paris even before they heard of Carlos himself.

It is standard procedure among police combating terrorists to send foreign nationals involved in the networks back to their own country. In this case, after the expulsion, both Böse and Weinrich appeared in Saarbrücken near the French frontier before a local German judge who knew nothing of the international ramifications of the group they belonged to. Böse admitted the mild offence of receiving a false passport, which in fact had been given to him by Carlos so that he could travel to Spain. His task was to provide information about the political scene there and the number of arrests made by the Spanish police among opposition movements in relation with the Carlos group. But the German judge knew nothing of all this and released Böse, who promptly disappeared. For this the German police blamed the French authorities who, according to them, failed to inform their German colleagues about their discoveries and suspicions at that stage.

Investigation of the detailed information now available about the movement of terrorists between Germany, France and other European countries demonstrates that strong links of international terrorism exist between the different bands operating in Europe under the auspices of the PFLP. It is strongly suspected in West Germany that although the Communist East Germans from across the border were not the prime movers in the terror campaigns they gave help by allowing revolutionaries to cross into East Berlin, where safe houses and bases were made available to them. Groups of Arab guerrillas have been welcomed for training as well as for rest periods at a special camp at Finsterwald on the banks of the Oder river in East Germany and special courses have been run there.

The possibility of even closer links between the terrorists and the East Germans seems highly likely to Herr Stumper. "I realise that Carlos and classic Communism do not seem to fit ideologically, but men like him move easily from one thing to another."

It is worth mentioning, finally, one other important occasion in the history of the Baader-Meinhof gang for the light it throws on the interconnexion of European revolutionaries. This was the visit of Jean-Paul Sartre to Andreas Baader in early 1975, when the latter was awaiting trial. It was Klaus Croissant, the German lawyer suspended from the Baader case for misdemeanours, who went to Paris and persuaded Sartre, elderly idol of trendy European militants, that he should do a little prison visiting. Sartre had a long record of speaking out in revolutionary causes; he had supported Algerian terrorist bombing against France in the 1950s. He supported Castro and Che Guevara and the French student revolt of 1968. Now he agreed to go to Mannheim and thus presented the new German anarchist revolutionaries with a propaganda victory for their ideas. He spent an hour with Baader in his cell before giving a press conference at the Zeppelin Hotel at which he made an appeal for outsiders to rally to the defence.

At this conference he used as interpreter Daniel Cohn-Bendit, the German whose role in the Paris revolt in 1968 earned him the name Danny the Red. And as he drove to the prison gates with Klaus Croissant, the chauffeur at the wheel of his car was none other than Hans-Joachim Klein, the man who had been connected in Paris with Carlos and who was to help Carlos capture the OPEC Oil Ministers and be wounded in the process. For Carlos and the terrorist groups among whom he flits, it is, indeed, a small world.

Chapter Twelve
The Japanese

CARLOS COULD HARDLY HOPE FOR BETTER ALLIES THAN THE SEKIGUN, the Japanese Red Army. Imbued with the kamikaze spirit, they are no less ready to die than were the fanatical airmen of the Second World War. And they are just as ruthless, even though their cause is diametrically opposed: World Revolution instead of Emperor and Country.

It is one of the strangest paradoxes of international terrorism that it should have roused these latent tendencies for suicidal action when, thirty years after the war, it was thought they were buried for ever in a Japan which had turned to the pursuit of the yen and the golf ball. But tradition will out, and Japan's militant youth, rebelling against the materialistic ambitions of "Ma-i ho-mu" (My Home) and "Ma-i Ka-a" (My Car) have reverted to age-old means to secure their revolutionary ends.

It is also traditional that any Japanese secret society should have a strong pitiless leader. The Red Army has just such a leader. But, in revolt against Japan's male dominated society, it has chosen a woman as its head. It is another of the phenomena of international terrorism that the women are often fiercer and crueller than the men. The late Ulrike Meinhof of the Baader-Meinhof gang, Leila Khaled of the Popular Front for the Liberation of Palestine, Marion Coyle of the Provisional IRA have all proved this. But none of them is more fanatical or cares less about human lives than Fusako Shigenobu.

An attractive dark-haired woman born just after the war, Shigenobu is a product of the economic miracle of the new Japan fashioned by

General MacArthur. She was a founder member of the Red Army and is one of the few original leaders still alive or outside prison.

The Japanese police did arrest her in May 1970 on several charges, including attempted murder, but she was soon released. The following February she married a student of Kyoto University, a breeding ground of left-wing militancy – and on the 26th of that month left for Beirut. There is some mystery about this marriage, for the executive of the Red Army, hard pressed by the police, had decided that its more notorious members whose names were on the police lists should, when travelling out of the country, go through marriage ceremonies with less well-known comrades and change their names, thus making it easier for them to obtain visas. It is not certain if Shigenobu's marriage was one of convenience or love. It is also not certain which of her comrades she married. The Israelis believe it was Takeshi Ukudairi, who was killed while taking part in the Lod massacre. But the Japanese say it was Osamu Maruoka who was recruited by Ukudairi and has since become one of the principal hit-men of the Red Army, virtually a Japanese Carlos.

There is no doubt where the real power lies. Shigenobu, who is called "Samira" by her Arab colleagues, is the head of the "Political Committee" of the Red Army and as such is responsible for the planning of operations, which are then carried out by its subordinate Military, Organisation and Logistic Committees. She is believed to have been responsible for planning the Lod massacre with George Habash's PFLP and it is probable that her close friend Leila Khaled also took part in the planning. She is wanted for questioning by the Japanese police on that score and a number of others, particularly the joint Red Army-PFLP hijacking of a Japanese Airlines Jumbo jet in July 1973.

Shigenobu spelt out her revolutionary philosophy in a letter justifying these two terrorist operations which was printed in the PFLP's own newspaper, *Al Hadaf*. It said:

These two operations were staged to consolidate the international revolutionary alliance against the imperialists of the world. We in the Red Army declare anew our preparedness to fight hand-in-hand with the Palestinians and wage joint onslaughts at any time to defeat the Israeli enemy. All of us should not be bound by international laws or by resistance within the framework of these laws ... because only revolutionary violence would enable us to defeat the imperialists throughout the world . . .

If the imperialists give themselves the right to kill the Vietnamese and the Palestinians, then we should have the right to blow up the Pentagon and kill the imperialists.

The refusal to be bound by recognised laws is common to all terrorist groups. Their attitude is that the "oppressors" made those laws and therefore they are invalid. Supported by this reasoning they can then argue, as did the members of the ancient cult of the Assassins: "Nothing is true and all is permitted." Once such reasoning is accepted then any act of terrorism, however cruel, however bloody, and whoever suffers, becomes justifiable.

It was in this sort of atmosphere and with this sort of twisted logic that the Japanese Red Army was born in 1969. It was formed among the disillusioned students who saw in the Paris student riots of May 1968 their blueprint for bringing about world revolution. The fact that the Paris riots failed to bring about that revolution did not matter. They almost succeeded, they showed what could be done, and militants in other capitals felt that they could have succeeded with more determination. The Japanese in particular believed that not only were they better equipped to do the job, but that their own political and social circumstances made their success inevitable. Kyoto University was one of the centres of this activity. And so was Meiji University, where Shigenobu was a student – one of the perpetual variety, more interested in revolution than in studying.

By October 21st 1969, International Anti-war Day, Takaya Shiomi, the original leader of the Red Army, felt he was ready to display his strength and took to the streets to do battle with the riot police. But his plans were never co-ordinated properly and the well-organised riot squads swept up the Red Army contingent with practised ease.

Shiomi was furious and disbanded his fighting organisation, telling its members that they would be allowed to return to the Red Army only if they carried out a bomb-throwing assault on the police as part of the campaign to prevent the Japanese Prime Minister from visiting the United States (one of the main targets of the various dissident groups was the US-Japanese Security Treaty).

In the event a few Molotov cocktails were thrown. They did little damage, but Shiomi's face was saved and most of the expelled members were re-admitted to Sekigun. Immediately after the consequent reorganisation of the Red Army, Shiomi turned his attentions to raising money for Japan's first terrorist spectacular: the Phoenix Plan. The money was raised even though the other members of Shiomi's political committee did not know what the Plan was. They might have guessed, for the Phoenix rising out of its own ashes is the symbol of Japanese Airlines.

On the last day of March 1970 a nine-man team of terrorists carrying swords, as well as pistols and explosives, and led by Takamoro Tamiya, took over a Boeing 727 carrying 131 passengers and seven crew as it flew over Mount Fujiyama. As hijackings go it was fairly uneventful. After an initial brandishing of samurai swords the jet landed at its original destination at Itazuke, Western Japan, for refuelling, and the hijackers demanded that it should be flown to the North Korean capital of Pyongyang. The captain tried to fool them by landing at Seoul airport in South Korea where hasty attempts had been made at disguise. But the hijackers were not duped, and the plane flew on to Pyongyang where the hostages were released and the hijackers given political asylum. Nobody in the West took much notice of this event. It was just another hijacking. Nobody was hurt and the plane was not destroyed. Judged by the standards of Palestinian hijackings it was indeed a non-event. But as part of the development of world terrorism it had two important results.

It gave the Red Army the cachet of success and the reputation for militant action among the young radicals who now clamoured to join an organisation which had actually taken a new direction instead of indulging in mutual head-beating with the riot police. It also brought the Red Army into contact with George Habash, leader of the PFLP, the man who once said that he regarded North Korea as the perfect revolutionary state, and who travelled to Pyongyang shortly after the hijackers arrived. It is significant that one of the hijackers was Takeshi Okamoto, elder brother of the Kagoshima University student Kozo Okamoto, sole survivor of the Lod killer gang. PFLP emissaries arrived in Tokyo to make contact with the Red Army. The Palestinians wanted doctors, nurses and technicians to serve in their Lebanese camps and the Japanese wanted to set up "international strongholds". Sekigun members began to make the pilgrimage to the refugee camps in Beirut where they discussed co-operation and took courses in guerrilla warfare. The link man between the Red Army and the PFLP was an Arab called

Bassam who was later said to have married Leila Khaled.

The next two years followed a confused pattern with the Red Army carrying out a number of robberies and kidnappings inside Japan, and after February 1971 Shigenobu started to build what is sometimes called the "Arab Committee" of the Red Army in Beirut. There was, however, no consistency in the membership or loyalties of the group in Japan. It formed and reformed in a number of minute factions, all dedicated to world revolution and almost equally dedicated to the destruction of rival groups. In January 1972 nine members of Sekigun joined forces with the twenty strong Keihin Ampo Kyoto to form the Rengo Sekigun, or United Red Army. And it was this splinter group whose actions caused the Japanese security forces to bear down on the revolutionaries and so cripple them that effective operations could only be mounted abroad, by Shigenobu's group.

In February 1972 the police, hunting for a group of the United Red Army who had been financing themselves by raiding banks and arming themselves by stealing guns and ammunition from sports shops around the fashionable holiday resort of Karuizawa in the mountains eighty miles northwest of Tokyo, flushed out five of the terrorists from their hiding place on the bitterly cold mountain.

The five, led by Tsuneo Mori, the twenty-seven-year-old son of a hotelier, and Hiroko Nagata, twenty-seven-year-old daughter of a businessman, fled from the police and seized a three-storey summer holiday lodge, holding the caretaker's wife, Mrs. Yasuko Muta, as hostage. Then, armed with a rifle, pistol, three shotguns and a supply of crude but effective Molotov cocktails, they settled down to withstand the police siege which eventually involved 1,200 policemen and lasted ten days.

At first the police decided against assaulting the barricaded lodge. They brought up armoured cars mounting powerful public address systems and pleaded with the terrorists: "Think of your own future. Surrender now." The terrorists replied by sniping at the loudspeakers. The next ploy of the police, determined to rescue Mrs. Muta unharmed, was to bring in three leading psychologists and ask them to study the scene and give their advice. But all that they could manage was to suggest that the police do nothing rash that would endanger the hostage. Shivering in the biting mountain cold, they also suggested that the police should keep warm. They retired, baffled, while the terrorists kept up their sniping to keep the besiegers' heads down. Next, the authorities flew in the mothers of three of the students to plead with their sons to surrender. Mrs. Yoshiko Bando, mother of the terrorists' crackshot, Kunio Bando, took up a megaphone and tried a political approach: "You know what Mr. Nixon is doing at this very moment in China. He's meeting with Chairman Mao and trying to do what you've long wanted to do. Come out. Your task is finished."

She was referring to the historic meeting between Nixon and Mao – before the American President was disgraced – in which the beginnings of a rapprochement were established between the leaders of the two great nations.

But her argument evoked no response, not even a shot from her son who boasted he could shoot out a policeman's eyes from a hundred yards. The police then settled down to wait out the siege while subjecting the terrorists to maximum psychological stress. They kept the lodge lit up by blinding searchlights and inflicted a barrage of noise on it with loudspeakers blaring out recordings of motor-cycle engines, bulldozers and soldiers on the march.

By this time television cameras were recording every minute of the siege and, according to the ratings 92·2 per cent of all viewers were tuned into the scene. The armchair strategists of the television sets inundated police switchboards with suggestions of a varying degree of helpfulness – one man wanted to hypnotise the terrorists by remote control. Gradually the whole nation became involved in the scene. For one young man the involvement was fatal. Offering himself as a substitute hostage, he broke through the police barrier and ran towards the lodge. The terrorists shot him dead.

And so it went on, noise, lights, the occasional shots, policemen stamping their feet in the bitter cold, the television cameras whirring, until after more than two hundred hours the authorities decided that the terrorists had been brought to the point of collapse.

The police brought up a wrecker's crane with a one and a half ton steel ball on the end of a chain. It rumbled up to the lodge and then began to swing its ball like a pendulum. It knocked great holes in the roof and walls and through these holes hose pipes poured in some sixty tons of water which froze almost as soon as it hit the building. The water was followed by hundreds of tear-gas canisters. Then specially trained squads of police stormed in through the holes. But the terrorists, far from being cowed, fought back with gunfire and bombs. Two policemen, one the superintendent leading the assault and an inspector, were shot in the face and killed. The attackers retreated, waited till dark and charged again. This time, the terrorists, holed up in a top-floor bedroom, surrendered with their hostage. Not one of them was harmed and it is a remarkable tribute to the Japanese determination to live down the reputation of wartime brutality that this was so. But there was to be one more death. Kunio Bando's father, unable to bear the shame brought upon his family, hanged himself from a tree. He left a note which summed up the traditional Japanese attitude towards family shame and the only way in which it can be expunged. He wrote: "With my death I offer apologies for the crimes committed by my son. Do not accuse the other surviving members of my family."

However, it was not until the terrorists had been interrogated that the full horror of their crimes became known. The United Red Army, supposedly in revolt from the regimentation of the capitalist society of Japan, had imposed its own regimentation; and its punishment for deviation was torture and death. The police found fourteen bodies buried in the wooded slopes of the mountains round Maebashi on the edge of the Japanese Alps. They had been stripped, tortured and then tied up in the open to freeze to death. Four of them were young women students. One of these was killed for wearing earrings – it was considered that this displayed bourgeois tendencies. Another was tied to a tree naked and left to freeze because she had committed the crime of marrying and becoming pregnant. She was accused of hampering the movement of the gang. She was eight months pregnant when she died. The women, in particular, were the victims of Hiroko Nagata, an unattractive, unstable woman who took particular care to make the "criminals" look as ugly as possible by shaving their heads as they lay on the floor helplessly bound.

Nagata and the handsome, arrogant, Tsuneo Mori dominated the group and organised the mock trials under what they called the process of "sokatsu". This word translates into English as "colligation" which, according to the *Oxford Dictionary*, is a process of logic, "the binding together of a number of isolated facts by a general notion or hypothesis". In fact it was an old-fashioned kangaroo court in which the accused stood no chance and in which the members were whipped into a hysterical frenzy by Mori and Nagata, whose self-confessed philosophy was: "Once the process of sokatsu starts, only death awaits." They committed hideous tortures on their friends. One man was stabbed to death by his nineteen- and sixteen-year-old brothers. Another bit off his tongue in his agony and bled to death. And cruellest of all, a woman was bound and gagged and shoved under the floorboards of the hut while the other members of the group went about their everyday tasks above her. She could hear them talking and eating and drinking. She took three days to die.

The details of this horrific story shocked a Japan which had "never had it so good". Christopher Reed, reporting from Japan for the *Sunday Times*, wrote:

Japan is in the midst of an agonised self-examination of how well-educated middle-class students could indulge in an orgy of killing more grisly than the Manson murders – and without the mind-distorting effects of drugs ...

The public, reacting in the Confucian ethic, has blamed the parents ... Popular opinion in Japan is understandably reluctant to blame its own society and the change in the nation since the Gross National Product became the new god. But a few left-wing sociologists and intellectuals are in no doubt that rampant hedonism had increasingly isolated a small group of students who set out in the beginning with genuine idealism.

Violence has bred violence as two decades of students (many now transformed into model businessmen) realised that peaceful demonstrations were achieving no change in the conservative government which has ruled Japan since the American occupation.

The radicals' sense of isolation is intensified in Japan through the nation's concept of the group society in which individualism is suspected, even feared ("The peg that stands up is the one that is hammered down," is a Japanese proverb).

The hopelessness and frustration of today's radicals is highlighted by the rebel student of five years ago who spoke to me recently. After showing me a photograph of himself helmeted with shoulder-length hair and brandishing a bamboo spear, the former militant, who now had a short back and sides and a conservative suit, explained that his ambition now was to be President of his company.

The combination of stern police methods made permissible by the "snow murders", the disgust of the public which withdrew its sympathy from the radicals, and the radicals' own defeated return to orthodoxy led inevitably to the destruction of the United Red Army as a revolutionary force able to operate in Japan. A hard core of supporters remained, but its function was mainly to supply "soldiers" to the one branch of the Red Army which was still capable of functioning, Fusako Shigenobu's Arab Committee working with the PFLP in Beirut.

Three months after the siege at Karuizawa, Shigenobu was able to prove in the most horrifying fashion that the Red Army, even if it was unable to bring revolution to Japan, could still kill in the cause of world revolution. Three of her "soldiers" carried out what at the time seemed an inexplicable act of terrorism. They killed twenty-six people and wounded seventy-two – mostly Christian Puerto Rican pilgrims – in the massacre at Lod airport. What happened is well established. Three young Japanese disembarked from Air France Flight 132 which had flown from Paris and Rome. They stood by luggage conveyor belt No. 3 and when their bags arrived they opened them and took out three Czech VZ58 assault rifles and a number of shrapnel grenades and opened fire on the excited throng of passengers. Within seconds the reception hall was a bloody shambles. Among the dead was the distinguished Israeli biophysicist Professor Aharon Katzir-Katchalsky. Two of the assassins also died, one mown down accidentally by a burst of fire from one of his companions and the other killed by one of his own grenades – it is still not known if he slipped and died accidentally or if he committed suicide. The third man, Kozo Okamoto, was captured. One hour after it was all over the PFLP proudly claimed responsibility for the massacre: "Our purpose was to kill as many people as possible."

What makes this story particularly relevant to this book is the way in which it was planned, the way in which it demonstrated that terrorism had become internationalised, and the insights into the thinking of young revolutionaries provided by the trial of Kozo Okamoto. It also showed once more the utter disregard for human life of George Habash and Wadi Hadad.

Okamoto told his captors that he had joined the Red Army in February 1970, just one month before his brother's band carried out their samurai hijacking. Two years later the PFLP, capitalising on George Habash's contacts with the hijackers in Pyongyang, sent Abu Ali, one of its leading members, to Tokyo to recruit three Japanese for a suicide mission. Kozo Okamoto, twenty-four-year-old drop-out from Kagoshima University, was one. The other two were Takeshi

Ukudairi, twenty-six, and Yasuiki Yashuda, twenty-four. They were both students at Kyoto University.

Okamoto was given money and airline tickets and left Japan on February 29th on a Canadian Pacific flight for Montreal where he stayed at the Hilton Hotel until March 4th. On that day he flew to New York and then on to Paris where he stayed at the Grand Hotel for two days before flying on to the Lebanon. In Beirut he met up with his two comrades who were masquerading as "Jiro Sugisaki" and "Ken Torio". Okamoto was known as "Daisuke Namba", a name which meant nothing in the Middle East but which was significant in Japan because Namba was a notorious figure, a revolutionary who was executed for the attempted assassination in 1923 of the then Crown Prince Hirohito.

The three Japanese were put through a commando course at Baalbek by the Palestinians, learning how to fire light automatic weapons and throw grenades. The PFLP instructors also taught them how to fire incendiary bullets at airliners. It was decided that they "should commit suicide at the completion of the task".

Their training completed, they left Beirut on May 23rd for Paris. They then moved on to Frankfurt where they were given forged passports. Two days later they left for Rome by train, staying in a hotel and a pension until May 30th. On that day they were issued with their weapons: three automatic rifles with twelve aluminium magazines each containing thirty rounds of 7.62 calibre, a few hand grenades of a particularly lethal variety which scattered shrapnel when they exploded. The courier who delivered the weapons was Fusako Shigenobu. That night they flew to Lod and stepped off the plane into the warm earth-scented night to do their killing.

When it was all over, with the cordite fumes hanging in the air, the dead terrorists were searched. In the pocket of one of them a copy of Rimbaud's memoirs was found. This was entirely appropriate, for the tragic figure of Rimbaud has been adopted by young revolutionaries all over the world as the expression of their own tragedy: "To whom shall I hire myself out? What beast should I adore? What holy images attack? What hearts break? What lies uphold? In what blood tread? Rather steer clear of the law. The hard life, simple brutishness, to lift with withered fist the coffin's lid, to sit, to suffocate. And thus no old age, no dangers."

Okamoto's own philosophy was less articulate but, as he expressed it in a rambling speech at his trial, it made absolutely clear why the young Japanese were prepared to kill and be killed in a cause which was far removed from their own.

"My profession is a soldier of the Red Army," he declared, when telling how he and his comrades had decided that their revolutionary mission had to be carried out decisively. "This was our duty, to the people I slaughtered and to my two comrades who lost their lives ... War involves slaughtering and destruction. We cannot limit warfare to destruction of buildings. We believe slaughtering of human bodies is inevitable ...

"When I was captured, a certain Japanese asked me: 'Was there no other way?' Can that man propose an alternative method? I believe that, as a means towards world revolution, I must prepare the creation of the world Red Army ...

"We three soldiers, after we die, want to become three stars of Orion. When we were young we were told that if we died we became stars in the sky. I may not fully have believed it, but I was ready to. I believe some of those we slaughtered have become stars in the sky. The revolution will go on and there will be many more stars. But if we recognise that we go to the same heaven, we can have peace."

The Lod massacre was to claim two more stars for Okamoto's heaven. Ghassan Kanafani, spokesman for the PFLP and the group's intellectual, bragged about PFLP's responsibility for the affair. A month later Kanafani, author of *Men in the Sun* and *That which Remains for You*, was blown to bits by ten pounds of plastique hidden under the bonnet of his car and detonated by a hand grenade. With him died his seventeen-year-old niece – another innocent victim of the war of kill and counterkill.

The Lod massacre brought forth universal condemnation except from those Arab states that were working with the terrorists and believed that any action taken against Israel was legitimate. Even the then Egyptian Prime Minister, Azziz Sidki, said: This incident indicates we are capable of achieving victory in our battle against Israel." Gaddafi, of course, went the whole hog:

Fida'i action must be of the type of operation carried out by the Japanese ... Fida'i action has not yet reached the level of the true spirit of the fida'in. We demand the fida'i action is able to carry out operations similar to the operation carried out by the Japanese.

Why should a Palestinian not carry out such an operation? You will see them all writing books and magazines full of theories, but otherwise unable to carry out one daring operation like that carried out by the Japanese, who come from the Pacific Ocean.

Kozo Okamoto was sentenced to life imprisonment by the Israelis but, ever since, the PFLP have made desperate efforts to get him out. The first of these efforts was made in December 1972 when a Black September gang seized the Israeli Embassy in Bangkok and demanded his release along with thirty-five other prisoners held in Israeli jails. However, this particular gang were lacking in resolution and were talked into releasing their hostages in return for a safe passage out of the country. So Okamoto remained in jail where he is to this day, still the cause of hostage-taking to secure his release.

The Red Army waited more than a year before carrying out another "spectacular" and then it was a most curious affair. Osamu Maruoka – the student said by the Japanese to have married Shigenobu – joined with three Arabs and a girl to hijack a Japanese Jumbo airliner thirty minutes after it left Amsterdam bound for Tokyo on July 20th 1973.

The operation was a disaster even before it started. As the girl, whose passport said she was an Ecuadorian called Mrs. Peralta and who was the leader of the group, sipped a glass of champagne in the first-class cocktail bar, she let slip a grenade which exploded, killing her and wounding the steward. The other hijackers were forced into precipitate action. Brandishing their pistols, they took over the plane and ordered it to turn south. That was simple enough, but it was the one simple thing about this hijack, for their leader was the only one who had been fully briefed and she was now lying dead, covered by a blanket in the bar. The other four had not been trusted with the proposed destination for the aircraft, or even what they were supposed to demand in ransom. They were lost, thirty thousand feet up, in command of a huge plane flying at 600 miles an hour with 123 passengers and 22 crew members at their mercy. They did not know where to go or what to do. There is still doubt about the identity of the dead leader. That well-informed British journalist, Chapman Pincher, later identified her as a Christian Iraqi with the English-sounding name of Katie George Thomas. Whoever she was, her carelessness with the grenade had led to her own death and had ruined a carefully planned operation.

The Jumbo, fully fuelled for its flight over the North Pole, trundled south over West Germany, Switzerland and Italy. Italian air force fighters intercepted it and escorted it out of Italian airspace. The Israelis called a Red Alert, fearful that the plane would be used as a kamikaze on Tel Aviv. As the Jumbo passed Cyprus the hijackers broadcast a message through Nicosia control tower. Its contents were predictable: "We are determined to fight Imperialism unto death." They were refused permission to land at Beirut. They tried to land at Basra but the runway was too short. Eventually they put down at Dubai where they spent three sweltering days sitting on the runway waiting for instructions from their headquarters. Wadi Hadad must have been going frantic trying to contact them. The wounded steward was allowed off the plane for treatment and the body of the dead leader was taken off. However, when the hijackers prepared to continue their Odyssey, they demanded that she be returned to them. Nobody wanted them. Saudi Arabia, Abu Dhabi, and Bahrein shut their airstrips and Beirut turned them away for the second time. Eventually they landed for re-fuelling at Damascus and finally, after another swing over the Mediterranean, were given permission to land at Benghazi for, said Gaddafi, "humanitarian reasons".

As the plane approached Benghazi the passengers were told that they had two minutes to get out of the plane before it was blown up. The terrorists were as good as their word. The plane landed at the far end of the airfield and as the passengers scrambled to safety down the Jumbo's fairground-like inflatable chutes the hijackers set their fuses. The passengers, most of them shoeless, ran for their lives while behind them the ten million pound aircraft started to burn and then exploded as the flames reached the fuel tanks. It formed an expensive pyre for the girl who should have paid more attention to her grenade and less to her champagne.

Nobody wanted to acknowledge responsibility for this disastrous affair. The hijackers had called themselves the "Sons of the Occupied Territory", an organisation never heard of before or since. There was an initial attempt to justify the hijacking by Gaddafi's Minister of the Interior, Major Khuweilidi al-Humeydi, who welcomed the passengers and crew to "the land of revolution" in the Benghazi hotel where they were quartered.

He expressed his regrets for what had happened to them but "what has happened is the result of the homelessness and oppression suffered by a people, the Palestinian Arab people, who are struggling by every means for the retrieval for their land which was usurped and occupied. These people are trying to draw the attention of the world, and alert the world's conscience, to their just cause.

"The hijacking was an individual action by the Palestinians. People of several nationalities from all over the world took part in the events of the past few days. As you may have noticed there were some Japanese, some Palestinians and some Ecuadorians, and this clearly shows that free men throughout the world now understand the cause of the Palestinian people . . ."

His reference to Ecuadorians is puzzling because it could only refer to the dead terrorist leader. Perhaps he had not been let in to the secret.

However, his justification of the hijacking was followed immediately by a denial of responsibility from the PLO and a threat that "the Revolution Command is carrying out a detailed investigation into the implications of this action and the motives of those behind it".

And a few days later Libya, too, changed its tune when the Minister of Information, Abu Zaid Durda, made a statement in which he described the hijacking of the Jumbo and its destruction as

a crime for which the perpetrators have not been able to give any justification . . . some hijackers seek to become rich by demanding a ransom for the release of their victims. Others seek fame and some want to travel free of charge. Some hijackers, however, try to justify their crime as being in the defence of a national cause . . . Just as it condemned robbery, megalomania and parasitism, Libya also condemned the reducing of methods of defending national causes to such a low level.

The Libyan Arab Republic has therefore decided to bring the hijackers to trial. They will be tried according to Armed Robbery Law No. 148 of 1972 which was enacted in line with Islamic law.

This may seem a somewhat strange decision in the light of what we know about Gaddafi's intimate involvement with terrorism. The likely explanation is that at that time he had quarrelled with the leadership of the PFLP over their addiction to Marxist doctrines. Every Arab, according to Gaddafi, must follow the true way of Islam. His choice of law under which to try the hijackers is also significant because it is part of the reversion to old Islamic laws that he forced on Libya. Under these laws a thief has his right hand cut off, an adulteress is stoned to death, and an armed robber is beheaded.

While the Libyans did not carry out that threat, they did imprison the hijackers. What happened to the Arabs we do not know, but Osamu Maruoka was kept in prison for a year. It was not too arduous a stretch. He wrote an article in the left-wing weekly *Shinsayoku* when he was released in which he reported that he had been treated as a special political prisoner and that his prison was equipped with colour television. He was released "because of a change in situation in the Libyan government".

He had now, he wrote, "returned to the front". The Japanese police were sorry about that. They still wanted to talk to him about his involvement with the planning of the Lod massacre.

Early the following year a complicated pattern of events was initiated which led to the close involvement of the Japanese with Carlos. The first of these events took place on January 31st 1974, when two Red Army members, Haruo Wako and Yoshiaki Yamada, and two unknown Palestinians, set off a bomb at an oil storage tank at the Shell refinery in Singapore. They were cornered but comandeered a ferry and sailed it into international waters with five hostages aboard. What they wanted was a plane to fly them to safety. The authorities chose to negotiate, hoping to wear down the terrorists and work them into a psychological state in which they would surrender. The negotiations went on for eight days. But rather than wearing the terrorists down, those eight days gave the PFLP time to organise a rescue strike.

On February 6th five Arabs stormed the Japanese Embassy in Kuwait and held Ambassador Yoshitaka Ishikawa and twenty-eight others hostage. They demanded a simple exchange: they would free their hostages if the Singapore authorities flew the four trapped terrorists and *their* hostages to Kuwait. The authorities had little choice. They capitulated. A Japan Airlines jet carried the Singapore terrorists to Kuwait, where they picked up their Arab comrades and then flew the whole party to that haven of terrorists, the South Yemen.

It was at about this time that Fusako Shigenobu led her troops out of Beirut and into Paris. The French capital was ideal for the Red Army. It has the largest number of Japanese students of any city in Europe and thousands of Japanese tourists visit it every year. While the French police were acutely conscious of the danger of Arab terrorism, the Red Army could lose itself in the Japanese sea of cameras and tape recorders.

Shigenobu had a specific object in mind with her move to Paris.

She wanted to establish her independence. Having worked as a nurse for the PFLP and then as leader of the Japanese contingent, she wanted more authority to mount her own operations. In order to do this she needed money. In February 1972, when the PFLP was short of cash, Wadi Hadad raised five million dollars by hijacking and holding to ransome a Lufthansa Jumbo. Even though the South Yemenis demanded a million dollars for "landing rights" PFLP still had enough left to stay in the terrorist business.

Shigenobu decided to follow Hadad's example, but her target was to be powerful Japanese businessmen living in Europe. According to the Tokyo District Public Prosecutor's Office the representatives of the Mitsubishi Corporation and the Marubeni Corporation in Düsseldorf were to be the first victims. The plan, code-named "Operation Translation", was to kidnap them and hold them to ransom for money to support a "simultaneous uprising" of all Red Army members in Europe.

The prosecutor, who got his information from a captured Red Army terrorist, said that the plot was first hatched in Beirut by Fusako Shigenobu and Taketomo Takahashi, the professor who was later arrested and deported by the French. The final details were arranged in the home of yet another Tokyo University professor in Paris.

The plan called for Yoshiaki Yamada – one of the Singapore bombers – to fly into Europe with the Red Army's treasury, $10,000, to finance the kidnappings. But once again things went wrong for the Japanese. The dollars were counterfeit and were of such poor quality that when Yamada was searched at Orly airport on his arrival from Beirut they were instantly recognised as forgeries and he was arrested. He was found to have three forged passports and a coded letter from Shigenobu. The letter was sent to the Japanese police for deciphering and the plot was "blown".

Acting on the information obtained from this letter the French police started to trawl through the Japanese community in Paris. They picked up a hundred people for questioning and eight were deported. They included a sociology professor, a film critic and a salesgirl at a Japanese department store. The salesgirl, Mariko Yamamoto, was the biggest catch, for she is one of Shigenobu's closest associates and in her flat the police found a coded notebook with the addresses of some fifty safe houses in European cities. She was also a key member of a ten-strong unit which called itself "VZ58" from the name of the assault rifle used in the Lod massacre.

All this activity by the French and Japanese police severely hampered the Red Army in its long-term planning. But there was one operation they had to undertake. According to the rules of the game, they had to mount an assault to "spring" Yamada. It is here that the Carlos connexion emerges. The Red Army planned to attack the French Embassy in The Hague and seize hostages as pawns in a bargaining game for Yamada.

But they needed help. It is the dead Moukharbel's little green notebook which shows how it was given, and the weapons which were left behind after the attack show what was given. Moukharbel's accountant-like mind led him to chronicle, in the terms of train fares and expenses for entertainment, the history of Carlos's European enterprises up till the day the chief executive shot the accountant.

Moukharbel noted that he and Carlos went to The Hague. On September 3rd 1974, ten days before the attack on the French Embassy, they travelled to Zürich to meet the three Red Army "soldiers" who were going to carry out the attack and gave them 4,000 French francs. And on the day before it was carried out, Carlos went with the Japanese to Amsterdam. It was all recorded in the notebook along with the train fare from Paris to Roosendaal on the Dutch border and bus fares from Roosendaal to Amsterdam.

Further proof of the Carlos connexion with The Hague affair was provided by the grenades left behind. They were some of that by now notorious batch of M26 fragmentation grenades stolen by Baader-Meinhof from the United States Army base at Niesau in 1971. They were handed over to Carlos and their use maps the spread of his network over Europe.

The chosen assault force, Jun Nishikawa, another drop-out from Kyoto University, Junzo Ukudaira, younger brother of one of the Lod killers, and Haruo Wako, who was Yamada's collaborator at Singapore, seized the Embassy on September 13th 1974. They wounded a Dutch policeman and policewoman who answered an alarm call and held the Ambassador, Count Jacques Senard, and eight other men and two women as hostages. They demanded that Yamada should be handed over to them, that they should be given a Boeing 707 to fly them to the Middle East and that they should be paid one million dollars. If not, they threatened, "the hostages will be executed at intervals". They got everything they asked for except the million dollars. That was cut to $300,000.

The ostensible reason for asking for money was explained on another occasion by Fusako Shigenobu: "We want to take back the money of the Japanese people which their government squandered in the name of condolence money for victims of the Tel Aviv [Lod] incident."

However, the terrorists were forced to give up the ransom when they landed at Damascus, after a tour of Middle East airports, and surrendered themselves to the Syrian authorities. It was part of the safe conduct deal they made by way of the plane's radio with the Syrians, who said later that the return of the money and the safety of the plane's crew were the principal condition for allowing the Japanese to land at Damascus. They were quickly allowed to move on to their base in the Lebanon. Their safe return was welcomed. But the loss of the ransom and the counterfeit money carried by Yamada was a hard blow.

Shigenobu was becoming desperate for funds. Her quarrel with the PFLP deepened because the Palestinians were insisting that their national needs should receive priority while she wanted to wage revolutionary war all round the world without any priority being given to the Palestinians, so she had been cut off from Arab funds. She had launched a campaign for money in Japan, and the kidnap operation, wrecked by the discovery of Yamada's forged notes, was another attempt to restore the financial situation. So the need to call on Carlos for help in The Hague operation was something of a climbdown. She was forced to accept that the Red Army could not operate without the support of the PFLP and the Carlos complex.

She was also running out of soldiers. They had dwindled until at the most there were only thirty operational members of the Red Army. There was still a great deal of support in leftist circles in Europe composed of those who had left Japan for ideological reasons and there were also the trendy supporters of revolution in Japan itself. But not many came forward to take part in hijacks and embassy raids.

It came as another great blow, therefore, when in March 1975 Jun Nishikawa, who had taken part in the successful Hague raid, and Kazuo Tohira, a new boy in the ranks of the terrorists, were arrested by the Swedish police when they were found watching, photographing and sketching the building in Stockholm which houses the embassies of Austria, Lebanon and four other countries. The Swedish police concluded that they were preparing an attack on one of the embassies, probably the Lebanese, in yet another attempt to obtain ransom money. However, the Swedes, not wishing to become the target for a Red Army rescue operation, simply put the two men on a Lufthansa plane and sent them off to Tokyo.

They were escorted by Swedish security men and as soon as the plane landed at Tokyo Japanese police went on board, arrested them and took them away for questioning. It was Nishikawa who confessed to the plot to kidnap Japanese businessmen in Europe and he also gave the police details of the way in which the Red Army had been reorganised in September 1974.

The controlling body, he said, was the Political Committee headed by Fusako Shigenobu. It was this committee that maintained relations with the PFLP and with the Carlos network. There were also three sub-committees, the Military Committee to which the commandos such as himself belonged, the Organisation Committee and the Logistics Committee.

Having confessed, he was charged with attempted murder during The Hague affair. It was he who had fired a shot over the heads of the hostages – and hit a picture of the then French President, Georges Pompidou.

Tohira also responded to questioning and he told the police that his group had been given orders to reconnoitre the Lebanese embassies in Copenhagen, Oslo and Stockholm in order to seize one of them, take hostages and demand ransoms to finance future operations. They had received their instructions and forged passports at a PFLP base in Beirut from Osamu Maruoka and Haruo Wako.

By this time the French and Swedish authorities were combing out the Japanese communities in both countries and a number of deportations were quietly carried out. Europe was getting very uncomfortable for the Red Army. Nevertheless, always more successful at follow-up rescue operations than in actual acts of terror – apart from Lod – the Red Army made it quite clear that they intended to secure the release of Nishikawa and Tohira. Shigenobu said that she planned to take action to release her arrested followers and in June of 1975 the Red Army published a book called *Form Ranks, A Declaration by the Japanese Red Army*, in which it said that it would surely be reunited with its two comrades and would accept them again as fighters for revolution.

They waited until August when, on the eve of Prime Minister Takeo Miki's visit to the United States for summit talks with President Ford, five Red Army terrorists seized the offices of the American Consulate and the Swedish Embassy in Kuala Lumpur and held some fifty people hostage, including the American Consul, Robert Stebbins, and the Swedish chargé d'affaires, Fredrik Bergenstrahle.

Shigenobu's demands for their release were simple: a DC8 to fly the raiding party and seven imprisoned Red Army members to sanctuary in Libya. The seven she wanted released were Junich Matsuura, a fund-raising bank robber; Hiroshi Sakaguchi, a revolutionary far to the left of even Shigenobu; Jun Nishikawa and Kazuo Tohira, the commandos captured in Stockholm; Hisashi Matsuda, another bank robber; Norio Sasaki, leader of the "Wolf" group of bombers whose targets were commercial enterprises; and Kunio Bando, sharpshooter in the siege of Karuizawa.

Two of these, Matsuura and Sakaguchi, refused to go: Matsuura because he was in poor health and was on parole with the prospect of release. The fires of revolution had gone out for him but not for Sakaguchi; his reason for refusing to be ransomed was that the Red Army was not sufficiently revolutionary. Shigenobu would not believe this at first. She thought it was a trick by the police to try to hold on to the militant. It was not until Sakaguchi, persuaded by the police, talked to the terrorists in Kuala Lumpur by international telephone that they reluctantly agreed to strike his name from their list.

The prisoners were taken from jail and put on board the plane at Tokyo for the flight to Kuala Lumpur, where the hostages were released and the joint party of raiders and ex-prisoners boarded for their flight to Libya. The aircraft was flown by Captain Tomio Mashiko, a veteran JAL pilot who is becoming quite experienced in ferrying terrorists to safety. It was he who flew the Singapore bombers to South Yemen in 1974. "I did not," he said ruefully, "expect to be asked to do this again."

The Kuala Lumpur affair was a success for the Red Army. Not only had they secured the release and recruitment of five expert terrorists; they had also brought off one of those spectaculars which all terrorist organisations need if they are to survive, for without continually forcing themselves violently onto the world stage, they are ignored, wither and die.

The affair, coming as it did on the eve of Premier Miki's visit to the United States, was shrewdly embarrassing for the government. Chief Cabinet Secretary Ichitaro Ide said it was extremely regrettable that

Japan as a constitutional state had to comply with an unlawful demand; "the government took the unusual step to release imprisoned radicals by giving top priority to the safety of the hostages." The police, while recognising that the whip hand was held by the Red Army, viewed the capitulation with distaste and foreboding: "It's something like turning tigers loose in the wilderness. It sows the seeds of trouble all over the world."

Curiously, in more than a year between the Kuala Lumpur raid and the time of writing this book, there has been no activity from the Red Army to justify this foreboding. There have been no hijackings, no killings, no kidnappings.

There are a number of reasons for this inactivity. In the first place, the Red Army, once so mysterious, is now well known. With only about thirty activists, the same names keep cropping up in every operation and by now every country in Europe knows those names and the faces that match them. Paris, once so secure for the Red Army, has become a hard city in which to work. Japanese features no longer provide anonymity but excite immediate suspicion. As the arrests in Stockholm prove, Europe has been virtually closed to the Red Army.

It has also been forced to retreat from the once safe PFLP bases in the Lebanon. The long civil war has made these bases dangerous, and has disrupted both training and planning.

So, lacking both security and infrastructure, the Red Army has now begun to look homewards, towards the East. Shigenobu has already threatened to step up operations against "Japanese imperialism" in Singapore, Malaysia and Indonesia. And in an attempt to re-establish a sound base in Japan, where money can be had and recruits, unknown to the police forces of the world, can be mustered, the Red Army is urging the hopelessly split radical factions in Japan to come together and establish a "Japan Council for a United World Revolutionary Front".

It is however significant that despite the debt the Red Army owes Carlos for the aid he provided at The Hague, there were no Japanese involved in either the OPEC affair or the Entebbe hijacking in July 1976. On both occasions the terrorists would have benefited from the inclusion of some experienced Red Army "soldiers" in their hit-teams. At Entebbe in particular the Arabs involved were mostly bureaucrats and not men of action.

Can it be, then, that the Red Army is a spent force?

One argument against this theory is that the Entebbe hijackers – German and Arab – demanded the release of Kozo Okamoto from the Israeli prison where he is serving his life sentence. It is argued that this means the Red Army is still part of the PFLP-Carlos alliance. But Okamoto has come to be something more than just a Japanese terrorist. He has become part of terrorist mythology, the only survivor of the bloodiest atrocity every carried out by the PFLP. Like the Russians with their spies, it has become a matter of honour and credence with the PFLP to get him out of prison.

It is in this situation, with the world wondering if it is defunct, that a terrorist organisation is at its most dangerous.

Chapter Thirteen
The Entebbe raid

THE SEIZING OF THE AIR FRANCE AIRBUS WHICH ENDED IN THE ENTEBBE raid adapted the famous dictum of Clausewitz, and proved that diplomacy could become the logical extension of terrorism. For, once the international band had seized the aircraft and forced it to land at Entebbe, Uganda, in the heart of Africa, they began a self-assured process of what they styled negotiations. To the outside watchers it looked like blackmail.

What they demanded was the release from prison of fifty-three terrorists, including the infamous Kozo Okamoto. They were all members of gangs with which the Carlos complex was associated. If they were not set free then 103 Jews and Israelis, segregated from their fellow passengers in the airport building, would be massacred. It did not end as the terrorists planned; for the Israelis struck hard, and released the hostages and not the terrorist prisoners. It was their raid, not the terrorists' strutting, which attracted the attention, even admiration, of television and news watchers throughout the world. For once, the theatrical coup came from the victims and not from the attackers who court publicity.

But the most significant conclusion to be drawn from this fascinating affair is the extent to which the Carlos network was used in a completely international operation. At least three national governments were involved in the planning and execution of the raid, while the gang themselves spoke as though they represented a *de facto* government of a sovereign state of war.

A similar pattern of swift violence, followed by long-drawn-out bargaining of a diplomatic nature, had been adopted by Carlos in his raid on OPEC at Vienna. The Entebbe affair was a logical development of the same technique practised by the same people, although Carlos himself was not present on the ground. The difference was that this time the terrorists were dealing not with Chancellor Kreisky, the liberal peace-at-all-costs leader of Austria, but with Israel which, after much havering, reached a diametrically opposed conclusion. Jews, the Israeli government decided, could not be allowed to be publicly persecuted; even risky action would be better than none at all.

The other new factor was that Palestinian-dominated terrorism had now penetrated deep into Africa, a continent where Israelis and Arabs had already fought out diplomatic battles to win influence for their respective causes. That development is a pointer to the future, for it may well be that international terrorist methods will soon be adopted by Africans themselves. Before long Carlos, backed by Arab money, may be teaching his techniques to the "freedom fighters" of South Africa and Rhodesia, who already find themselves in a position analogous to that of the Palestinians.

In the 1960s, the Israelis, anxious to win influence in Black African countries, to gain support and build friendly outposts in those new nations hemmed in to the north by the Arab Mediterranean states, sent technical aid groups to Africa. Development experts, irrigation engineers and agriculturalists went to help – and also to propagandise for the cause of Israel in a "hearts and minds" campaign.

They also set up an intelligence network with the idea of using it to penetrate the Arab countries to the north. Some of the experts provided help and support for dissident movements fighting against Arab countries. They were particularly active in encouraging the Blacks in southern Sudan in their long struggle against the Arab government in Khartoum, justifying this with the claim that Israel would help any group fighting against tyranny.

They also sent military aid teams to those countries that would accept them. These teams taught Israeli methods of dealing with guerrillas and their blitzkreig methods of combining aircraft and tanks in swift forays. They went even beyond Africa and modernised Singapore's forces for Harry Lee. But nowhere were they better received than in Uganda – the country which had once been proposed as a national home for the Jews. President Amin still wears his Israeli paratrooper wings – if, that is, he is still alive when this book is published. Israeli pilots taught Ugandans to fly at Entebbe airport which was modernised and enlarged by Israeli engineers, whose blueprints were to prove invaluable to the commando rescue team. The head of the military mission, Colonel Bar-Lev, became a close friend of Idi Amin.

In the years following victory in the Six-Day War, it seemed that nothing could interfere with the happy relationship between Israel and those black countries which form a cordon across Africa where Arab rule ends.

But the Israelis had reckoned without the oil money pouring into Moammer Gaddafi's treasury and the strong traditional links between the Moslems of the black countries and their co-religionists in the Arab states – even though those links had originally been the chains between the slave and the slave master. Gaddafi set out to win back Africa from the Israelis. With a mixture of promises of millions of pounds, of guarantees of military aid and exhortations to support the true faith, he succeeded remarkably quickly. Uganda fell to him in 1972. The Israelis were kicked out. Idi Amin, a Moslem, was converted overnight to supporting the Palestinian cause. He acquired a Palestinian body-guard. He acquired Migs and Soviet armoured vehicles. Palestinian pilots trained at Entebbe, taking off from the new runway built by the Israelis. And when Amin fought his little war with the deposed Milton Obote's supporters in 1972 it was Gaddafi who despatched an airborne force of Libyan soldiers to help him. (It is this expedition which is at the root of Gaddafi's enmity for President Numeiri of the Sudan, for Numeiri refused to allow the Libyans to use Khartoum's airfield facilities. The Libyans missed the war and Gaddafi was once more enraged.)

All over Africa the Israelis took a terrible diplomatic hammering – except in South Africa whose friendship only served to widen the split between themselves and the black countries. The PLO opened offices wherever the Israelis left. Close associations were built between the Palestinians and the black guerrilla movements fighting the Portuguese and the Rhodesians. The Organisation of African Unity became solidly anti-Israeli and the United Nations, with a now co-ordinated Arab-African Communist vote, became almost hysterical in condemning Israel and all its works.

In a parallel process, the PFLP also began to look towards Africa. It was a move dictated by both necessity and opportunity. Europe was becoming increasingly dangerous for Wadi Hadad's men. The anti-terrorist squads set up by European police forces in the wake of Munich and with especially close co-operation between the Common Market countries, were keeping their home-grown terrorists in check. Most of the Baader-Meinhof leaders were dead or imprisoned. The Japanese Red Army, at odds with the PFLP, was being harried from one country to another. Carlos himself had been "blown" and was on Interpol's wanted list. At the same time the civil war in the Lebanon had virtually closed down PFLP's international operations out of Beirut. Fresher, safer territories were needed. Hadad moved out of Beirut to the safety of Aden and looked south. There he saw not only easy communications across the Red Sea, but also an established network of PLO offices in countries which were sympathetic to the Palestinian cause and in which terrorism was regarded not as evil but as the holy right of the under-privileged.

The stage was set for Entebbe. But, before that drama was played, a little act was put on in Nairobi, rather like that of buskers entertaining outside the theatre before the main performance.

In January 1976, less than a month after the OPEC attack, three Arabs went to the British Consulate in Beirut and asked for visas allowing them to enter Kenya – Britain acts for Kenya in Lebanon. The British saw no reason for not issuing the visas and when they forwarded the three names to Nairobi there were no objections. This is not surprising because the three men were undoubtedly travelling on false passports.

However, somebody was watching the progress of this trio, for when they reached Kenya they were arrested. Under interrogation, they confessed that they were members of the PFLP and were planning to make yet another attempt to destroy an El Al airliner with a SAM 7 missile.

Gaddafi was once again trying to exact revenge for the Libyan airliner shot down by the Israelis into the Sinai. And once again he and PFLP had failed. They failed because they were forced to choose the one country in Black Africa where El Al still operated, Kenya, which almost alone maintained relations with Israel. The Israelis, through the arcane processes at which they are so expert, learned of the plot and warned Jomo Kenyatta's security service, the General Service Unit. Duly grateful, the GSU picked up the three terrorists, questioned them rigorously, and handed them over to the Israelis. They took care, however, to keep the whole affair secret. The PFLP commandos, wondering what had happened to their missile-team, sent in two of their German colleagues to make contact. But they, too, were arrested and one of them, a woman, was found to have instructions in secret ink written on her stomach. They disappeared without trace. It is not known what has happened to these two, but it is likely that it was the handing over of the three Arabs to the Israelis which led to stories after the Entebbe raid that the Israeli commandos had captured three of the terrorists and taken them back alive. Certainly these five figured on the list of terrorists that the hijackers wanted released, and their inclusion in the list caused much confusion, for, until that time, few people knew of their mission.

Nobody could say that about the hijacking of Flight 139. It was a true terrorist spectacular and into it went months of preparation and international organisation. It is quite remarkable that Wadi Hadad, operating from the Yemen, could have mounted such a complex affair only six months after the OPEC raid. Consider the difficulties. First, the target had to be chosen, and the choice was limited. It would have to be a plane carrying a large number of Israelis. It would accordingly have to be flying to or from Israel. It would further have to be a non-Israeli plane because all El Al airliners are protected most stringently, as will be discussed more fully in a later chapter. Finally, it would need to pass through an airport where security was lax so that the hijackers, whose pistols and grenades would be revealed by the electronic devices and body searches at the stricter terminals, could board the aircraft fully armed.

Athens was ideal. It was inundated with foreign tourists and security was negligible because of a strike of searchers and guards. It had the other essential in that it is a staging post for planes coming up from Arabia and passengers from those planes simply move into the transit lounge in order to change onto planes arriving from Israel. One other condition was that the hijackers should be able to carry their weapons on board the plane which would deliver them to the Athens transit lounge. And this is precisely what happened. The original four hijackers boarded a Singapore Airlines flight at Kuwait carrying their pistols and grenades. They held valid tickets routing them to Athens where they were to change planes and pick up the Air France airbus out of Tel Aviv en route to Paris.

They behaved like any other passengers, taking their hand baggage with them and waiting in the transit lounge for Flight 139 to arrive. Normally even transit passengers are searched but, because of the summertime confusion at Athens airport and the strike, no searches were made. The terrorists must have known this, just as they knew that they could board the plane at Kuwait without any trouble. Kuwait is beginning to figure more and more in terrorist planning. It is administered by Palestinians who earn rich money as technicians in the oil fields and as civil servants who attend to the boring business of making the state work while the native-born Kuwaitis enjoy their oil money. Most of these Palestinians, who number 200,000 out of a total population of 800,000, are conservatives who pay their tithes to the PLO but shun active involvement in the fight against Israel. However, after Israel, the feudal oil states of the Gulf are prime targets of the Marxist terrorist groups, and the militant Palestinians are attempting to turn Kuwait into another Lebanon, a host country in which they can operate freely.

The next step in the planning of the hijack was to pick the "soldiers". It was essential to have a team of mixed nationality. Four Arabs hanging round the transit lounge might have roused the suspicions of the Greeks. Hadad called on Carlos. Obviously Carlos himself could not go on the mission. His face and his fingerprints have been spread round the world by Interpol. And anyway, it was not his type of operation. Israeli targets do not interest him any longer. He chooses only the big men for his personal targets, the Teddy Sieffs and the Zaki Yamanis of this world. So Carlos turned to his Baader-Meinhof associates, Wilfried Böse, who worked with him in Paris, and Gabriele Kröcher-Tiedemann, the enthusiastic killer of the Vienna raid. Two Arabs were selected to go with them. Later in this chapter we shall discuss the importance of identified individual Arabs who were shot by the Israelis.

As with every military operation, once the target had been selected and the personnel chosen, these two elements had to be married by reconnaissance and training. There was at least one dry run to get the timings right and the "feel" of the mission. There were communication procedures to be established and memorised. There were maps to study and reports from Athens, Kuwait and Tel Aviv on timings and security precautions. Then there was the actual takeover of the airbus. That had to be rehearsed. During the hijack itself, the gang identified themselves by numbers. They had their routines practised to perfection. They searched the passengers for documents, and they separated the Jews from the non-Jews. Nothing was left to chance. It was all organised and the planning and rehearsals must have taken weeks.

Talking with one of the hostages who asked him how he knew the pilot had obeyed his instructions, and was flying to Benghazi, Böse smiled and said: "I learned the subject thoroughly in several Arab countries. I spent several months learning to read maps and instruments. I knew where the plane was flying."

This was no slapdash "cowboy" raid, but a highly organised military-type operation backed by large amounts of money, involving a number of highly trained agents, and set up in a safe base with extensive facilities.

There was also the question of indoctrination, the justification of this particular act of terror. Already the two Germans were steeped in revolutionary doctrines of violence and their Arab comrades naturally believed passionately in the Palestinian cause. Nevertheless, the conversations which Böse, the hijack "captain", had with the hostages showed that he had been carefully tutored in what to say. Although the PFLP at first denied any connexion with the hijacking, Böse, speaking in English with a heavy German accent, announced to the hostages: "My name is Ahmed el Kubesi of the Gaza Strip–Che Guevara commando unit of the Popular Front for the Liberation of Palestine," and he then made a long speech about why the plane had been hijacked, and the crimes the Israelis had committed against the Palestinian people.

The theme of his announcement was that in March 1970 the Israeli army wiped out PFLP forces operating in the Gaza Strip, and killed one of the PFLP heroes, Mohammed Mahmoud Al Aswad. He had been built up in Palestinian propaganda as the "Guevara of Gaza". So we have the situation where a German anarchist, hijacking a French aircraft from a Greek airport, identifies himself absolutely with the mainstream of PFLP terrorism, and with the romantic myth of the Cuban revolutionary.

Having picked the target, and chosen, trained and indoctrinated the hijack team, Hadad had to set up the inter-governmental aid which made the operation possible. It is most unlikely that the Kuwait government was involved. The Kuwaitis are opposed to terrorist activities because they know full well that they are themselves potential targets. All that was necessary was for PFLP sympathisers among the airport staff to allow the terrorists to board the Singapore Airlines plane with their weapons or, as has been done before, conceal the pistols and grenades on the aircraft.

There was no need to involve anybody at Athens, for the reasons already given. It is interesting, however, that Rolfe Pohle, one of the Baader-Meinhof anarchists freed from prison the year before in exchange for the kidnapped politician, Peter Lorenz, was in Greece at the appropriate time. He was picked up by the police in Athens after the raid and was found to be carrying a Peruvian passport and yet another false Ecuadorian passport. It is intriguing to note how many times Latin-American passports figure in this story.

It was after the hijack had taken place that international co-operation on a government basis became essential for the success of the terrorist enterprise. The plane had to be refuelled; and from past experience the hijackers knew that most airports in the Middle East would shut off their landing lights and roll bulldozers onto the runways at its approach. But they also knew that one would always remain open to them. They headed unerringly for Benghazi, and accepted the customary Libyan courtesies for terrorists.

President Gaddafi has since argued that he authorised the plane to refuel only because of humanitarian feelings for the hostages. But why is it that all aircraft hijacked by the PFLP make for Libya? Why is it that Carlos, after the OPEC raid, set course for Libya? The answer to these questions can only be that the terrorists were assured of help when they landed there.

The next and most important step was to ensure the co-operation of His Excellency Al-Hajji Field-Marshal Dr. Idi Amin Dada, VC, DSO, MC, life President of the Republic of Uganda. This was not too difficult. He was grateful to his friend Moammer Gaddafi for military and financial help and he had made his position on the existence of Israel quite clear in September 1972 when, in a message to Kurt Waldheim, Secretary-General of the United Nations, he praised the Munich killers and said: "Hitler was right about the Jews, because the Israelis are not working in the interests of the people of the world, and that is why they burned the Israelis alive with gas in the soil of Germany." It is not known exactly how much Amin was told about the hijacking before it took place, but he was fed enough to make him believe that he was going to emerge from the affair as a heroic world figure, a master of international diplomacy, a champion of Palestinian rights and saviour of the hostages. He would win a great victory to mark the end of his term as Chairman of the Organisation of African Unity.

There is no doubt at all that Entebbe was always planned as the ultimate destination of the hijackers, and that Amin and his army were fully prepared to receive the aircraft, the hostages and the terrorists.

The most telling evidence is that as soon as the plane landed the hijackers were greeted by a group of their own senior colleagues, heavily armed with sub-machine guns and explosives, one of whom took over command of the operation from Böse. They were on the airfield waiting for the airbus to arrive.

Chaim Herzog, the Israeli Ambassador to the United Nations, later detailed to the Security Council the various points that proved Ugandan collusion. He stated:

The entire story is one of collusion from beginning to end on the part of the Ugandan government. Let me spell out only a small proportion of the facts as recounted by members of the Air France crew and the hostages who were released.

On advance complicity:

A. The Captain of the Air France plane has stated that the German hijacker, Wilfried Böse, knew in advance that Entebbe was the plane's destination.

B. When the plane landed at Entebbe, the German woman hijacker declared: 'Everything is okay; the army is at the airport."

C. Böse announced to the passengers when they landed that they had arrived at a safe place.

D. Immediately on arrival, Ugandan soldiers surrounded the plane. They were accompanied by five armed Arab terrorists who embraced and kissed the hijackers on the plane. After that the terrorists' reinforcements took part in the guard duties and in the negotiations.

E. Before landing, while they were still in the air, the hijackers advised the passengers that buses would come to collect them.

F. After the passengers had been concentrated in the terminal's large hall, President Amin was seen embracing and shaking hands with the hijackers.

G. As the plane landed and was taxi-ing along the runway, a black Mercedes car drove up, two terrorists emerged and one of them took over control of the operation. He boarded the plane, embraced

Böse, the German hijacker, and talked to him.

H. Michel Cojot, a French company executive who acted as a go-between for the passengers and the hijackers, reported that when the airport director brought supplies for the hostages, he, the director, said he had prepared supplies, as he had been told, to be ready for approximately 260 passengers and crew.

Now on the detention of the hijacked passengers:

A. In the first twenty-four hours, guard duty was done by Ugandan soldiers, and the hijackers were not in sight. When the hijackers returned, refreshed, the Ugandan soldiers supplied them with sub-machine guns to guard the hijacked passengers. I ought to mention here that the Foreign Minister of Uganda had said that the hijackers were armed with sub-machine guns, what he omitted to mention was that on the plane all they had were pistols and grenades. The sub-machine guns were supplied to them when they landed at Entebbe.

B. In the following days the Ugandans were on guard outside the building, while a large force of them was concentrated on the first floor of the building.

C. Ugandan soldiers escorted the hostages to, and guarded them in, the toilets.

D. The terrorists came and went as if they were at home, with two cars driven by Ugandans, one of them in uniform, at their disposal.

E. The hijackers received logistic aid and were supplied with arms – sub-machine guns, pistols and explosives – at the airport. They also received a mobile communications set.

F. The terrorist who took control of the operation in Entebbe took hostages aside, under Ugandan guard, for interrogation.

G. Every time President Amin appeared in the area of the terminal and before the passengers, he was closeted with the terrorists in a most friendly atmosphere.

H. At the outset of the negotiations President Amin dismissed the French Ambassador and prevented him from establishing contact with the terrorists. This contact was conducted by him [Amin] in person.

I. President Amin warned the hijacked passengers not to dare to try to escape.

J. Apparently for reasons of bravado and to frighten the hijacked passengers, two jet aircraft overflew from time to time the terminal in which they were being held. Near the building an armoured vehicle was parked, and close to it stood two helicopters.

K. A mixed guard of hijackers and Ugandan Army men guarded the hostages; contact between them was constant and free. The Ugandan soldiers were on guard both inside the hall, on the second floor of the terminal, and on the plane.

L. The hijackers were unconcerned and very relaxed during the period on the ground. They left the airport building from time to time, and acted with an obvious feeling of assurance that the Ugandan Army would not attempt to overpower them. Mr. Tony Russell, an official of the Greater London Council and one of the Britons freed from the hijacked Air France airbus, said that President Amin had been in a position to release all the hostages if he had wished. "Once we were moved from the aircraft," he said, "the terrorists were not in a commanding position. I have the feeling that if Amin wanted to free us after we were transferred to the airport building, it could have been done. The terrorists had had no sleep for thirty hours, and had no powerful weapons at their disposal."

M. The commander of the hijackers in Entebbe spent all his time in the company of President Amin, who, incidentally, recounted this fact by telephone to Colonel Bar Lev [onetime commander of Israel's military mission to Uganda] who spoke to him from Israel.

N. While the passengers were being held, Radio Uganda broadcast an announcement of the hijackers praising Amin for his stand against Zionism and Imperialism.

O. And finally, the hijackers were buried with full military honours together with soldiers of the Ugandan Army.

Perhaps Herzog over-egged his pudding, but he did present an overwhelming case in proof of the charge of collusion against Amin. And, in truth, the hijacking would have had no chance of succeeding without Amin's co-operation, or at least his acquiescence.

There remains the sinister involvement of Somalia. This "Democratic Republic" denies all complicity in the hijacking and when, early on in the business, the Somali Ambassador to Uganda, Hashi Abdullah Farah, was seen to be conducting negotiations with the terrorists, it was felt that here was a humane man working for the good of the victims. Alas, it was not so. In spite of an indignant denial by the Somali Ambassador at the United Nations, the Somalis were in the plot up to their necks. Wadi Hadad set up his operational headquarters for the hijacking at Mogadishu, the Somali capital, and nothing happens in Mogadishu without permission of the Soviet-style government. Indeed, Somalia is now so heavily infiltrated by Russian advisers that hardly anything happens there without the Russians themselves being aware of it. It was also noticed in Entebbe that one of the first Palestinians on the scene was the head of the PLO office in Somalia. The conclusion must be drawn that the Somali Ambassador to Uganda was acting on the orders of his government and that they were fully in accord with the aims of the terrorists.

How did all these different elements come together? Why did they get involved in this desperate enterprise?

For Wadi Hadad and George Habash the decision was simple. It was their operation and it, or something like it, had to be carried out. The civil war among the Arabs in Beirut was destroying the Palestinian cause. The Israelis were able to point to the destruction of Beirut and ask: are these the people we are supposed to invite into our country? Yasser Arafat, after his moment of glory in addressing the United Nations to secure PLO recognition, had done nothing to weld the PLO into a government which could be accepted by the world as representative of the Palestinian people. The Palestinians were rent by disputes. They fought with each other and they killed each other. The situation was slipping away from them, the atmosphere prevailing before the Munich massacre was returning. Something had to be done to maintain Palestinian credence as a powerful force in the world. The OPEC raid had been spectacular but it had been aimed mostly at fellow Arabs. Now something was needed that would shock the world and harm the enemy, Israel. The function of terrorists is to terrorise, and if they do not carry out that function they cease to have a *raison d'être*. Therefore, the PFLP had to launch their raid.

Gaddafi, obsessed with desire for revenge against Israel, would naturally go along with Hadad's scheme. Gaddafi had little to lose; all he had to do was allow the airbus to be refuelled. If the operation was a failure he could claim, as he did, that he had no option but to give the hijackers the facilities they demanded. If it succeeded he could claim the thanks of his grateful Arab brothers.

Carlos's people who took part in the hijack would also go along willingly. To them it was another blow against the present order, a blow for the Palestinians against the Israelis, the puppets of the imperialistic, capitalist Americans. For their Palestinian colleagues it was a coup for their nation against the hated enemy. For the Somalis, flexing their new-found Sovietised muscles, it was an opportunity to display their support for the Palestinian cause – especially as the Palestinians were starting their move into Africa. For poor, bamboozled, Big Daddy Amin it was a glorious opportunity for self-aggrandisement.

One of the puzzling aspects of the hijacking is that the terrorists took two days to present their demands – it seems that Böse did not even know what those demands were to be. When they did, what they asked for seemed an almost modest return for such a complicated operation, with so many lives at stake. They wanted fifty-three imprisoned terrorists, forty held in Israel, six in West Germany, five in Kenya, and one each in Switzerland and France, to be flown to Entebbe and freed. If these demands were not complied with then the hostages would be executed. But the point is that it did not matter what the terrorists demanded; the real prize was in the act of terrorism itself, the humiliation of Israel and the proof to the world that the Palestinians could force the Israelis to give in. "Flight 139 was taken," said a PFLP announcement, "in order to remind the world of our intention to expel Zionists so that we may replace Israel with a social democracy . . ."

That was the hub of motive round which everything else revolved. And how close the adventure came to overwhelming success.

The terrorists had allowed most of the hostages to go free, keeping only the Israelis. Israel was once again isolated, and even inside Israel nerves were beginning to fray. A committee formed of relatives of the hostages addressed emotional appeals to Prime Minister Rabin asking him to give in to the PFLP's demands. He appeared to waver in response to these appeals, and it was announced that a ministerial team had been empowered to open negotiations with the hijackers. The feeling of defeat spread in Israel and in Entebbe success seemed assured.

But there were some people who remembered another occasion – that of May 8th 1972, when four Black Septemberists hijacked a Sabena airliner and had the audacity to have it flown on to Lod airport where they demanded the release of 319 imprisoned feda'in. The Israelis opened negotiations, using the Red Cross as their link with the hijackers. The talks dragged on for twenty hours and it seemed as if Israel would give way. But suddenly the doors of the aircraft burst open, and in a flurry of shots from the Israeli assault squad the two male hijackers were killed and their two female companions captured. One passenger was killed.

Could the Israelis do something like that again? It seemed impossible. Entebbe was over 2,500 miles from Sharm el Sheikh, Israel's southernmost airfield. The lands in between were hostile, bristling with radar and SAM missiles. Entebbe airport was guarded by the Ugandan Army. There were combat-ready Migs on the field. There was no way in which an assault team could fly there and back without refuelling. The situation seemed hopeless.

But there were several factors working in Israel's favour. In the first place, whatever their governments said and however weak they appeared, the anti-terrorist forces of the world were united in their determination to do all they could against terrorism by helping the Israelis. The extent of this help has been overlooked. In fact the Telex lines to Tel Aviv were full of information elicited from non-Israeli hostages released by the hijackers, from men who knew Entebbe well, from soldiers who had served there. Nor should we denigrate the part played by Great Britain, who, because of her long association with Uganda, was able to provide a large part of this essential information. The British army and air force also made contingency plans to take part in a rescue attempt and it may be that these plans, based on military agreements with Kenya, formed the planning basis of the Israeli rescue raid.

Secondly, the intelligence network that the Israelis had left behind in Africa proved its worth, funnelling back vital information to join the library of knowledge that was being assembled at Army HQ in Tel Aviv. Colonel Bar Lev helped in this process by holding long telephone conversations with his old friend Idi Amin, thus enabling experts who were listening to evaluate his moods and intentions.

Thirdly, Amin's aggressive posture towards Kenya, his threats to send his army marching over the border, and the assistance he had given the Palestinians who had plotted to shoot down an El Al airliner at Nairobi, had done nothing to allay the Kenyans' suspicions and fear of their bombastic neighbour. They were therefore eager to help the Israelis.

Fourthly, the process by which the Israelis were selected to remain as hostages while other nationalities were released brought back dark memories of the Nazi concentration camps. It was the Jews who were under attack once more, the evil spirit of the pogrom was abroad. And the Israelis reacted with all the ferocity built into their souls by two thousand years of oppression.

The story of the rescue operation has already been the subject of a number of books. It has become, as Prime Minister Rabin said it would, "the subject of research, of poetry and legend". We do not propose, therefore, to deal with it in detail but to examine its results in the context of the main theme of this work.

The most immediate and dramatic effect was on Idi Amin. He was shattered. His prestige was destroyed. For the first time there were serious open protests about his bloodthirsty, inefficient rule. He threatened his revenge and took it by behaving like a latter-day T'Chaka, the Zulu chief who slaughtered anyone who displeased him. Amin had the radar operators at Entebbe shot and poor Mrs. Dora Bloch, a seventy-five-year-old hostage, murdered. Mrs. Bloch had been left behind by the rescuers because she had choked on a piece of food and had been taken to hospital to have it removed. On the day after the rescue Mrs. Bloch, who held a dual British-Israeli nationality, was visited in hospital by Mr. Peter Chandley of the British Embassy. When he returned to take food to her *an hour later* he was told that she had been returned to the airport the night before. In fact, as soon as he left the hospital after his first visit she had been dragged screaming from her bed by four men, taken away and slaughtered. Mr. Chandley was called a liar and kicked out of Uganda.

The Ugandans resorted to what Ambassador Herzog called "damnable lies", insisting that Mrs. Bloch had been returned to the airport "when she got better". But whatever support Amin ever had among civilised countries was destroyed by this murder. More important, the swift and terrible raid by the Israelis pricked the bubble of his pretence of invincibility in his own country. He was exposed for what he is, a dangerous, bloodthirsty buffoon.

In less flamboyant fashion the damage done to Wadi Hadad was almost as great. What had seemed to be building into the most successful vindication of terrorism as a political weapon ever achieved was turned into the worst defeat ever inflicted on the PFLP in just ninety minutes of action. Hadad already had serious doctrinal differences with George Habash over the use of terror. While Habash has no compunction about using terror when it suits him, he has come to believe that to rely entirely on it is a mistaken policy, and after the hijack apologists were putting it about that Hadad and his international team of hit-men were alone responsible and were not acting in line with official PFLP policy. What is more likely is that Habash, a sick man with a weak heart, permitted Hadad to go his own way while he himself pondered the subtleties of doctrine. But whoever was responsible, the hijack caused enormous embarrassment to Arafat and the PLO. The Israelis were quick to point out that Habash, Hadad and the PFLP were still members of the PLO and that Arafat was the chairman of it. Therefore, they argued, Arafat must bear his share of responsibility for the hijack, and from this they have inferred that, despite his appearance at the United Nations and his acceptance as leader of the Palestinian movement, he was still a terrorist and therefore unfit to be treated as the leader of a nation.

If the raid embarrassed the Arabs, it did nothing but encourage the Israelis. In the summer of 1976 the Israelis had still not recovered the self-confidence which they lost when the Egyptian and Syrian armies hit them as they had never been hit before in the early days of the Yom Kippur War. An air of depression lingered, the heady aroma of success borne on the news of buccaneering military adventures was sadly missed. Then, when the nation was in the depths of its depression at the apparent impossibility of rescuing the hostages, one bold stroke put the world right for them.

The cumulative results of the hijack must therefore be judged as a disaster not only for Hadad but for the whole Arab cause. But the damage done to Hadad should be counted not only in political terms. Also to be considered is the loss of valuable men. The original team of young hijackers was met and reinforced at Entebbe by three of Hadad's most senior agents, and the group was made up to ten a few days later when a Ugandan plane flew three more high-ranking terrorists from Mogadishu.

Among the men who met the hijackers at Entebbe was none other than Antonio Degas Bouvier, and according to the Israelis he "took command of the entire action at Entebbe". The presence of this veteran terrorist, Carlos's teacher in Cuba and his accomplice in London, provided the proof, if any more were needed, of the international links in this affair. The Israelis were extremely sorry not to find his body among the men they killed. He was one of the three who got away. He and two others were off duty away from the airport, eating and sleeping till their turn came to guard the hostages.

Among the seven who were on duty and who died, the most important was Fayez Abdul Rahmin Jaber, a forty-five-year-old veteran of Arab militancy who was born in Hebron on the Israeli-occupied West Bank of the Jordan. The Israelis were astonished to find a man of his seniority at Entebbe, for he was one of the founders of the PFLP and a close friend of George Habash. His history provides a classic example of the life and death of a Palestinian terrorist. His birthplace, Hebron, is revered by both Arab and Jew as the holy place where Abraham and Sarah, Isaac and Rebecca, Jacob and Leah and also Joseph are buried. It has been said that "nowhere else in the world do the Moslem and Jewish faiths intermingle so intimately as here where the Hebrew Patriarchs are revered as prophets by the followers of Mohammed. The tribal wanderer from Chaldea, to whose seed God promised the Land of Canaan, is claimed as their ancestor also by the Moslem Arabs, who call him 'El Khalil' (The Friend of God) – the Arabic name for Hebron. The Jaffa Gate in the Old City of Jerusalem, from which one sets out for Hebron, bears an Arabic inscription that says, 'There is no God but God and Abraham is the friend of God' " (Joan Comay: *Introducing Israel*).

But the friendship of ancient times degenerated into enmity. In 1929 a mob of Arabs whipped up by the Mufti of Jerusalem – to whose family Yasser Arafat belongs – attacked the Jewish quarter of Hebron and killed sixty Orthodox Jews. From then until the Six-Day War in 1967 there were no Jewish residents in the town of Abraham. Their return after the war with the occupation forces brought renewed conflict. There were riots and bombings as the Arabs fought not only against the Israeli army but also against the Orthodox settlers who sought to reoccupy their holy places. It was in this atmosphere that Jaber came to prominence. He had already, in 1964, founded a group of young commandos known as "the Heroes of the Return", which was responsible for Jerusalem's "Night of Grenades".

In this affray his younger brother was killed trying to throw a grenade into an Israeli administrative building in East Jerusalem. In December 1967 he took his own group into an alliance with two other small groups to form the PFLP with George Habash, the Greek Orthodox doctor, as its leader. Jaber became head of PFLP's internal security and was then appointed commander of special operations "in the external sphere", meaning outside Israel. Given such an appointment it seems likely that he was sent to Entebbe in order to report directly to Wadi Hadad. His death was a grievous blow to the PFLP.

The loss of Jayel Naji el Arja was equally harmful, for he was a political man, second in command of the PFLP's Department of Foreign Relations, and he had special responsibility for South America where he spent much time raising funds and propagandising among the Arab communities. But more important than that, he was a skilled recruiter and probably the man who.had made the initial contact with Carlos. He was in Entebbe as the liaison officer between Bouvier and Hadad. Although, as the Israelis ruefully admit, they had once jailed and then released him, he had no record of active service and his presence at Entebbe indicates how politically important the operation was considered by Habash and Hadad. Like Jaber, he was in his forties and came from a religious centre, Beit Jala, near Bethlehem on the occupied West Bank.

We have less personal information about the three other Arabs killed at Entebbe, Abdul Khaled el Khalil, Abdul Razag – known as Abu Dardai – and Abu Ali. Abu Dardai had a reputation as one of the PFLP's operational commanders who had carried out a number of missions in Europe, and there is an intriguing possibility about the man called Abu Ali. It is a common name meaning father of Ali and in Arabic slang a man is said to be an Abu Ali when he is loud-mouthed and boastful. One cannot therefore pin down his identity. But it was a man with the same name who made the initial contacts in Japan between the PFLP and the Japanese Red Army and the likelihood is that they were the same man.

The full sweep of the international network represented by the hijackers at Entebbe now becomes apparent. There was Bouvier, Carlos's friend, with his South American, European and Russian connexions; Jaber, one of the founders of the PFLP; el Arja, "ambassador" to South America; and Abu Ali, probably the man who established the Japanese connexion. And, to complete the picture, the two Germans: Wilfried Böse and Gabriele Kröcher-Tiedemann.

All the rescued hostages are agreed about Gabriele. The young woman who had boasted of killing two men in Vienna behaved, they said, like a true Nazi. Sarah Davidson, an Israeli housewife who was on Flight 139 with her husband and two teenage sons, kept a diary. In it she noted that "the sadistic German female terrorist, who was marching around with a pistol the whole time, reminded us of the Nazis".

Another hostage diarist noted about Gabriele: "She's the sort who gets things together fast. Anyone who wants to go to the toilet lifts a finger, she shouts an order to go; in one case, when two passengers get up at the same time to go to the toilet, she screams like a veritable animal." It was the sort of behaviour that brought back the fear of the concentration camps to elderly Jews among the hostages who had survived Hitler's holocaust. This fear was heightened when Böse began the concentration camp process of "selekzia" in which the Jews were selected for "special treatment". Mrs. Davidson, who had several conversations with Böse, wrote that he "told the group that the hall was too crowded and that for the benefit of everyone it had been decided to split us up into two groups. He emphasised that there was no significance in the way the selection had been made. But we soon realised that only the Israelis and other Jews had been left in the hall."

It was this process of selection which made the rescue operation inevitable because it became clear that the real targets of the operation were the Jews. It evoked too many awful memories for the Israelis to give in without a fight.

Böse, a far more subtle character than Gabriele, handled the situation with skill. He achieved a measure of rapport with many of the passengers who were only too happy to agree with any suggestion which would keep them alive. They clapped Böse every time he made a speech, especially when he said: "No harm will come to you. The whole history of hijackings proves that we did not kill the passengers. We shall negotiate. We have demands. If they are met, we shall release you and you'll return home."

Sarah Davidson was sickened by the clapping, but it brought realisation to her:

All these years I could not comprehend the holocaust. Year in, year out, I read what is written on the subject, and I see the films and hear the horrifying testimonies, and I don't understand. Why did the Jews enter the gas chambers so quietly? Why did they go like sheep to the slaughter when they had nothing to lose. I needed that nightmare at Entebbe to comprehend, and now, but only now, do I comprehend. It's easy to trick people when they so want to live. The Jews in the holocaust did not know what was in store for them, and believed the lies about work camps and the showers. We were also easy to deceive. The German woman was like a wild animal. Frustrated as a person and as a woman. But she was less dangerous because she was frank about what she was, and wore no mask . . . She was an open enemy.

The German man adopted a pleasant manner. He was a concealed enemy, pretending, tempting his victims to believe in his good intentions. He was so quiet, so pleasant, so affable that, after my conversations with him, I found myself accusing myself: You believed him. He succeeded in deceiving you. If he had said to march in a certain direction where his colleagues were awaiting us with machine guns, ready to mow us down, we would have gone . .

Instead, it was Böse and Gabriele who were mown down along with their Arab colleagues when the Israeli rescuers charged into the old terminal building at Entebbe. It was the most devastating blow ever struck at the PFLP and the Carlos complex.

Chapter Fourteen
The reasons why

On a summer day in 1914 in Sarajevo, Gavrilo Princip assassinated Archduke Franz Ferdinand, the Hapsburg heir to the throne of the Austro-Hungarian Empire. At his trial he was given an opportunity to explain why he had done so. He replied: "I am a south Slav nationalist. My aim is the union of all south Slavs, under whatever political régime, and their liberation from Austria."

Questioned about how he meant to accomplish this political aim he replied: "By terrorism." Nothing could be more succinct. His aim was legitimate, and he had chosen this particular form of warfare to achieve it because it was practical and, he believed, effective. What he succeeded in doing was to detonate the explosive charges of nationalism under an entire continent and to provoke the beginning of the First World War.

What makes this historic incident applicable to a consideration of international terrorism today is that, as Princip's trial demonstrated, the young idealists who plotted the assassination were not acting in isolation. Arms had been provided for them by Colonel "Apis" Dimitrievitch, head of military intelligence in Serbia, who also helped them to plan the coup. And behind him again was the Imperial Russian military attaché in Belgrade who financed the affair.

That is the point about terrorism. The planning of an act of violence involves so many different interests that there is no telling where it will lead, or what the final result will be. The process starts with a man, or group, fired by a political objective and by the belief that it is a good and necessary one. It cannot be achieved through argument and the conventional means of persuasion. The opposition is too powerful and too entrenched. So a short cut has to be taken. The zealot, often neurotic and self-obsessed, never pauses to reflect that perhaps his aim is unreasonable, and unacceptable to a majority of other citizens. So he and his group take the fast road marked terrorism. When other people become involved in organisation the consequences cannot be contained, even if the original objective is gained.

This last point was strikingly displayed in the Entebbe affair. The objective was realistic – to secure the release of various terrorists captured in earlier actions. Yet the raid itself led to a whole range of consequences which the group involved could never have imagined possible, and which were not necessarily in their interests. The Israeli army made an unexpected counter-strike killing most of the terrorists and liberating their hostages. In revenge President Idi Amin's men slaughtered totally uninvolved citizens from neighbouring Kenya who lived in his country. War between Kenya and Uganda threatened. Relations between Uganda and Great Britain became extremely tense, and British missionaries in the country were in danger of their lives.

There are many reasons why ripples from one act of terrorism spread right across the pool. The main one is the confusion of aims in the terrorist plotters' collective mind. Although in the case of the Entebbe hijack the tactical aim was a clear one – to obtain the release of fellow terrorists – the strategic aims overshadowed and complicated it. The Palestinians, on whose behalf it was carried out, saw it as an encounter in the continuing campaign to destroy Israel. The subsidiary aims were to impress Arabs who live under Israeli control, to prove to them that Arabs can effectively strike at Israel, even if they cannot do so within Israel itself, and, finally, to attract the sympathetic attention of the world outside.

But when Israel struck back, the whole effect boomeranged. Far from feeling sympathy, the outside world was bored and fed up with terrorist attacks and threats directed against people who have nothing whatsoever to do with the Arab-Israeli conflict. The reaction was one of excitement at the Israeli counter-raid and of relish at the defeat of the international brigade of killers.

Terrorism is the strategy of the weak, and historically the only successes of this form of war are recorded when the aim is precise and the conditions right. Robespierre, in the French Revolution, sent thousands to the guillotine during the Reign of Terror. Publication of names on his death list was enough to stifle opposition. With only a score of supporters he held power over the state by fear. But not for very long. A time came when Fouché rallied the intended victims and overthrew the head terrorist.

Again, in the years before the Russian Revolution, a great deal was heard about the Terrorist Brigade composed of Socialist-Revolutionists. Yet it was not they who made the revolution that toppled the Tsar. That task was accomplished by the Bolsheviks, who won the support of workmen and soldiers. The Terrorist Brigade fought a forlorn though bloody battle which makes it appear now more closely related to the factions of present-day international terror than to genuine Communism.

The essence of terrorism is to sow fear, to make heroes out of murderers, and thereby to convince opponents that the terrorists' cause is right and that the authorities are in the wrong. During the past fifty years such tactics have succeeded in a few special cases.

In the 1920s the southern Irish won their independence by terrorism, but that terrorism was supported by a much stronger form of war, the guerrilla campaign. For there is a difference between the two. Guerrilla warfare is conducted by unconventional means but with real military aims and targets; whereas terrorism is indiscriminate in both. It is planned for public effect, not for military objectives. Yet even in Ireland, the Black and Tan counter-insurgency force which fought against the rebels was an effective and successful one. Michael Collins, the Irish leader, said to a British official at the peace negotiations: "You had us dead beat. We could not have lasted another three weeks."

In that instance, of course, the methods of the repression force caused such an outcry in a free society that they were the ones who finally appeared as the villains. How different the situation would have been had the events taken place in the Soviet Union. Even now the Black and Tans would still be receiving praise as "honoured security men who so effectively helped to solve the Irish minority problem".

We believe that what brought about the success of the Irish at that time was not so much terrorism itself, but a symptom induced by terrorism which may be called "fatiguism". Public opinion grows tired of endless news about killings and bombings, and eventually comes to believe that the nation is faced with an insoluble problem, and that the struggle does not justify the bloodshed. As Kipling said: "If blood be the price of Admiralty, Lord God we ha' paid in full."

"Fatiguism" was certainly the final factor in a number of colonial guerrilla wars fought by the British in Egypt, Cyprus and Ireland. And the same symptom affected the French in North Africa. There, in Algeria, the rebels built upon the foundation of terrorism a state which did not until then exist at all. By murder and massacre the minuscule National Liberation Front first eliminated rival nationalist movements and then turned to bombing and machine-gunning compatriots at large. The French reacted by sending in more and more troops, by withdrawing units composed of Algerians, and by rounding up Algerians and treating them as though they were a separate people, even though Algeria was proclaimed to be French Algeria. The French army became a target, and the mass of Algerians who originally had little sympathy for the terrorists came to view them as patriots. Around them a new nation finally rallied. Simultaneously, as the terror campaign spread to metropolitan France with the bombing of apartments and public places, "fatiguism" set in, and liberal opinion sympathised with the terrorists who by now had become national leaders – a government in exile.

It is not surprising to find President Boumedienne sheltering Carlos, for his government came to power by terror, and the President himself assumed office through an armed coup when his agents seized ex-President Ben Bella, who has never been heard of since. There was no question of putting him on trial or invoking the processes of law.

It was the Algerian war which stimulated the thought of one of the most important source philosophers of the new terrorism, Frantz Fanon. A black doctor born in Martinique, Fanon went to work as head of the Psychiatric Department at Blida Hospital in Algeria in 1952 as the war was beginning. He threw in his lot with the National Liberation Front, and he died of leukaemia shortly before the Algerian victory in 1962.

Fanon was not disposed to violence himself (though he was once wounded by an exploding French mine on the Tunisian border) and never went further than to offer refuge to terrorists in his home and hospital at Blida and to support FLN groups. But, led on by his blazing hatred of colonialism and racial oppression, he elevated violence into a mystique. "Violence alone, violence committed by the people, violence organised and educated by its leaders, makes it possible for the masses to understand social truths and gives the key to them," he wrote in his book, *The Wretched of the Earth.*

Fanon preached that violence was not simply a means of ending colonial rule, but also an improving element in itself. "Violence is a cleansing force," he wrote (a sentiment to be echoed by Gaddafi, among others). "It frees the native from his inferiority complex and from his despair and inaction; it makes him fearless and restores his self-respect."

One of his justifications for such beliefs was that European affluence was in itself scandalous, being derived from robbery of the Third World soil and from slavery. There was to his mind an immense debt to be repaid and one that justified the armed struggle by the wretched of the earth against deportations, massacres, forced labour and slavery, "the principal means used by capitalism to augment its reserves of gold and diamonds, its wealth . . ." Although Marxist in thought, Fanon had nothing but scorn for Western workers, whom he accused of benefiting from latter-day colonialism. At the time of the Algerian war he even criticised Jean-Paul Sartre, a philosopher he otherwise admired. Simone de Beauvoir reported: "He could not forget that Sartre was French and he blamed him for not having expiated that crime sufficiently."

The violent teachings of Frantz Fanon are important, not simply in the context of the Algerian war but because they helped to set a pattern of thought among leftward-looking young intellectuals in the Western world. Only by understanding his work and that of the other philosophers of terror is it possible to comprehend the actions of Carlos and his connexions.

Fanon helped to instil that sense of guilt, that feeling that the Third World of the ex-colonies must be right, which has provided so much support for international terrorists. The Germans of the Baader-Meinhof groups and the French students, whose revolt in Paris in 1968 coincided with a climax of anti-Americanism over the war in Vietnam, drew inspiration from Fanon's emotional pleading for the colonially exploited. He helped to set the scene for international terrorism by justifying the resort to it as a legitimate way of attacking injustice.

For those who sympathised with such views, Israel was firmly placed among the capitalist powers, condemned by Third World supporters as a neo-colonial power under Western protection, and as the exploiter of Palestinian Arabs.

Now that Israel itself is the target of Arab terrorism, it is easy to forget that terrorism with limited aims, carried out by Irgun Zvai Leumi, a small group of militants from a Jewish terror organisation, played a notable part in the foundation of the state of Israel. After 1945 this group, with no more than 1,500 members, set about mounting a deliberate campaign of bombings and killings in Palestine, then governed by Great Britain under a mandate from the old League of Nations.

It forced the British into sending troop reinforcements, a costly business that the post-war government could ill afford. Irgun Zvai Leumi then attracted outside sympathy, much of it from the United States, by publicising British counter-terrorist measures and repression. In the end, it was the Israelis themselves who took action against their own terrorists. In 1948 Ben Gurion used the swing of public opinion against terrorist killings, and the need to unify all Israel's forces into a regular army, to justify the disbanding of the Irgun. The terrorists had lost public sympathy, and with the emergence of a Jewish government had lost their *raison d'être*.

Palestinian Arabs now use the example of Jewish terrorism in order to justify their own acts in the same style. Terrorism breeds terrorism, and the more it succeeds the more attractive it appears to potential supporters.

These examples of recent terrorist campaigns which achieved differing degrees of success in Ireland, Algeria and Israel were all conducted in colonial or semi-colonial situations. The kind of terrorism we are mainly concerned with in this book has developed in different circumstances. This is something which international terrorists of the Carlos breed tend to ignore when they draw upon the history of terror in justifying, and sometimes in planning, their own actions.

One great advantage that modern terrorists enjoy over their violent predecessors lies in the speed and range of air communications. Because of this, and of instantaneous press and television coverage of news, superficial relationships between nations and situations throughout the world are much closer and more immediate than in the past. For many people dramatic events in Vienna or Entebbe can be far more urgent and real than something which is going on within a mile of their own home. Thus the impact of terrorism is more speedily apparent.

Because of this speeding up, the philosophers of terror have assumed that one of their principal aims, the creation of a climate of repression in liberal societies, would become easier. They hoped by this repression to achieve what they call the alienation of the masses which then prepares the way for revolution. But in Europe and the United States the theory has not worked out. To take only two examples of states under constant attack, the Americans from a host of different forces and the British from the Irish; neither country has taken to repression, and neither has notably changed its style of government in face of bomb and machine gun. The police state, a step on the road to revolution, has failed to emerge.

Where terror did create repression was in Uruguay, once regarded as a model Latin-American democracy. Constant Tupamaros attacks did indeed destroy democracy there, but it was replaced by a military dictatorship which succeeded in destroying the Tupamaros themselves. At present, even in Uruguay, there is no sign of the masses performing their allotted duty of rallying to the banner of revolution. Indeed Régis Debray, the French intellectual and writer, who was one of the apostles of revolution and a keen supporter of Che Guevara, acknowledged this when he said: "By digging the grave of liberal Uruguay, they [the Tupamaros] dug their own grave." He himself has now had second thoughts about the whole theory of terrorism.

What the terrorist really does is to apply the well-tried techniques of the gangster and the blackmailer to political situations. In the process he dresses it up and packages it as a splendidly contemporary piece of ideological finery. Those whose campaigns we have examined are certainly élitist, and show nothing but contempt for the masses they claim to serve.

There is nothing new in the discovery that young people chafe under the rules and regulations of their elders. It just becomes more apparent when a lot of them band together. But in fact few take their rebellion to the point of violence and among these are frequently the most affluent students at the universities. Those from working-class families are too busy carving careers for themselves to have time for revolutionary activities. Among the terrorist bands hardly any recruits come from the shop floor, where life is already real and earnest. It is the others, like Carlos, who have time for fantasy and action.

Intellectuals of the left are always tempted to get in on the act of violence since they have little experience of hard, physical life. For this very reason they are anxious to display their political virility and to show that they are not simply men of words. They want to prove that they can fight and suffer like their theoretical heroes, the peasants and workers, people they know only from books and theories. It is the bourgeois, to borrow their own revolutionary terminology, who plan and in many cases execute terrorist violence.

It was in Latin America that hijacking of aircraft, the first manifestation of the new wave of international terrorism, began. As far back as 1958 Cuban revolutionaries seized a Cuban airliner on a flight from Miami. It crashed in the Oriente province killing seventeen people. After the Cuban Revolution the following year there were more hijackings and the campaign reached its climax in 1969, during which year sixty aircraft were diverted to Cuba by force. As airlines and governments reacted and produced stricter security, the number of successful aircraft hijacks fell dramatically. And when Castro decided that hijacking was no longer in his interest, there were no more Cuban hijackings.

The doubtful honour of re-launching the ancient technique of kidnapping in the cause of terrorism also goes to Cuba. In 1958 supporters of Fidel Castro grabbed the racing driver Juan Fangio, thus setting the fashion for seizing, in search of publicity, people of international eminence. For similar reasons terrorist groups in Latin America also picked on foreign diplomats, as in 1970 when the Guatemalan government refused to give in to the demands of terrorists who then murdered the West German ambassador there, Count von Spreti.

The tactics of modern terrorism were made in Latin-America. A revolutionary group in Brazil run by Carlos Marighella, now regarded as one of the founding fathers of modern terror, set the pattern for urban guerrilla activity. In his *Handbook of Urban Guerrilla Warfare* he wrote:

Bank raids are the most popular form of action. In Brazil they are very common; we have almost made them a kind of entrance exam for apprenticeship in the technique of revolutionary war ... In this particular activity, revolutionaries have two types of competitors – bandits and right-wing counter-revolutionaries. This to some extent confuses ordinary people, and therefore the guerrilla will try to make clear the political purpose of his action, in two ways: he will refuse to behave like a bandit, either by misguided violence, or by taking money or personal possessions from customers who may be in the bank; and he will back up his expropriation by some form of propaganda – writing slogans attacking the ruling classes and imperialism on the walls, handing out pamphlets, or giving people leaflets explaining the political purpose of what he is doing.

This passage gives the flavour of the naive instructions handed out. It is tragic that a whole generation of students failed to perceive how richly comic they were.

In Brazil Marighella's followers ruthlessly carried out the suggestion, and in less than a year took the best part of half a million pounds from banks in Rio and São Paulo. The same technique was meticulously copied by Baader-Meinhof in West Germany. But in the course of their "entrance exams" a number of Brazilian comrades were taken by the police.

In September 1969, to rescue fifteen of them, Marighella's group kidnapped the United States' ambassador in Brazil, Charles Burke Elbrick. To avoid bloodshed and diplomatic embarrassment the government gave in, but despite this surrender the terrorists went on to other acts, gradually escalating their demands for the release of prisoners. Five were handed over for the life of the kidnapped Japanese consul, forty more for the West German ambassador and finally seventy for the Swiss ambassador.

These actions proved to the Brazilian government that it did not pay to give in to kidnap blackmail. But equally they proved that Carlos Marighella had been right to recommend the tactic in his handbook. There he wrote:

We can kidnap and hide policemen, North American spies, political figures, or notorious enemies who are a danger to the revolution . . . To kidnap figures known for their artistic, sporting or other activities who have not expressed any political views may possibly provide a form of propaganda favourable to revolutionaries, but should only be done in very special circumstances, and in such a way as to be sure people will accept it sympathetically.

Kidnapping American personalities who live in Brazil, or who have come to visit here, is a most powerful form of protest against the penetration of US imperialism into our country.

Starting from the precept that the duty of a revolutionary is to make the revolution, he went on to outline the personal qualities of an urban guerrilla – courage and initiative, good tactics and a good aim with a gun, the use of skill and cunning. He then continued, to the delight of his young followers:

The urban guerrilla does, however, have one enormous advantage over the conventional soldier and the policeman: he is defending a just cause, the cause of the people – whereas they are on the side of an enemy the people hate.

Though his arms are inferior to those of his enemy, his moral superiority is incontestable, and it is this which enables him to carry out his major tasks: to attack and to survive.

Although he himself was killed in 1969 in the wave of repression which the actions of his supporters had provoked, the ghost of Marighella in the form of his teachings survived among latter-day terrorists. Ilich Ramirez Sanchez may well have had his name, as well as his teachings, in mind when he chose the forename Carlos as his principal pseudonym. Marighella's book was considered such powerful medicine that when it was translated into French in 1970 the French government forbade its distribution and sale.

The handbook became a standard work for all ambitious terrorist leaders. Some of Carlos's recorded conversation shows that he was familiar with its teachings. It also became required reading for romantic students in American and European universities, who fancied themselves as men of action. It helped to popularise the term "urban guerrilla", which has been such a pest ever since. He declared that urban guerrilla warfare started in Brazil in 1968.

The significance of Marighella is that he was an old Communist Party warhorse, already in his sixties when he decided to abandon the Party's rigid bureaucracy to take to real revolution. "The only way out for Brazil is through armed struggle and preparation for the armed insurrection of the people," he wrote.

His military theories are neither sensational nor very new. They were derived from Chairman Mao's instructions to Communists on how to take over China from the Nationalists. Mao passed on his military wisdom to the Vietnamese, who already in the 1950s had successfully put that teaching into practice by ousting the French from Indo-China. As America became unsuccessfully involved in Vietnam, it began to seem to revolutionaries throughout the world as though Mao Tse-Tung had produced a magic formula to defeat capitalism and imperialism in the field.

Yet when similar theories were applied in Latin-America by Guevara they met with far less success. Conditions in the assorted republics of that continent were very different from those prevailing in China and in Indo-China. Mao had asserted and proved in battle that Communist guerrillas could strangle the cities from the countryside. The "encircle-ment of the city by the countryside" theory became holy writ.

But in many parts of Latin America, and certainly in Western industrialised societies, a high proportion of the population, sometimes as much as four-fifths, inhabit the cities. In such places it is hardly possible for the country minority to "strangle" the city majority, and the Mao principle falls flat on its face.

By the time Marighella broke with orthodox Communism, counter-insurgency forces with new techniques and good training were in the process of destroying the rural guerrillas in Latin America. Guevara had over-reached himself in Bolivia with his ambitions to provoke an American military intervention and thereby spark a perpetual war like the one in Vietnam so that revolution might thrive. Rural guerrillas in Brazil had proved a disastrous failure.

The rural "foco" – or "focus" advocated by Guevara was a guerrilla-occupied base of activity in the countryside to which recruits theoretic-ally poured in to form a miniature revolutionary state. In fact, the idea failed in Latin America because the rural guerrillas could not secure the support, promised by theorists, of farmers and peasants. Marighella simply adapted the "foco" principle to urban activities. The attraction of the towns was that the terrorists were urban people; in the towns, intellectuals and students stood a better chance of survival, if not of victory, by practising the more flashy arts of terrorism.

For these reasons new forms of terrorism evolved from the guerrilla campaigns in Latin America, and their origins were multiple: the Chinese Communist battles, the terror and guerrilla wars waged against the occupying powers in what had been European colonies. As decolon-isation came to an end, it brought a decline in strictly guerrilla wars that might easily be won by nationalist fighters – a new faith was needed to inspire them.

In the Latin-American campaigns the turning point came with the death of Che Guevara in Bolivia in 1967. During the early 1960s, insurgent movements had spread in Guatemala, Brazil, Peru and other countries in the hemisphere. The inspiration for these wars came from Cuba, where Fidel Castro and his revolutionary guerrillas had succeeded in defeating the old-established dictatorship and installing themselves as the government. From his island base Castro encouraged similar movements among his Latin neighbours. Tyranny and capitalist imperialism, personified by the United States, were the enemies. And Castro provided the example of how to overthrow them as well as furnishing the weapons and the know-how.

The man who taught Castro and Che Guevara the rudiments of guerrilla warfare was an elderly Spanish officer who had retired to Mexico after serving as a Republican in the Spanish Civil War. His name was Alberto Bayo, Colonel by rank, General by designation, and he had great practical knowledge of his subject, brought up to date by reading the works of Mao Tse-Tung. With Castro money he bought a farm at Santa Rosa, near Mexico City, and there established a training school for guerrillas under Spartan conditions. He was a mercenary of the Cuban revolution, being paid 8,000 dollars down, and Che Guevara was his star pupil, though Fidel Castro, whom he also taught, has achieved more worldly success.

Guevara, a physician born in Argentina and an ambulant revolutionary, became the theorist of revolution in this part of the world and the missionary of it. "I was born in Argentina, I fought in Cuba, and I began to be a revolutionary in Guatemala," was how he put down his own potted autobiography. He came from a Spanish-Irish family, he was a sporadic student and a constant traveller who learned the theory of subversive war, and then became famous by writing *Guerrilla War* in 1960. After Cuba, none of his campaigns succeeded; he made mistake after mistake and even his book on how to conduct this kind of warfare was derivative, being based on a modest manual written by Colonel Bayo and on Mao Tse-Tung. But Guevara provided the new trimmings of political theory and philosophy.

He became a great influence on foreign guerrillas and ultimately on terrorists of the Carlos kind, even though he himself favoured military activity in the field as opposed to terrorist attacks. Indeed, he warned against the dangers of terrorism because it hindered "contact with the masses and makes impossible unification for actions that will be necessary at the critical moment".

His policy was to avoid harming the population, so as to encourage the recruitment of more people for the cause. Cuba had shown the ability of people to free themselves from oppression by civil war; and therefore, however small the resources of guerrillas, and however great their disadvantages, that was no excuse for not starting the war. Guevara distilled a distinctly knightly aura, that of a social reformer in arms, who only operated with the support of the oppressed people.

His best pupil, Régis Debray, the French intellectual and philosopher of revolution, took over his ideas about the revolutionary power of the focus and spread them in Western Europe.

For Che Guevara the idea of East-West co-existence was anathema. He preached proletarian internationalism like a heretical Communist. His message was, forget about the parties and doctrines and get on with the fighting, and from this will emerge the political beliefs. Capitalism could only be defeated, he strongly believed, by a world-wide series of attacks on the United States. Destroy first, see what develops later, was the message: and it caught on.

Having helped Castro to succeed in Cuba and to consolidate revolutionary power there, Guevara broke with his revolutionary comrade-in-arms, abandoned his comfortable office of state, and went off questing for more action. In the autumn of 1964 he told Castro that he was off to liberate Latin America, and that he intended to start in Bolivia.

Already he was too late. The guerrillas were failing everywhere in that part of the world, out-fought and out-manoeuvred by the counter-insurgency forces already in being. In the field Che Guevara was a blundering though enthusiastic commander. As he fought his forlorn battles in Bolivia, other guerrilla forces in Latin America were being wiped out by regular armies with the benefit of equipment and technical training from the United States. Such as survived did so miserably in jungles and remote mountains.

Then in the autumn of 1967 the Bolivian 8th Division, some of its men disguised as peasants, surrounded Che Guevara and his band in the Santa Cruz district. Pinned down in a ravine and himself wounded, Guevara was captured leaning against a tree and taken to the tiny village of La Higuera. General Joaquin Zentano Anaya, then a Colonel, received orders from La Paz to shoot the captured guerrilla leader. Che Guevara's death, in highly romantic circumstances, generated as we shall see its own hagiography and mythology, though it also marked the end of an era in the violent history of Bolivia and of Latin America. "Che Guevara lives" became a rallying call for rebellious leftists throughout the world. His most obvious memorials are the dashing posters showing him in full guerrilla gear which still decorate thousands of student halls and rooms. His tattered bands of insurgents are no more.

As a footnote, it may be recorded that General Zentano, at the age of fifty-five, and by then Bolivian ambassador to Paris, was himself shot down and killed, as he stepped into his car near the Bir Hakeim Bridge over the Seine, by an unknown gunman in the spring of 1976. He was the fifth person closely connected with the execution of Guevara to meet a violent end, and a group calling itself the "Che Guevara Brigade" claimed responsibility for the murder. It is symbolic that revenge for the death of Guevara should take the form of a terrorist attack in a foreign capital, for it shows how the international terrorist movement developed at least partly from the Latin-American guerrilla wars of the previous decade. Carlos himself, conscious of recent Latin-American history, developed as a leader under the influence of Castro, in whose camps he trained, and of the Guevara myth. The same myth became manifest again when the ill-fated Entebbe terrorists announced that they were called the "Che Guevara-Gaza Group", taking their name from a Palestinian terrorist who styled himself the Che Guevara of Gaza.

Carlos, too, was familiar with the transformation of defeated guerrillas into urban terrorists. And in the Western hemisphere it was not long before small bands of terrorists, uniting with like-minded people in other countries, turned from national to international targets. United States influence was strong in Latin America, the CIA and the US armed forces helped to train counter-insurgency officers and troops, and it was by a natural development that the terrorists began to launch attacks, first against American officials and advisers, and then against businessmen, who were put down as capitalist oppressors. Finally, and in order to impress outside opinion, they kidnapped ambassadors of other Western countries.

As Che Guevara died, the revolutionary Red Guards were already rampaging in China. Immediately news of his death spread youths marched through half a dozen Italian cities and to the war cry

"Guevara lives" fought the police. In Bonn, others of the same generation bombed the Bolivian Embassy and swore vengeance for the death
of their hero. Within months, the students and the New Left were
storming and barricading the boulevards of Paris. Their leaders, Rudi
Dutschke and Danny Cohn-Bendit, used the martyr image to inspire
their revolutionary followers.

The new radicals from the Western universities found it easy to
identify with the man in the beret who had died in the Bolivian mountains. Students who occupied buildings in London and Berlin, who
clashed with the Chicago police at the Democratic Convention there,
were all emotionally at least followers of Che. Like him, they were
white, from prosperous families, but in one way or another intent
on changing the established world by violence and revolution. Even
Jean-Paul Sartre, in a moment of high elation, proclaimed of Guevara:
"This man was not only an intellectual, but the most complete man of
his age."

Many followers in their enthusiasm got the ideas of the Latin-
American revolutionary slightly wrong. An anonymous American
student quoted in a *New York Times Magazine* article on May 5th
1968 entitled "Seven Heroes of the New Left", declared: "Amigo, I
want there to be more Vietnams, as many Vietnams as possible. Wars
without number, murders, executions, surprise raids, night attacks,
bombings and burnings and beatings." Of course, the whole of the
younger generation in the United States was by then obsessed with
Vietnam, but the significant point in this quotation is that it shows that
the idea of violence and terror as a solution to world problems had
taken hold. And that message had spread from South America.

A new nihilism was taking over and action for action's sake became
the motto. As Guevara died, Régis Debray, his French sympathiser,
who was to make him even more famous in death than he had been
in life, was under arrest in Bolivia, charged with aiding the guerrillas.
He was sentenced to thirty years' imprisonment, but was released within
three years.

Who was to lead the revolution? asked Debray in his works on the
subject. And he concluded: "The irony of history has willed . . . the
assignment of precisely this vanguard role to students and revolutionary
intellectuals, who have to unleash, or rather initiate, the highest forms
of class struggle." In expounding more skilfully the theories of Guevara,
Debray continually stressed the need for the armed struggle on the

Cuban pattern. The importance of this in the development of terrorism was that it involved the young people of Western Europe and the United States and gave them the idea that they must take up arms against the "system".

Robin Blackburn put it rather well in his Introduction to Debray's *Strategy for Revolution*:

"Along with other guides to guerrilla strategy, Debray's writings have helped a new style of revolutionary politics to spread from the Third World back to the metropolitan heartlands of imperialism. The sort of immediacy which the foco strategy can achieve has also been attained in the actions of the revolutionary movement of Europe and North America – in factory and university occupations, black uprisings, squatters movements and so forth.

From the concept of the idealised guerrilla hero it is a short step to the trans-national terrorist hero, the role taken on by Carlos. To die under the flag of Vietnam or Venezuela, or Guinea, or Bolivia would be, as Régis Debray explained, "equally glorious and desirable for an American, an Asian, an African, or even a European".

The path to this kind of glory led, so far as the Americans and Europeans were concerned, through student uprisings and violent occupations. For the New Left and the violent radicals, the inspiring philosopher was Herbert Marcuse. The examples to stir them on were the Red Guards in China and the memory of Che Guevara, and the uniting situation was the American war in Vietnam. It was not by accident that the Paris student revolt in 1968 coincided with the opening there of the Vietnam peace talks. At the time, speaking to a Vietnamese leader there, one of the authors of this book asked him whether he was not upset by the noise of exploding tear-gas bombs and screams outside his hotel. He replied: "On the contrary, it is a pleasure to be in Paris in an ambience truly 'révolutionnaire'."

At the time the name of Marcuse was on every student revolutionary lip, for he had predicted that students were destined to lead the revolutionary forces against capitalism. And there in Paris they were putting into effect his theory of Red Bases in the universities, by occupying the Sorbonne and throwing barricades across the boulevards, fighting the forces of repression personified by the grim, armed and helmeted members of the Republican Security Companies (CRS). Herbert Marcuse, born in Berlin in 1898, philosopher, theoretician and sociologist, was by then Professor of Political Thought at the University of California. His examination of the new industrial societies had led him to the belief that scientific and technological revolution had changed the structure of the working class and thereby altered a number of Marxist assumptions. In the new technologically-based society of the West a labour aristocracy had developed, and a new alliance had grown up between big business and the working class which was no longer revolutionary or intent on overthrowing the established order.

This development created a situation in which only what he called the "outsiders" were now the true revolutionaries. The outsiders were those forced from the system because they were unemployable by it; those persecuted for their colour; the exploited masses of the Third World, and the students and intellectuals disgusted by comfortable consumerism in the West.

In particular the greatly expanded student population consisting of young white people, by and large middle class in origin, could see the spiritual void of the new Western world. They were aware of the faults in the society they had grown up in and conscious too of outside disasters, both natural and man-made, in the Third World.

Marcuse had observed that in the 1960s many young people were already in revolt against their elders and their ways. He codified and explained the reasons for their discontent, and by his flattering suggestion that they were the vanguard in the fight to build a new world he provided them with a philosophy that encouraged them to take action.

In the United States the student movement concentrated on the Vietnam war and its consequences. They protested against its cruelties, but also against the use made of universities both for recruitment and for military research. They expressed their Third World guilt complexes and sympathy for fellow outsiders by demanding Black studies in the universities and the end of colour discrimination. The big monopolies were also a target in their attacks upon ostentatious wealth and exploitation.

The themes of this student revolt spread to Europe with few modifications. It was a desire to change higher education which ostensibly sparked off the Paris revolution; but the real aim was to give a lead to the workers, by now considered incapable of making their own revolutionary struggle to overthrow capitalism. By striking, the workers did join in, and for a while it looked as though General de Gaulle's

Fifth Republic would be overthrown by them. Through his extra-ordinary energy and the magic of his personality the Republic survived and he was finally voted out of office in democratic fashion. Significantly the workers abandoned their occupations of factory and office in return for more money and better conditions.

It would be a mistake to suppose that the Paris revolution was all student thought and high-minded idealism. From the moment that law and order started to break down, all manner of criminals, idlers and political adventurers flocked to the Sorbonne and joined in its occupation. Journalists discovered a whole *bas fond* of gangsters, Foreign Legion deserters, whores and other such characters squatting in the centre of learning, some of them mouthing slogans of revolution, but a larger number intent on their own affairs. General de Gaulle, drawing on his barrack-room vocabulary, described them all, students included, as "Ce chie-en-lit" (These shit-a-beds). Beneath the romanticism and high ideals was another world ready to pounce on civilisation.

May 1968 in Paris was the high point of student revolt. The Red Bases may have failed to make a successful revolution but they created a new mythology, and the failure of the bold attempt left behind bitterness and a feeling that even more drastic action was needed, in future, to put things right. It also brought together all the new radical themes: the violence preached by Fanon; the foco theory of Guevara and Debray tried out in action in the streets rather than the jungles; and the student vanguard idea of Marcuse's outsiders.

Yet when all the banners which had fluttered from the barricades were furled again, the world seemed more or less unchanged. As Marcuse had predicted, the workers, although they had made the ritual noises of revolution, had returned happily enough to the comforts of home life. Perhaps they really were in league with the capitalists. There could be no further point in the young student revolutionary supporting the conventional left of the Communist Party.

Many turned to the fringe parties of the left. The Paris revolution and the age of student protest left behind in the minds of those who had taken part, or who had been at universities during that time, a certain attitude to life and politics. In many cases, as we have seen in this book, people giving support to terrorist groups did so out of sympathy for their propagandist aims of serving the cause of "outsiders" through terror. We do not suggest that the ardent and generous young reformers moved straight from student revolt to international terrorism. But many people of that generation, still inspired by the heroic figures and leaders, retain a sneaking respect for the ideal terrorist as a man of conviction risking all for the cause.

Like the student revolutionaries who paved the way for them, the terrorists claim to fight for, and speak on behalf of, the working class. Even though that class rejects them, most of them do start out indoctrinated with ideological beliefs and are convinced that what they are doing is right. It is their arrogant assumption that they know best, and therefore have a right to kill and bully. They have learned to think in this way from the works of Marx and Lenin. Did not Lenin himself abandon the prospect of becoming a lawyer in order to make the revolution? It is very easy for the young and inexperienced to drift into such patterns of thought, which lead them into unlikely situations.

Gabriele Kröcher-Tiedemann started her political career as a German student revolutionary. She was trapped into violence by way of the Baader-Meinhof group, and found herself shooting down two men in the OPEC raid. They were innocent people; but the terrorists do not accept that there are any neutrals in the continuing war against society. Eventually, in the cause of fighting for the "outsiders", she ended up sub-machine gun in hand, separating Jewish from non-Jewish hostages on the airfield at Entebbe, shouting "Schnell, schnell" with the same brutality as her Nazi elders, who sent Jews to the gas chambers.

Certainly so far as her friend Carlos is concerned his first political experiences came in the excited world of Latin-American left-wing ferment, at the time of the guerrilla wars and in the early stages of the student revolt. His Baader-Meinhof helpers were people whose terrorism sprang from the failure of the university movements, and so too were the Japanese. Their violent campaigns developed from a way of thought nurtured by the events and philosophies we have just analysed.

The Carlos complex was also heavily influenced by events in another part of the world where violence had originated in ancient quarrels, more religious than philosophical. In the Middle East the logic of events and the confusions of the post-war world were pushing other similar groups of young men and women along a converging revolutionary path. In the Middle East, too, there were defeated guerrillas who in their despair, and as terrorism began to flourish in Latin

America, turned to acts of terrorism in order to make their political voices heard.

In the Arab countries there is a venerable tradition of guerrilla warfare. For the Arabs, inspiration, both political and religious, springs from the desert, the great purifier. Raiding parties from one tribe in the wilderness used to make stealthy war upon their neighbours. Saudi Arabia and its ruling dynasty was founded by a small group of forty men on horses and camels moving quietly across the desert from Kuwait to seize Ryadh, the capital, by ruse. For centuries such methods have been considered a legitimate way of making war. Lawrence of Arabia, in the First World War, harnessed the old skills when he led Arab groups in raids upon the Turkish occupying power and cut its lines of railway communication. In words which were prophetic of later Arab terrorist activities, he remarked that his men seemed to judge the degree of success of their operations by the amount of noise their weapons made.

Bringing up to date the tactics of their forebears and those used by Lawrence, the Palestinian terrorists made their first attacks on world air transport lines of communication. They hoped thereby to isolate Israel and to terrify the outside world into supporting their cause.

Raiding was the form of warfare adopted against the emergent state of Israel by Palestinians, Jordanians and other Arab neighbours when the Jews began carving out a homeland state in Palestine. The Israelis' determination, with the help of the outside world after the war, brought them victory in the first round of Arab-Jewish wars and Israel became established on the *de facto* borders of an armistice line. It was an irrational frontier full of loops and bends with an anomaly every kilometre, which divided villages and even houses in half. Even Jerusalem was split in two. The Palestinians nurtured a deep sense of injustice. An Arab in a village near Qualquilya showed Payne the place just across the unmarked border where his land was: "Those are my oranges in that grove," he said. "Why should there be foreign soldiers there eating them?" This was a feeling that had nothing to do with high politics, simply with injustice.

Arab terror developed at a significant time, just as the nations of North Africa such as Libya and Algeria, and the older monarchies of Saudi Arabia and the Arabian Gulf, were becoming millionaire oil masters to the world. Huge sums of money began flowing into their treasuries from the industrial countries paying for their oil at ever-increasing prices. Partly to assuage their feelings of guilt at having failed to give military aid against Israel, and in some cases as a form of danegeld to protect themselves from terrorism, the oil countries lavishly financed "liberation groups" dominated by men as intent on world revolution and achieving personal power as on the liberation of Palestine.

Rich Arabs contribute as naturally to Palestine liberation funds as Irish Bostonians donate to the Irish Republican Army to provide bombs and machine guns for use against folk-enemies. Apart from voluntary contributions huge sums are also raised by threats and blackmail, money paid by Western governments to get their airliners back, and protection money. For there is gangster financing as well as contribution financing. Lufthansa paid three million pounds to get a hijacked aircraft back from Aden.

Armed men force payments from the Palestinians themselves, even in the refugee camps, and those members of the community who settled abroad and prospered in the Middle East have more substantial levies to pay. President Gaddafi ordered a six per cent deduction from the salaries of Palestinian exiles working in Libya to help finance Yasser Arafat.

As a result, terrorism pays and has become big business. A spokesman for the Rejectionist Front boasted in 1975 that the income of the Palestine Liberation Organisation was as great as the national income of an Arab nation such as Jordan. Although hard figures are difficult to come by, it has been estimated that in 1974 terrorist revenue amounted to more than £120 million. With such sums at their disposal the terrorists have begun to act like multi-national companies and make legitimate investments through world stock exchanges. One calculation is that the PLO has £50 million invested in London alone.

John Laffin, a British journalist, wrote: "Terrorism is big business, with low investment costs and immense profits. On a commercial basis it is among the best paying industries in the world ... The terrorist leaders are entrepreneurs, and terror is merely the commodity in which they principally deal."

Terrorism has acquired a political and military infrastructure; and in the process it has become self-perpetuating with its own bureaucracy. There are office staffs, $5,000-a-month men equipped with company cars and secretaries. Some are concerned only with money matters or public relations, but others still on the planning staffs dictate memos to girl secretaries urging plans for assassination and bombing, and assessing what might be the effects of various bloodthirsty activities. Until the civil war in the Lebanon made things too uncomfortable and dangerous for terror planners, they worked in opulent air-conditioned office blocks in Beirut. Now they have been forced back to safer bases in Aden and Tripoli for their conferences. Some leaders have made themselves rich with villas and numbered bank accounts in Switzerland. The 1970s have opened the era of the fat terrorist, sometimes reluctant to take violent action himself, who controls a work force of well-rewarded international operators such as Carlos, the mercenaries of violence. The time of the lean revolutionary is past.

With such resources at their disposal the Palestinian terrorists have no difficulties in purchasing sophisticated arms and equipment (more fortunes are made thus). They can also pay for operators in the field, bribe officials for information, and behave in the opulent style of a government-financed superior intelligence service. And fortunately for the terror masters, they have no trouble in recruiting young men and women in search of adventure as well as idealists to do the dirty work in the field, while they themselves edit triumphant communiqués and visit the training camps.

The Arab terrorists have followed the revolutionary trends set in the philosophies we have examined in this chapter, and their wilder groups now preach world revolution as well as Palestine for the Palestinians.

Although many of the people who compose this branch of the Carlos complex started out as genuine idealists full of moral fervour and a determination to reform people and institutions, they have now, like it or not, become a pool of mercenaries. They are in the terror business for the money and for the excitement. Drawn from the broad university movements of anti-establishment conviction, they now work side by side with criminals and pyschopaths. And Carlos has something of all these varied types in his make-up.

He recruits his followers from small bands of fanatics in many countries. The phrases they mouth are cliché-ridden, the faintest echo of the philosophers who originally inspired their thought. It is tragic that so many people have been deluded into taking their appeal at face value, and that generous-minded people of goodwill try to understand their ways in the hope that understanding will satisfy them. In fact they crave only attention and power. The proof of their insincerity in demanding change is that there is no example of international terrorists striking at those parts of the world where left-wing tyrants rule with a heavy hand. Violent protest never hits the real tyrannies, whether they are effective right-wing governments or Communist dictatorships. Their target is democracy and liberal thought.

Chapter Fifteen
What is to be done?

"WHAT IS TO BE DONE?" ASKED VLADIMIR ILICH LENIN IN 1902 IN the historic essay in which he advocated the establishment of a network of professional revolutionaries, united in doctrine and in aim, devoting themselves absolutely to the accomplishment of revolution. "Give us an organisation of revolutionaries – and we will overturn the whole of Russia." We ask the same question about the man named after him, Ilich Ramirez Sanchez, and the organisation of revolutionaries he has established to overturn the world.

What is to be done about Carlos and his nihilistic followers? What is to be done about Wadi Hadad and his dedicated, ruthless Palestinians? What is to be done about the enigmatic Moammer Gaddafi? What is to be done about that malady of our times, international terrorism?

Operationally the problem may be divided into two sections: the tactical and the strategic. The tactical is directed to two main situations – hijacking and the holding of hostages. Bomb attacks and assassination attempts do not really come into consideration because little can be done to prevent a determined man or woman, prepared to die, from throwing a bomb or firing a gun even in the most hostile environment. It is a situation which is well known to security officials, and unless a potential target is kept completely isolated nobody can guarantee absolute safety. One has only to study the stories of the Tsar killers of the nineteenth century, of the murders of Trotsky and the Kennedy brothers, and of the attempts on President Ford, to realise how impossible it is for important men to be kept safe from vengeful opponents, terrorists or lunatics.

Random bomb throwing is equally difficult to guard against. There is little that can be done to prevent a terrorist, or a deranged man like the "Mad Bomber" who terrorised New York in the 1950s, from planting a time bomb or throwing a grenade at a bus queue. Neither can much be done about the kidnapping of individual businessmen and officials. There are not enough police in the world to protect all the men who might be held to ransom. Such people, in the end, must arrange their own protection.

Hijackings and sieges are different because they extend over a period of time and are carried out to give publicity to a cause, however wrong-headed. They need a stage, a setting, and actors. In fact, paradoxically, one of the freedoms the terrorists threaten, namely freedom of speech and of the press, is here their essential weapon. The Munich massacre was planned and carried out to ensure publicity for the Palestinian cause. If the world had not been watching, if the deed had been done in secret, Black September could have murdered the entire Israeli team and yet it would have failed utterly. Freedom of the press is essential to the success of terrorism. For that reason terrorism could never succeed in the Soviet Union. There, unless there are political reasons for reporting a piece of news, as in the case of the amateurish attempt by a group of Jews to flee from Russia in a hijacked plane on June 15th 1970, it is simply not reported.

The next paradox is that it may be better to sacrifice hostages' lives in order to save more lives later on – in other words, innocent people may have to be martyred so that terrorist blackmail can be seen not to be effective. But that type of decision takes more courage or more ruthlessness than most statesmen possess. Some, like Chancellor Kreisky, refuse to stand firm and give in to all demands in order to secure the freedom of hostages. Understandably, this appeals to the hostages then involved. But does it appeal to the hostages who are taken by the same terrorists in later atrocities? Until the killings in the rue Toullier, the French also preferred the soft line. When the Japanese Red Army occupied the French Embassy at The Hague, the Dutch prepared a force of Marines to storm the building but the French, with their ambassador and others threatened with death, would not hear of it and capitulated to the terrorists. Neither country was overly pleased with the other's conduct.

We do not know how Britain would react in a similar situation with international terrorists holding hostages. The government did order the release of Leila Khaled, but the circumstances which obtained then, with 425 hostages being held in the desert and the Middle East on the verge of war, were exceptional. The only cases we have to go by are the Spaghetti House siege, in which a number of hostages were held in the cellars of an Italian restaurant in Knightsbridge, London, in a purely criminal enterprise, and the Balcombe Street siege, where four IRA terrorists, who had spread chaos and death through central London with a campaign of bombings and shootings, were trapped with two hostages. In both cases the authorities played for time, talking softly to the terrorists but at the same time letting them know that the only place they were going when they emerged was prison. In both cases the terrorists threw down their arms and surrendered. But, in the case of the Balcombe Street siege, plans had been made for an assault by anti-terrorist experts of the Special Air Service. Even if it had cost the lives of the unfortunate hostages, there was to be no way out for the IRA killers. Israel, as we have seen, will not treat with terrorists unless there is absolutely no possibility of attacking them. They are prepared to shed blood in order to kill or capture men who, if allowed to fly away, will have succeeded in their customary objective of securing the release of their imprisoned colleagues and will go on to mount bigger, bloodier acts of terror.

They took, for instance, this tough line at Ma'alot. Sixteen schoolchildren were killed and sixty-eight wounded when the Israeli army stormed a school held by a group of Arabs who had crossed the border from Lebanon. They took it in storming the Savoy Hotel on Tel Aviv's waterfront when it was occupied by a Fatah suicide squad. And they were prepared to take it when they went to Entebbe. They were so sure there would be heavy casualties that the raiding party included no fewer than thirty-three doctors. The late Richard Crossman, a supporter of Israel, wrote bluntly after the Munich affair that exploits like that massacre "can only be prevented by a state prepared to risk the lives of innocent bystanders, including women and children, in order to prove that terrorism does not pay ".

The Israelis, of course, have special emotional, political, and military reasons for never giving in to terrorist blackmail. But the decision to sacrifice innocent people would be one that would haunt the statesmen of any other country for the rest of their lives. It is a thought which already haunts the families of American diplomats, for they have been told quite plainly that they will never be ransomed if they are captured by terrorists. That is what happened at Khartoum when a Black September gang occupied the Saudi Arabian Embassy. The Americans refused to agree to the terms for the release of Ambassador Cleo Noel and his Deputy Chief of Mission, George Curtis Moore, who had been attending a farewell party for Moore at the Embassy. The terrorists demanded the release of Sirhan Sirhan, the killer of Senator Robert Kennedy, and a number of terrorists imprisoned in Jordan, Israel and Germany. President Nixon told a press conference in Washington that America "cannot and will not pay blackmail". The two Americans and the Belgian chargé d'affaires, Guy Eid, were then murdered. A year later the eight murderers were sentenced to life imprisonment – and set free on the same day. President Numeiri of the Sudan has since shown himself to be less compassionate when the attempts have been against himself. He has had several hundred of his opponents shot.

As far as the protection of airliners is concerned, the weapons to hand are absolute vigilance and a set of security procedures which, while adding nothing to the comfort and dignity of passengers, ensure a measure of safety. Here the Israelis are once again the most rigorous. Their airliners all carry members of the "007 Squad" who have orders to fight it out in mid-air if an El Al plane is attacked. They carry low velocity .22 pistols so that any bullets missing their targets will not cause an explosive decompression of the airliner. The airliners themselves, in a series of hair-raising experiments over the Sinai deserts, had grenades exploded in their specially strengthened fuselages to determine whether or not a grenade would be fatal to the plane in a mid-air fight. The results showed that the aircraft would survive and so the Israeli sharpshooters are prepared to do battle at thirty thousand feet even when their opponents have pulled the pins from their grenades. Once more, they are prepared to pay the price in passengers' lives.

The Israelis are equally stringent with their pre-flight security checks. Passengers must now book in two hours before flight time and this interval is taken up by a minute baggage and body search. When thick-soled shoes were fashionable the security agents could be seen using a large awl to make sure the soles were not filled with plastic explosive. Both the authors of this book have had their cameras and typewriters stripped down to ensure that they did not conceal explosives or parts of a pistol. The result of these precautions is that travel on El Al is tiresome and frustrating – but safe from hijacking. It is because of the difficulty of smuggling weapons on El Al planes that the Entebbe hijackers chose a French aircraft. Carlos in Paris tried to destroy El Al airliners from the outside by Sam 7 rockets and, a few weeks after Entebbe, two Palestinians threw a grenade at El Al passengers waiting to board their aircraft at Istanbul – out of rage at the airline's near-impregnability.

It is interesting to note that both the Palestinians carried Kuwaiti passports and had waited in the transit lounge after flying from Libya. The price of freedom is eternal vigilance and nowhere is this more true than at airports. Entebbe only happened because of complicity at Kuwait and laxity at Athens. Given the vulnerability of large aircraft carrying over three hundred people, there can be no excuse for sloppy security – even if the passengers complain.

The Israelis have also taken the lead in protecting their embassies. Remotely controlled television cameras, reception rooms which can be turned into killing rooms, tough young men and women armed with weapons brought in by the diplomatic bag, reinforced concrete and barred windows, have turned Israeli embassies all round the world into miniature fortresses. Again, that is why the terrorists have turned to indirect targets. They no longer dare attack Israeli embassies.

All these counter-measures are essentially defensive. They are reactions to actions taken by the terrorists. But there comes a time when a defence is so good it becomes offensive. The SAM anti-aircraft system of the Egyptian army, for example, was essentially defensive. But in the Yom Kippur War it assumed an offensive role by making the sky dangerous for Israeli planes for fifteen miles in advance of the front line. Under this forward-thrust umbrella, Egyptian tanks and soldiers were able to develop their offensive on the ground in comparative safety while the Israelis were forced to look for ways through or round it.

This is precisely what happens when strict anti-terrorist measures are adopted. They force the terrorists to look for other ways to achieve their objectives; they force them into the open, to take chances, to waste men and money on difficult missions; they make their enterprises much more complicated and dangerous. But this offensive-defensive posture can only be effective if every country adopts correct security procedures and co-operates with other countries – particularly in the exchange of information about the movements of suspected terrorists, new methods and new weapons.

This leads us on to a discussion of the strategy required in dealing with terrorism. It is unfortunate, but in the nature of national states, that some governments have been reluctant to give the full co-operation just mentioned. The French were particularly at fault in this respect and the Germans, too, were hesitant. The French, sensitive about trade and oil, had no wish to make it appear to the Arab countries that they were taking part in a European purge of the Palestinians, and the Germans, still trying desperately to divest themselves of the Nazi legacy, played the game gently until forced by events and constant urging from Britain to join in what amounts to an anti-terrorist Interpol without the political restraints imposed by the Interpol agreement.

Fortunately that has now changed, and the British-German-French alliance has been embodied in a Common Market convention. But even before the governments came to their agreement, the security forces of the three countries had worked out their own operational arrangement backed by constant unofficial contact in all three capitals and in Brussels and Geneva. There was an extensive exchange of information, which has now been legitimised. The Germans concentrated on their Arab students and workers and the Baader-Meinhof revolutionaries, the French on their Arab migrants, especially the Algerians, and the South Americans, and the British on the Irish, while feeding in information from the efficient network they still maintain in the Middle East. The British Foreign Office, apart from its punctilious diplomatic procedures, is a remarkably efficient information-gathering organisation. Many of its members under a number of guises devote their time to fighting terrorism.

In this international anti-terrorist community, the USA is a weak sister. After the Munich massacre, the Americans set up an "Inter-Departmental Working Group on Terrorism". Ostensibly this was a high-powered governing body consisting of the Secretary of State, the Ambassador to the United Nations and the heads of the FBI and CIA. However, it does not seem to have made much of an impact and enquiries at its office in the State Department are told rather plaintively: "Why don't you ask the British or the French, they know much more about terrorism than we do." The British and the French for their part tend to rely on their long-established contacts within the CIA. These contacts, keeping their heads down during the current problems in the agency, are taking care not to attract any attention but feed their European counterparts with useful information.

Most information, naturally enough, comes from the Israelis. At one stage the French were complaining that if they acted on every piece of information passed to them by the Israelis their whole police force would spend its time simply checking the names given to them by Mossad, the Israeli secret service. The Israelis, on their side, were enraged when the French allowed known terrorists to slip through their fingers.

But the French have stopped complaining since the rue Toullier killings and the Israelis are impressed by the co-operation they are now getting in Europe – except when, as in the notorious case of Abu Daoud, the quartermaster of the Munich massacre according to his Jordanian interrogators, the D.S.T. is overruled by the government in the cause of political expediency. The Israelis have pulled off some notable coups simply by dispensing information. They warned the Kenyans about the attempt to shoot down an El Al plane at Nairobi. They thwarted an attempt by Abu Iyad, the Black September leader, to assassinate King Hussein at the Arab leaders' summit in Rabat in October 1974, and they were able to warn the French about a car filled with explosives which they had traced all the way to Paris from the Lebanese border, and which the police picked up just before it was due to explode in front of the Israeli Embassy. It is exploits like these that make it certain that the Israelis have infiltrated the high echelons of terrorist groups. Their information is too precise, too detailed, to come from any other source.

This co-ordination of information is invaluable; the various security authorities are no longer stumbling round in the dark. The Germans, for example, would not release another Wilfried Böse if he was handed over to them by the French. The French would not make the mistake of simply expelling him without passing on his dossier, and the Germans would have their own dossier of his activities outside his own country. Once again this is the offensive-defensive posture. But what purely offensive action should be taken now that all this information is available?

Here we come to another paradox. Because of politics, both international and domestic, action has to be restricted to the defensive rather than the offensive. In the authors' various assignments to Northern Ireland they are always told the same thing by the soldiers: "We could clean this lot up in twenty-four hours if the politicians would allow us to." At this point a Public Relations Officer usually appears from thin air, sends the offending soldier on his way and mutters platitudes about "young men not really understanding the subtleties of the problem". But the young man in question is not usually concerned about the subtleties. He is concerned with being shot by an Armalite, which will tear his arm off, or blown up by a culvert bomb. He knows the killer with the Armalite, he knows the man who makes the bombs and he knows where he can "lift" them. He is not allowed to because any such campaign would raise a fierce political storm. Similarly, action taken against suspected Arab terrorists in Europe would rebound. The most that can be tried is a quiet deportation unless actual criminal charges can be made – and there is no country in the world that wants Arab terrorists in its prisons.

The Israelis tried it the hard way with their campaign of assassination. They tried to kill Hadad with rockets aimed at his Beirut flat. Their fighters intercepted an Iraqi Caravelle flying from Beirut to Baghdad on August 10th 1973 and forced it to land at one of their own military airfields. They knew that George Habash was booked to fly on it. And they wanted him. But Habash had had a recurrence of his heart trouble while waiting to board the aircraft and had cancelled his flight. They landed a commando force in Beirut and killed three leading Palestinians. Technically these operations were highly professional and they had justification because they were aimed at ridding the world of men who commissioned murder. But the political results were counter-productive, and since the time when they killed the wrong man at Lillehammer the Israelis have abandoned direct action, except where, as at Entebbe, the lives of their own nationals are at stake. They would prefer to avoid the international opprobrium of carrying out anti-terrorist actions which themselves smack of terrorism. Until the Arabs started to do the job for them by killing each other in the Lebanese war, the Israelis maintained their air raids against the refugee camps which housed terrorist headquarters and continued to harry the groups operating in the "Fatah land" of South Lebanon. But even these reprisals were beginning to be demonstrated as counter-productive for, as Martin Luther King used to say, "You can kill the hater but not the hatred."

There is a delicate balance in terrorist affairs by which, if the security forces are thought to be too repressive, the balance of public opinion swings against them. This is a fact well known to the forces of revolution who deliberately conduct operations which they know are going to bring down the full weight of the police and military against them and incidentally against the civilian population. This has happened many times in Ireland and each time the revolutionaries, while perhaps losing some men, have gained in local support and worldwide propaganda.

The balance also comes into play when deciding how much freedom a democratic country should be asked to surrender in order to fight terrorism. When the House of Commons was asked to approve new anti-terror measures which included the exclusion of United Kingdom citizens from Northern Ireland – as well as Great Britain – when they were suspected of terrorism, there were several Members who spoke against what to most people seemed a very small step towards defeating the IRA. Mr. Ron Thomas, the Labour Member for Bristol NW, argued that the measure went against civil liberties. People would not know what the evidence against them was, he said, nor would their families or MPs. "This House should be the watchdog of civil liberties, not the Home Secretary's poodle." The new laws were passed by 140 votes to 21, a good enough majority. But the 21 votes cast against reflected the British hatred of surrendering any fragment of the freedoms won at great cost throughout Britain's history.

The paradox here is that it is necesary to surrender some of that freedom in order to preserve the whole. But how far do you go? When the British army held a number of exercises round Heathrow airport in which light tanks were used and road blocks were set up, the authorities explained that these were vital security exercises designed to protect the airport in the event of a terrorist attack. This was moreover at a time when a number of American anti-aircraft missiles had been stolen from a NATO arsenal and it was feared that an attack would be made on aircraft at Heathrow. But, despite these explanations, there was a great deal of suspicion in left-wing and trade-union circles that these were excuses designed to cloak exercises in the use of the army in the event of large-scale strikes and mass demonstrations.

Where does support of law and order become repression? How much freedom should be surrendered in order to fight terrorists? There is the sad example of Uruguay already quoted, where the Tupamaros sought to instigate a revolution through terrorism. Their excesses brought a coup by the army and the establishment of a harsh right-wing régime which not only destroyed the Tupamaros but also every vestige of freedom in the country.

There is a happier example from Canada where Premier Trudeau invoked the War Measures Act in 1970 and moved in the army to deal with the Quebec separatists who had kidnapped James Cross the British Trade Commissioner in Montreal and Pierre Laporte, Quebec's Minister of Labour and Immigration. When he was criticised for this move he replied: "There are a lot of bleeding hearts around . . . All I can say is let them bleed." The FLQ killed Laporte but Cross was released and although the kidnappers bargained their way to safety on a flight to Cuba, Trudeau's firmness stopped the FLQ's terror campaign, and the freedoms that were temporarily sacrificed were later restored in full.

The FLQ's position was also eroded by Trudeau's decision to react politically as well as militarily to the separatists' campaign of violence. He instituted a long-term government investment policy in the separatist areas and compulsory French courses for English speakers, thus destroying much of the support for the FLQ in the French-speaking community. The terrorists were no longer able to swim in the sea of the people, although it must be admitted that they were small fish swimming in waters that were never too hospitable.

Trudeau's success demonstrates that a proper balance of firmness, vigilance and political flexibility can destroy a revolutionary group's ability to terrorise a nation. But, as Paul Wilkinson says in *Terrorism versus Liberal Democracy – the Problem of Response*, a paper he wrote for the Institute for the Study of Conflict: "Part of the price we pay for the survival of democracy is the freedom of ideas. Hence in a working liberal democracy it is both dangerous and naive to hope to destroy a subversive movement utterly."

Violent action brought concessions for the French Canadians, it will mean more power for the Roman Catholics in Northern Ireland, and it should lead to some form of Palestinian state in the Middle East. Yet whatever is achieved will fall far short of what the extremists demand, and therefore terrorism in one shape or another will inevitably continue. There will always be a French Canadian ready to throw a bomb or an Irish Republican ready to shoot a political opponent.

It is argued that terrorism could not exist unless it is rooted in genuine grievances and that, therefore, the way to stop terrorism is to cure the grievances. But if this road were to be followed then Canada would be split in two, Northern Ireland with its Protestant majority would be handed over to the Roman Catholic minority, and the state of Israel would be destroyed. These are all impossibilities and, anyway, old grievances would be replaced by new.

Furthermore, new directions and developments must be allowed for. In particular, if all the Palestinian demands were granted, if every evicted Palestinian was given back his house and his farm, if every Jew who arrived in the Holy Land after 1939 was returned to Russia or Poland or wherever he came from, and if an Arab government sat in Jerusalem, terrorism would still not cease. For the Palestinian cause, the foundation on which the edifice of terrorism of the Carlos conglomerate has been built and furnished, has become merely the excuse, the emotional vindication, for acts of terror which are aimed not at bringing justice to the Palestinians but at worldwide revolution. The initial cause bears little relation to current objectives. Terrorism is being conducted by the generals of revolution, who are using the victims of the refugee camps both as their camouflage and as their cannon fodder.

We are by no means arguing that the Palestinian problem was created for the purposes of spreading revolution, but the situation that has resulted is ideal for that purpose and is being used with the utmost cynicism. George Habash is using the Palestinian problem to realise his dream of the great Arab revolution with the feudal leaders of the oil states overthrown and North Korean style governments established in their place. Gaddafi is using it to pursue his vision of becoming leader of an Arabia which has returned to the fundamental tenets of Islam. The international terrorists who have grouped round the PFLP and Carlos are using it to satisfy their own nihilistic ideas for the destruction of the present world order. And the Soviet Union, the most cynical power group of all, is using it to try to maintain its influence in the Arab world with all its strategic importance.

The Kremlin, always eager to meddle in troublesome situations, has enlisted the aid of its satellites. Czechoslovakia supplies arms to the terrorists, East Germany trains them and provides easy access to Western Europe. Palestinians are taught guerrilla warfare in several camps inside the Soviet Union. Officially, the Russians abhor terrorism and urge the various groups to work for "support among the masses" rather than carry out acts of terrorism. But they use the terrorists as proxies, establishing their men in the various Arab groups to take over the leadership when the old leaders go. They use long-established agents such as Curiel to funnel back information. And we believe that while Carlos owes allegiance to Wadi Hadad and the cause of world revolution, he is also a Russian agent.

Given these powerful backers, it is highly unlikely that the terrorism of the Carlos complex will disappear, whatever political settlements are made in the Middle East. The PFLP and Carlos are already looking to new opportunities in Africa.

Perhaps the most disheartening aspect of all is the way in which the United Nations has been used to condone terrorism. Not once has the Soviet Union condemned terrorism in the Security Council. Not once has the United Nations General Assembly passed a resolution outlawing terrorism. The most the combined Arab-Communist-African majority has allowed the United Nations to do is to pass a feeble resolution expressing "deep concern" over the increase in acts of violence.

Even that small concession to morality was further weakened because the resolution went on to express support for the national liberation movements and to condemn "the continuation of repressive and terrorist acts by colonial racist and alien régimes" – an impeccable-sounding sentiment, but one that in the context of the resolution meant that the United Nations was in favour of terrorism.

We have asked: "What is to be done about terrorism?" It is obvious that the United Nations with its double standards will do nothing. It has abandoned its responsibilities and allowed itself to be misused in a cynical exploitation of the principles of democracy by totalitarian states.

Daniel Moynihan, the rumbustious former United States ambassador to the United Nations, has called for the establishment of an international force to fight what he describes as "The First International of Terrorism". But, quite rightly, he stipulates that it should be run by the democracies and not by the United Nations.

Terrorism has brought members of the United Nations close to war twice in the past six years. In 1970, when the hijacking by the PFLP of four airliners and 425 hostages to Dawson's Field eventually provoked King Hussein to turn on the Palestinians, Syria sent an armoured column into Jordan in support of the guerrillas and the Israelis moved their army up to the Jordan, ready to invade if the Syrians did not retreat. Hussein's air force and armour gave the Syrians a bloody nose and they fell back. But the world came close to war that morning. Then again, after Entebbe, Idi Amin, enraged by the help given to the Israelis by the Kenyans, came close to sending his forces over the border.

The danger is that someone like Carlos could become another Gavrilo Princip and by an act of assassination plunge the world into war. One hesitates to speculate on what might have happened if Carlos had carried out his intention to kill Sheikh Yamani after the OPEC raid. One may be sure, however, that the Saudis would have used their vast resources to avenge his death. And Carlos is not the only professional killer whose services can be bought.

There is another grave danger arising from terrorism and its proxy use as a weapon of coercive diplomacy, and that is the threat posed by the possession of modern weapons of war by revolutionaries. These young men and women are often unbalanced and would not hesitate to use such weapons, however devastating their effect. We have already seen the use or planned use of SAM 7 missiles on at least four occasions, at Nairobi, at Rome, and twice at Paris. What next?

Chemical weapons, a flask of poison in a town's water supply, a radio-active container hidden in a sports arena – this is the stuff of television melodrama, but it is also a real possibility. And what is more than just a possibility is the stealing, building, or buying of an atomic bomb by the forces of revolution. Colonel Gaddafi, for example, is on record as saying: "Tomorrow we will be able to buy an atomic bomb. The nuclear monopoly is about to be broken." However, when Ronald Payne asked him for more information about his atomic plans he piously replied: "You know that efforts all over the world are being made to use nuclear power for peaceful purposes. Certainly backward countries want to use it for peaceful purposes and our efforts are exerted in this direction."

Pressed further about the military side of nuclear development, he became even more bland: "I think such questions should not be presented to countries trying to build themselves up and to develop." The fact that the Israelis were reported to have atomic weapons, he said, was their policy and their responsibility and no concern of his.

But that was Gaddafi talking for the Western world, and not the Gaddafi who gloated over Munich, praised the killers at Lod and paid Carlos a million pounds for the OPEC affair. The fact is that Gaddafi wants an atomic bomb and it is not too difficult, given the amount of money he has, to obtain one.

Professor Theodore Taylor, an American physicist who has been arguing for years for stricter control of atomic materials, says that any bright student of physics could make an atom bomb, hide it in the boot of a car and detonate it with enough power to destroy the centre of New York or London. Early in 1975 a twenty-year-old student at Massachusetts Institute of Technology proved Professor Taylor's theory by designing a crude but explodable atom bomb in just five weeks with the aid of published technical works. He did it in answer to a challenge by an American television programme. The producer of the show on seeing what he had brought about said in stunned disbelief: "We found it was frightfully easy."

Basically it is simply a matter of bringing two chunks of plutonium together with sufficient force for them to "go critical". Once the mathematics have been worked out, this can be done by an alarm clock timing device and a chemical explosive primary charge which could be set by any accomplished terrorist bomber.

It was this situation that caused two hundred leading scientists meeting at the Pugwash Conference on World Affairs in Oxford to issue a warning that "there is a danger that, to some degree, fissile products may fall into the hands of irresponsible and even criminal groups. The need for national and international actions to safeguard against this must be emphasised."

All terrorism is blackmail in one form or another: Release these prisoners or we shall blow up this aircraft ... Broadcast this declaration or we will kill this ambassador ... Pay us a million pounds or we will execute this capitalist hyena. But possession by the terrorists of an atomic device would be the ultimate blackmail.

What then is to be done?

Tactically, more stringent precautions must be instituted at airports and embassies and other danger points, even though this means more tedious delays and a certain restriction of freedom for the public. The public must be made more aware of the danger of international terrorism. In specific operations the press and television could be asked to co-operate with the authorities in keeping an act of terrorism secret until it has been foiled. But normally this would not be possible as in most cases the act itself is too public, too violent, too international for secrecy to be possible or effective. It would, moreover, bring the curtailment of liberty close to the point where it became unacceptable. In fact, one must soldier on, using increased awareness along with the weapons and techniques that are being continually improved through experience.

Strategically, there is hope to be gained from the co-operation which has been established between the Common Market countries. If this co-operation could be extended with more and more countries agreeing that there can be no hiding place, no support for terrorists, then their sphere of operation must inevitably shrink. The perfect example of the effect of such co-operation even between political enemies is the agreement between the Americans and the Cubans governing hijackings. Before this agreement was signed, no pilot in America knew when he took off if he would land at his real destination or Havana. Since the signing not one aircraft has been hijacked to or from Cuba.

But that agreement was signed only because Castro found the hijackings to be politically embarrassing. And it is here that the strategy for dealing with terrorism breaks down. Too many countries not only do not find it embarrassing but actively support it when it is directed at their enemies or if it is thought that by causing trouble for the democracies their own purposes will be served. Russia and its satellites, for cynical political reasons, and the Arab states, for emotional reasons stemming from the long war against Israel, are the guilty nations and there are disturbing signs that the support for international terrorism – apart from cross-border raids by black nationalist groups – is growing in Africa.

The sad fact is that international terrorism will continue while it suits these countries to give aid and shelter to the terrorists. And in the present climate of political immorality, reflected by the double standards prevailing at the United Nations, there is little likelihood of their agreeing to join the democracies in stamping it out. So the danger will remain and Carlos or somebody like him will continue to plague the world.

Index

compiled by Robert Urwin